Dedicated to Angela, Re

CONTENTS

Foreword	Page 7
Story	**Page**

The Linlithgow Gypsies – Result hanging Alexander McDonald and Charles Jamieson – Theft at Kilsyth 1 December 1769 (victim Alexander McDougall) — 9

Process of Scandal by Hannah Smith against Andrew Aitken 1786 — 16

Process of Scandal – Libel of Declatory of Marriage Alexander Caitchen against Lilias Peebles of Linlithgow 1789 — 17

Escape from Linlithgow Prison 6 January 1820 - *Thomas Wilson, Alexander Harvie and Daniel or Donald Cameron* — 20

Riot in the streets of Linlithgow 19 April 1823 - *David Morrison and Alexander Wardlaw (victim John Law)* — 22

Charles Macewan from Ireland assaults Hugh Robinson, biting off his nose - *South Bridge Street, Bathgate 22 May 1824* — 24

Culpable homicide on the High Road from Edinburgh by Broxburn, between Kilpunt and East Mains Farms on 15 March 1825 - *John Todd of Mauchline (victim George Halliday)* — 29

Furious driving of carts along the King's highway to the terror of the servants of John Mowbray Esq of Hartwood, West Calder 14 July 1825 - *James Bartholomew, William Sommerville, John Meikle and James Watson (servants – William Finlay, Ann and Barbara Knight)*   34

Poaching at Moss Planting, Torphichen 10 January 1827   40
John Russell (on lands of William Downe Gillon Esquire)

Passing counterfeit money at Bathgate 31 December 1829-13 January 1830 - *William and John Braidwood (victims Alexander Arthur, Margaret Russell or Arthur, Margaret Brock, Archibald Marshall)*   43

Assault at Bargaber Bridge, East Whitburn 16 April 1831   46
James Brown (victim Peter Love)

Returning from transportation at Linlithgow Bridge December 1831 - *David Milliken Scott, alias David Millican or Milligan*   51

Theft at Bathgate 8 December 1832 - *David Dobbie (victim Isabella Hamilton or Young)*   55

Theft by housebreaking at Polbeth 9 April 1833 - *John Fleming and James Mitchell (victim James McLeod, farmer)*   58

Theft at Bathgate 17 September 1834 - *Joseph Auld from Ireland (victim Terry Herring)*   62

Attack at Uphall 22 June 1835 - *William Addie and William Hamilton (victim David McCulloch)*   64

Culpable Homicide at Selms Farm, Kirknewton 20 July 1836 67
James Bell (victim John Kerr)

Assault at Broxburn 16 May 1837 - *Robert Fairfowl (victim Helen Alexander, or Allan)* 72

Assault of David Purves with intent to rob at Bathgate 26 June 1837 - *Charles Crease from Edinburgh* 74

Embezzlement and breach of trust at Mid Calder 4 November 837-January 1838 - *William Trotter (victim Robert Borthwick, baker)* 77

Theft at High Street, Linlithgow 9 December 1837 - *George Yorkston (victim Mrs Jean Johnston or Gibb)* 80

Theft by Housebreaking at Howden Park, Mid Calder 29 March 1844 - *Robert Ferrier and Mary Porteous (victims William Auld and James Murray)* 86

Culpable homicide at Mounteerie, Bathgate 19 May 1844 90
Dundas McCriner (victim Marion Wardrop or McCriner)

Theft at Carriden and Linlithgow January/February 1845 97
Janet Callender or Hastie (victims Ann Young and Alexander Callender)

Theft with previous conviction at Kirkliston and Dechmont 29/30 May 1848 - *Margaret Mackenzie or Burns with various aliases (victims James Baillie, Janet Douglas or Kerr, James Russell)* 100

Wilful fire raising at Glasgow by Elizabeth Forrester of Bathgate 18 April 1849 *(victim William Kidston)* — 104

Assault and robbery at Boghead Farm Steading, Bathgate 28 November 1849 - *James Watson, George Scoular and John McNie (victim David Black)* — 107

Theft at Drumshoreland Store, Uphall 15 January 1850 — 115
Michael Fannon alias William Thomson (victim John Bruce)

Assault at Cairniehead, Whitburn 28/29 September 1850 — 117
Alexander Graham (victim John Corkle)

Theft at Cochrane Street, Bathgate 9/10 July 1851 - *Mary Hunter and Jean Anderson (victim Christian Wardrobe)* — 121

Child murder at Houstoun House, Uphall 29/30 May 1852 — 124
Mary Paterson

Passing counterfeit money at Broxburn 22 November 1852 — 128
Alexander Alexander and Mary Alexander (victim Mary White, Agnes Gilmore)

Theft from a Royal Mail bag between Torphichen and Linlithgow 11 June 1853 - *Thomas Scott* — 134

Theft of a horse from Easter Inch, Bathgate and a dog and ropes from Bathgate 14/15 October 1854 - *David Drysdale (victims John Pollock, Henry Fairley, John McDonald)* — 142

Assault and robbery at the Meadowhead Tavern, Bathgate 17 November 1854 - *Matthew Boyd (victim Laurence or Larry Hart)* — 148

Murder and assault at Bathgate 15 November 1856 - Result hanging - *Peter McLean, William Mansfield, Christina Peters or McLean (victims John and Thomas Maxwell)* — 154

Assault near Russell's Row, Armadale 7 August 1859 – — 160

William Mansfield (victims Luke Haughey, Lawrence McAlinden, Patrick McAlinden

Litigation Thomas Crawford of Limefield, Bathgate 4 June 1863 *(against Jane Kerr or Neilson)* — 164

A vagrant comes to town – fraud and wilful imposition at Linlithgow 16 November 1869 and Bathgate 18/19 November 1869 *Donald McLeod alias James Stewart, John Stewart, James Campbell, Alexander Campbell, John Maclachlan* — 167

WEST LOTHIAN – *THE DARK SIDE*

Foreword

The historical search room in General Register House (National Records of Scotland), the handsome Robert Adam designed repository in Edinburgh, has a hushed ambience, as everyone investigates their documents. Obtaining the indictments and witness statements for the following High Court cases was like opening up Pandora's box. The old, hand written documents are tied with string and many of them had not been touched for over 200 years. Using this source, I have written short stories about people who either originated from West Lothian or whose crimes were committed around the area, mostly in the earlier part of the nineteenth century. I have also included several additional short stories based on "scandal".

Gypsies, tramps, thieves – and murderers! There are a great many thefts, but it is interesting to note how serious these crimes were considered when the articles being stolen are taken into consideration. Most people had few possessions, unless they were relatively wealthy, and these articles had to be used for many years, unlike today's throwaway society. It is difficult to believe, for instance, that for stealing articles of clothing from a shop an eighteen year old girl could be transported to Tasmania. People knew down to the last handkerchief exactly what they owned and generally where they had seen it last. Looking at one page of the Linlithgow Prison Register of Criminals for the year 1845, the articles being stolen included silver plate, cotton lace, a horse, hay, bundles of cut grass, potatoes and turnips, a bell pull from a door, eighteen herrings and a bundle of willow!! Other crimes on the same page included desertion from the 92nd Regiment, malicious mischief, breaking into a garden and refusing to aliment (maintain) an illegitimate child.

Some criminals were incorrigible and looking at the prison register confirms this. For instance, Richard Greenwood, a tailor, seemed a very dubious character. His appearance on 1 February 1845 in front of the Magistrates described him as being aged thirty seven, born at Linlithgow, of dark complexion, light hair and hazel eyes. He had was dirty, but sober, and was wearing ragged clothes. He had already been in the Linlithgow Prison seven times before. On this occasion, he was tried on 24 February 1845 – his crime being *"exposing his person naked in the streets of Linlithgow"* – and was sentenced to imprisonment for six weeks. Moving forwards to 13 June 1845, Greenwood was in prison again for assault and breach of the peace and on 9 April 1846 he was back for theft of a top coat. On 3 June the same year he was once again convicted of assault - by striking his mother with a wooden shelf! [National Records of Scotland reference HH21/18/1] Clearly, this was a man who would not change his ways.

The demon drink! It is immediately obvious, and would no doubt be welcome reading to those in the temperance movement, that most of these incidents occurred due to *"taking a dram"* – or some form of alcohol. One must keep in mind that it was probably safer to drink beer in the nineteenth century, as diseases could be spread by drinking the polluted water which was available then. Alcohol was fairly cheap and many took advantage of this. There were a great many public houses in Scotland around this time. Anti social crime due to drinking alcohol is certainly not a new phenomenon, as the following pages will testify to. The Edinburgh Evening Courant of Saturday, 20 December 1851 under the heading of **New Year's Drinking** notes, for instance,

"New Year's drinking is again coming round and while it brings the many enjoyments peculiar to itself, it also brings the drunkenness which is its not less invariable accompaniment. This odious vice may well indeed be reckoned the curse of this country. We are happy to learn that the Scottish Association for Suppressing Drunkenness, among other efforts to arrest the progress of this degrading propensity, is publishing this New Year a short address to the people of Scotland written by the Rev. Dr. Guthrie, portraying in vivid colours the miserable condition of the drunkard."

A mutchkin of whisky is often referred to in this book. It is a Scottish unit of capacity equal to a quarter of the old Scottish pint, or roughly three quarters of an imperial pint (0.43 litres).

This book gives an insight into the lives of people in West Lothian, in general, over the space of about a hundred years from 1769 to 1869 and includes 2 cases which resulted in hanging.

The upstanding and respectable Sergeant John Kerr appears in many of these stories. According to the Register of Defaulters (police disciplinary records), John Kerr was a native of Perthshire and was stationed at Bathgate in 1858. (The 1851 census lists him living with his wife and family at Academy Street Police Station.) He was aged 43 in 1858, and was 5 feet 7 inches tall, with grey eyes, dark hair and a swarthy complexion. He had served in the police force for 17 years prior to that year. Did he also go over to the *"dark side"*? On 13 July 1859 he was found to be drunk on duty, for which he was suspended and fined ten shillings, but he was allowed to remain in the same position. On 8 November the same year he was fined two shillings and sixpence for appearing at the High Court in a top coat - this not being his uniform coat - which was in contravention of General Order 9. Then, on 10 July 1863, things definitely began to deteriorate. He was found drunk on duty again and had been disobedient to Sergeant Buglass. For this he was suspended. He was reinstated on 12 July but a short time later, on 27 July, he was found to be in neglect of duty, and was swearing, insolent and drunk. He was reported by the Chief Constable. For this he was finally reduced to a First Class Constable, removed from the station on 7 August 1863 and transferred to Bo'ness. He was found drunk on duty once again on 21 March 1864 and finally he was dismissed. (*Reference ED6/12/2 Edinburgh City Archives*)

THE LINLITHGOW GYPSIES - ALEXANDER McDONALD AND CHARLES JAMIESON

THEFT AT KILSYTH - 1 DECEMBER 1769

It was on 1 December 1769 at Kilsyth when Alexander McDougall's shop was broken into and a large quantity of goods stolen. Mr McDougall had been confined to bed early that evening, having been kicked by a horse that day. He had been asleep in his house which was situated next door to the shop. He had only found out about the burglary early next morning when his neighbours across the street had come to advise him that his shop door was lying wide open. (The door had not been broken, but the lock picked.) They had assisted him to walk to the shop where he was horrified to discover that a large bundle of goods, which had already been made up bound for Kirkintilloch, was missing. There were various printed linens, blue and black shalloons for linings, cotton velvets, blue plush, white linen, thirtieths and bombazines, striped cotton for vests, as well as other goods. Some fabric had been purchased from Duncan Blair, a merchant in Bucklyvie, the printed cloth from John Buchan, a shop keeper in Crieff, and the total value of the missing items was one hundred and twenty pounds. After searching in vain for the goods at Kilsyth, Mr McDougall had gone to the house of William Shaw, the weaver, who lived to the south of Kilsyth, as it was well known that a gang of thieves frequented barns and outhouses by his home. On being questioned, Shaw had originally said nothing to McDougall about the gang's whereabouts that night, because he was terrified of what they might do to him. However, he did later admit that he had seen Charles Jamieson in McDougall's shop on a previous occasion and was highly suspicious that it was he who had actually picked the lock.

McDougall remembered that Jamieson and his wife had come into his shop some time before the break in, as she was searching for fabric to match another piece which was to be made into a garment for her. However, what had struck McDougall about the visit that day was Jamieson's intense interest in the door of the shop and its lock. He had seen Jamieson at fairs previously and it was common knowledge that he was one of *"McDonald's Gang."* A man named Taylor had also been in the shop at the time and after Jamieson's departure, McDougall had told him how uneasy he had felt that day.

Eighteen year old James Bilsland related that he and Robert Glasgow had stayed late one Thursday night the previous winter, about Martinmas, at Alexander McDonald's house at Linlithgow Bridge. Glasgow had left the following morning and McDonald and Bilsland had left for Maddiston, with McDonald saying that they might *"get something"* at McDougall's shop at Kilsyth. They had gone to Charles Jamieson's house, where Adam McGregor was present, to finalise planning the robbery. Jamieson had already *cased* the shop and they had all set off at dusk. Passing New Merchiston, they had called in to collect Robert Glasgow. Bilsland was riding on the back of McDonald's grey mare, Jamieson was on a small black mare and McGregor on a small brown sheltie and all were wearing dark blue clothes. Glasgow had left them at Falkirk and he, according to Bilsland, had not been party to the plan. They had passed the Toll Bar to the east of Falkirk on their way to Kilsyth, and Bilsland said that they had taken a dram there. They had met a carter and another individual who had told them to beware, as half of the Bridge of Bonny had disintegrated, so they were obliged to walk the horses along the remaining part, where they paid the toll and eventually arrived at Kilsyth at around eleven o'clock in the evening. They had tied their horses to a bush about a half mile up the road and the four of them had proceeded into town on foot. As some house lights were on near Alexander McDougall's shop, which was in the middle of the town near the Cross, they had kept hidden for a while.

The plan was that McGregor was to stay outside to the west to keep watch, with Bilsland to the east, whilst Jamieson and McDonald were to break in and enter the premises. Jamieson had picked the lock, whilst McDonald had remained at the bottom of the stairs, but proceedings had suddenly been interrupted when a dog barked and Jamieson had quickly exited carrying only a pair of stockings. They had all hidden outside again, returning a short while later. Jamieson and McDonald had then re-entered the shop, leaving shortly afterwards with a very large bundle. The swag had then been divided into packs, taken back to where the horses had been left and the four had ridden away with them, with the packs hooked and hidden by the tails of their blue great coats. Bilsland had no pack, but was riding behind the others. It was around three o'clock in the morning when they reached the part of the road between Light Water Bridge and Camelon and they had met some carters there, who asked about the fallen bridge. They had ridden on a bye road to Falkirk to avoid the Toll Bar and the goods had been hidden in the Falkirk Wood, following which the robbers had parted – Jamieson and McGregor going to Jamieson's house, and McDonald and Bilsland to McDonald's house at Linlithgow Bridge.

On the Sunday evening the four had met up again at Jamieson's house and rode to the woods for the packs, returning to McDonald's house where they were opened. There was a great deal of fabric, according to Bilsland, and he was able to describe it in detail. When Bilsland was shown a woman's white dimity petticoat and calico gown at the trial, he was only able to say that he had seen such fabrics in the pack, but could not verify that these garments were made from the stolen cloth. McDonald and Bilsland had subsequently sold part of their share of the stolen goods – calico and red mankie - to Deacon Andrew at Linlithgow, with other parcels being sold to other individuals. Bilsland had received thirty shillings as his part of this share.

William Liston, a carter in Glasgow, confirmed that he had passed Peter Steel at the Toll at Callender at about eight o'clock on the Friday night that Bonny Bridge fell. The toll keeper – Robert Ewing – had informed them that as they were going westwards, they should be on their guard as McDonald's gang had already passed that way, so they should protect their carts if they contained anything valuable. They had proceeded to John Brock's house at Falkirk and between them they had watched the carts all night. It was actually the following morning when they had heard from the post boy about the bridge falling, so they had engaged James Brock, John's son, to lead them by another route by Dunnipace. They had set off at approximately three o'clock that morning and just past Camelon, before Light Water Burn, they had encountered five men, four on horseback, with two men on two horses – one grey, the other black. James Brock had said, *"There's McDonald and the gang!"* Liston had responded that they had never harmed *him* before and hoped they would not do so now. It was dark and Liston could not identify faces, but he could see that the men were *"riding wide"*, as though there was something bulky between them. They had only spoken a brief, nervous *"good day"* on passing, but on reaching Kilsyth, two different people had informed them that Alexander McDougall's shop had been broken into, with almost everything stolen from it.

Peter Steel, a carter in Glasgow, fully corroborated this statement. Seventeen year old James Brock lived with his father, John, at his inn at the West Port of Falkirk. He recalled the night that the Glasgow carters had come to his father's house (when Bonny Bridge had subsided) and how they had sat up the whole night guarding their carts because they had been told about the *"Lithgow Bridge Gang"* being in the vicinity. He had led the carters away early next morning and at Light Water Burn they had met McDonald (whose voice he knew well) and four others there. The gang, who had a black horse and a grey horse, appeared to have packs around them and young Brock admitted to feeling acutely anxious in their presence, having heard about their exploits. He had later found out about McDougall's shop being broken into.

Walter Robertson, a tenant at Bonny Water, who lived in close proximity to the Bridge of Bonny, confirmed that the bridge had fallen on Friday, 1 December. He recalled Alexander McDougall, a Kilsyth merchant, coming to his house next day asking if any strangers had passed by, as his shop had been burgled. John Dobbie, a millwright at Bonnybridge, confirmed that a large part of the bridge had fallen down about an hour and a quarter past sunset. Only a man on horseback could have used it afterwards, but a cart would have been too wide to pass on the remaining structure. William Allan, who kept an inn at New Merchiston, recalled that McDonald and Jamieson had called at his premises two or three times between Martinmas and New Year's Day. He remembered particularly that they had been there at Martinmas because of the two significant events which had taken place – Bonny Bridge falling and Alexander McDougall's shop being burgled.

Alexander Taylor, a Maddiston butcher, had been told by his wife that McDonald and Jamieson had taken a dram at his house the night McDougall's shop had been robbed. His wife, Mary Thornton, recalled that night also. She remembered that Charles Jamieson's wife, Eupham Graham, had come to her shortly afterwards offering to sell a piece of dimity cloth cheaply, but thinking it may have been stolen, she did not buy it. She had been offered it for eighteen pence, when she knew full well it was worth at least two shillings a yard! She had heard that Catherine Walker had bought it, though, and had had it made into a coat. She was acquainted with Charles Jamieson, who used to cast smoothing irons.

Catherine Walker, who was the wife of Peter Wyper, a coal miner in Falkirk, and who lived at Brightons, recalled that about Christmas "*Newstyle*" Eupham Graham, who lived in a house on the side of a hill near Maddiston, had offered to sell her a piece of white dimity and a piece of printed cloth. She had paid seventeen shillings for it, but on hearing about the burglary and the description of the stolen material she had informed the Justice of the Peace in Falkirk, who had advised her to return the items. The purchase of these items had been witnessed by Agnes Wyper, the wife of William Gillespie, a coal miner at Maddiston. Agnes had not bought anything, apparently, but she did remember Jamieson's wife throwing some goods into her house around this time (on the day a search was ongoing for her husband), asking if she could leave them until she returned. They included two pieces of green drugget striped with yellow, two pieces of black cotton velvet, two pieces of black shallon, a piece of blue worsted plush, a piece of green durante, two pieces of printed calico, a blue shallon petticoat and a black mankie petticoat. She vehemently denied that she had ever disposed of goods for Charles Jamieson's wife.

Margaret Forgue, the wife of Alexander Livingston of Maddiston, had often bought items from Charles Jamieson's wife in the past and she certainly recalled that she had bought calico from her for three shillings on the Handsell Monday previous. When Abraham Leishman, a Falkirk merchant, had gone to Charles Jamieson's house on 15 January around midnight to arrest him with some others, Jamieson had already left, but a shirt and piece of striped cotton cloth had been left there. This story was corroborated by James Tibbeth, innkeeper at Falkirk, who also described that a woman had run towards the house crying out in alarm when they had arrived. They had gone to McDonald's house to search for him, but neither he, nor any stolen goods, had been located.

James Hart, a Linlithgow tailor, confirmed that he knew Alexander McDonald, (whose only occupation seemed to be making horn spoons) as he had lived at Linlithgow Bridge the previous winter. He confirmed that he had often made clothes for McDonald, but the fabrics were bought from Linlithgow merchants. At the end of the previous year Alexander McDonald had brought along a piece of striped cotton druggate to be made into a waistcoat and this had been duly delivered to him. However, Alexander McDougall had come to Hart's shop later, saying that his shop had been burgled, whilst describing the type of fabrics which had been stolen. On hearing the description of the materials, Hart had confirmed that a waistcoat had been made for McDonald from the striped cloth.

Another hardware shopkeeper in Linlithgow, Robert Andrew, confirmed that he was acquainted with Alexander McDonald, as he had lived for approximately two and a half years at "*Lithgow Bridge*". He recalled McDonald coming to his shop at the end of the year to buy tobacco and dram glasses and at the same time a man called Bilsland had arrived, offering to sell two remnants of printed material. He did not deal in this type of merchandise, but as a corporal's wife lived in the upstairs flat, he had sent his son, Alexander, with Bilsland to her in case she wanted to buy it for a gown. The fabric had been purchased for twenty two shillings and the money left at the shop for Bilsland to collect. McDonald had returned with Bilsland when he had collected the money.

Thomas Fleming at Cockhill confirmed that he had known McDonald for eight years and that he had put him up in his house on many occasions when he travelled the country. He described that he had seen McDonald selling white iron work and occasionally selling horses. He had heard nothing detrimental about McDonald's character and he knew that he paid his way in the neighbourhood. He only knew Jamieson slightly and on one of the occasions he had seen him, he had been selling smoothing irons. James Law, a farmer at Nethertown, Cambusnethan, knew that McDonald often used to stay at Cockhill and that he had sold horses at markets and fairs, one of which had been sold to the Laird of Wishaw. He recalled that McDonald's wife had been arrested in the spring of the previous year and that McDonald himself had come to see one of the baillies, enquiring as to the reason for her commitment. He would not leave the town without her, and he was also arrested on that occasion.

Lieutenant Arthur Fitzgerald, who lived at Pentland, confirmed that he was well acquainted with Charles Jamieson, having served in the same regiment as him from 1756 to 1759, and said that he had a very good character all that time. In 1759, however, Jamieson had been moved to join the Regiment commanded by Stuart Long Morris, which was being newly raised, as Major Signet had recommended him for the posting, Jamieson having been trained to be a corporal or sergeant.

As well as being indicted for the break in and robbery, McDonald and Jamieson were indicted by the 13th act of the 20th parliament of King James 6th 1769 entitled "**Act against Egyptians** for being vagabonds, forners and common thieves, commonly called Egyptians or habit and repute such without any visible fortune or lawful employment for subsisting honestly, and being frequently seen haunting and keeping company with gangs and numbers of idle and vagrant persons of bad fame and reputation."

What of Jamieson and McDonald themselves? What had they to say about the matter? Charles Jamieson gave his first statement on 26 June 1770, in which he confirmed that he was a brazier and founder who travelled up and down the country. He had stayed for approximately ten weeks at Maddiston, renting a house from John Turnbull, and had made many a smoothing iron for people in the neighbourhood. He had left the house before the end of the tenancy (from Martinmas – 11 November – to Whitsunday) because he had heard that he was to be arrested for thefts at

Falkirk. He denied knowing any individual named Bilsland, however, saying that he only knew a collier named Gillespie, not McGregor. He said that McDougall had come looking for his goods at his house, but had found nothing there. Jamieson denied ever having been in the company of McDonald, McGregor (alias Gillespie) or Bilsland or having been involved in the break in at McDougall's shop. He had bought a halfpenny worth of cloth at the shop, however, around Lammas (1 August).

On being interrogated on 13 July he changed his story. On the previous Christmas day he had shared some boiled beef and a mutton pie with Alexander Taylor, John Turnbull, Alexander McDonald, William Gillespie and their respective wives. He had paid no rent to Turnbull for his house, in which there were no windows. Jamieson refused to describe the colour of McDonald's horse, or answer questions relating to the death and funeral of McDonald's father, or if he had been at a house at New Merchiston on a Friday evening last winter (Linlithgow market day) with Bilsland, McDonald and Glasgow, or being in the Kilsyth area the night that Bonny Bridge fell, or about his wife throwing a bundle of goods into William Gillespie's house. In fact, he completely refused to answer any more questions at all!

On 18 May Alexander McDonald gave his first statement, saying that he had lived at Linlithgow Bridge for around four years until about last Christmas, when he had relocated to Cockhill, Cambusnethan, where he took a house from Thomas Fleming, tenant of Sir James Stewart of Coltness. All his furniture had been left at Linlithgow Bridge, because of debts owed there for his father's funeral, as well as to John Roberts in Stirlingshire and Mrs Wood, innkeeper at Linlithgow. He said that he had been in the habit of leaving Linlithgow Bridge around the Candlemass (Christmas) and going south or west to avoid debts. He had sometimes stayed at Cockhill and he sometimes stayed with someone named McDonald at Moffat at the Cross Keys at Lockerby, or at Ecclesfechan. When at Dumfries he would stay at the Stank of Riddell in a public house. He was a white iron smith by profession, but had followed the jockey trade for a while and sometimes *"louped to five or six horses per week"*. He confirmed that Bilsland had been in his house a few times, but had never stayed overnight, but he *had* stayed nearby for two days just before Christmas when McDonald's father's corpse was laid out. He denied ever having any business with Bilsland or being acquainted with Charles Jamieson, or McGregor who lived near Maddiston. He denied having anything to do with the break in at McDougall's at Kilsyth, as his father was lying dead at the time. He said that the only time he had been in prison was at Lanark and Edinburgh.

On being interrogated on 13 July McDonald changed his story. He said that around Christmas day he *had* been at Charles Jamieson's house at Maddiston where he had drunk some whisky and ale. Turnbull and his wife had been there, as well as Alexander Taylor, from whom McDonald used to buy his coats. On that day he had received a message delivered by a boy sent by Daniel Wood, innkeeper at Linlithgow, to say his father was extremely ill. His father had subsequently died on the Saturday and was buried on the Monday following. He denied ever having been in a man named Allan's house at New Merchiston, or being involved in the robbery at Kilsyth, or giving Robert Glasgow a ride from New Merchiston to Falkirk. He denied having met carters at Light Water Burn about the time Bonny Bridge fell and when asked how he had spent his time between the end of November and 3 December last he replied that he had nothing more to say about the matter and would answer no more questions!

At Edinburgh on 14 August 1770 a *"great plurality of voices"* found the two accused guilty of the crime of shop breaking as libelled. They were to be carried to the Tolbooth of Edinburgh, detained till Thursday 20 September, following which they were to be delivered over to the Sheriff depute of Edinburghshire and transmitted under a sure guard until they were brought to the confines of the county of Linlithgow. They were then to be taken from the Tolbooth and carried to the most convenient place for execution within the county of Linlithgow, near to Linlithgow Bridge, and then and there between the hours of two and four o'clock in the afternoon to be set upon a gibbet and to be hanged by the neck by the hands of the common executioner till they be dead. All their moveable goods were to be brought to his Majesty's use.

Linlithgow Bridge and Avon Viaduct

National Records of Scotland reference JC26/192/1; JC3/37

ANDREW AITKEN

PROCESS OF SCANDAL BY HANNAH SMITH 1786

Andrew Aitken, a schoolmaster in Bathgate, was furious when his cousin, Hannah Smith, announced her marriage to William Glen of West Mains of Linlithgow in November 1784. (The proclamation states that William Glen of Mains in this parish and Hannah Smith in the parish of Wilston proclaimed in order to marriage Nov 28th) He let it be known that he had a previous claim on her and that she had actually been engaged to him first. The claims he had on her, apparently, were for debts owed to him. When Hannah's marriage was proclaimed on 28 November at Linlithgow, he had written letters to the minister who was to marry them and *"many dark and insidious insinuations to defame her character"* had been made. He did not, however, seem to state any objection to her marrying – even in his letter written four days after the wedding.

Aitken had apparently gone round the whole of Bathgate trying to make other people testify that what he was accusing her of was accurate, but eventually he was made to retract his statements relating to her. He was even made to appear before the Kirk Session. The offensive impression which he had created on the minds of the public had to be eliminated. He had still persisted in his accusations against her, however, saying that he had letters in his possession which would destroy her character. The words he used had been very explicit and he had tried to describe her as being of an *"abandoned and dissolute disposition"*. He had actually implied that in the July and August of that year he had been in bed with her and carnal dealings had taken place. *"Familiarity had passed between them, which was against all decency"*!

Was Andrew Aitken just jealous? Regardless, he was found guilty of scandal and had to pay over the sum of five pounds in damages and expenses and was fined the same sum.

William Glen and Hannah Smith went on to have seven children whose births were registered at Linlithgow between 1786 and 1794.

National Records of Scotland reference CC8/6/762

Old Parish Register for Linlithgow 668-0050 fr 2016

LILIAS PEEBLES OF LINLITHGOW

PROCESS OF SCANDAL – LIBEL OF DECLATORY OF MARRIAGE 1789

Lilias Peebles was born at Linlithgow on 2 March 1754 to William Peebles, a tanner in Linlithgow, and Helen Struthers. In February 1789, having instructed Mr James Balfour WS, Alexander Caitchen had her served with a summons of scandal and she was ordered to appear at the Commissary Court in Edinburgh on 18 March. It appeared that Lilias had accused him of bigamy and that she had *"disturbed the peace and harmony of any person, sowing dissention between man and wife"*

Lilias had been telling people, mostly at Newlands parish, near Peebles, where she now lived, but also at other places, that she had been married to Caitchen seven years previously. At that time, both had been working for Mr Kennedy of Romanno – with Lilias being employed as a chambermaid. According to her, Alexander Caitchen had courted and followed her for several years before she had consented to be his wife. On 19 May 1781, they had subsequently gone to Edinburgh, where, at the house of Mr Potter, a stabler, they had been married – without the usual proclamation of banns. A minister had been procured, he had solemnly married them and a certificate to that effect was produced at court. The certificate headed *"Edinburgh, May 19th 1781"* stated that *"These are to certify all whom it may concern that the parties following viz Alexander Caitchen and Lilias Peebles were this day duly married by mutual consent, having first declared that they are both free unmarried persons"* and was signed by four people, including the "minister".

Consequently, the couple had consummated the marriage there and had been acknowledged by all as man and wife. She had explained, however, that they had agreed to keep the marriage secret on their return to their workplace, until they could set up home together. Soon afterwards, Lilias had left Mr Kennedy's employment to work for a private gentleman and his family eighty miles to the west and because she could not write, she had had no further communication with Alexander Caitchen. She stated that she could not have anyone else write on her behalf, due to the secrecy they had agreed upon. She had not heard from him for several years (which seemed very odd) and had no way of knowing what was going on at Romano, so she had been – according to her – dumbfounded when she had returned to the area sometime in 1787 to find that he was now "married" with a child. She had resolved there and then to prosecute him for bigamy, although at that time she had left her marriage lines with a confidential friend so could do nothing until she was able to collect them. As far as she was concerned, he was her lawful husband, and while she was deliberating on her own action, she herself had been served with a summons from him to put her to silence.

Clearly, Lilias had been in dire circumstances as regards her finances. A Certificate for Lilias Peebles - Poor circumstances 1789 stated,

"We the ministers and elders of the Parish of Linlithgow do certify to whomsoever it may concern that the bearer, Lilias Peebles, daughter of William Peebles, tanner in Linlithgow, and reputed spouse of Alexander Caitchen, servant to Mr Kennedy of Romanno, is in poor circumstances and unable to pay the expenses of prosecuting an action of declaratory of marriage at the instance before the Commissaries of Edinburgh against the said Alexander Caitchen, as witness our hands at Linlithgow the 8th day of April 1789.

John Scotland, minister

William Napier, Elder

Stephen Mitchell, Elder

James Andrews J P"

Apparently, her action had been considered to be a viable one, as a letter dated 22 April 1789 was included which stated, *"The subscriber's solicitors for the poor, having in obedience to above remit, considered the petition of Lilias Peebles with the certificate of marriage, and are of opinion that the petition has a probable cause. 24 April the commissaries, having considered the above, admit her to benefits of the poor's roll."*

As far as Alexander Caitchen was concerned, he stated that her accusations had also been made recently to the Reverend Doctor James Moffat, minister of the gospel in Newlands parish, although she had made no objections when he was publically proclaimed three several Sabbath days in the Newlands Kirk prior to the celebrations. The complaint to the minister had resulted in Caitchen and his wife being withdrawn from church privileges, and their child being refused baptism until this matter was resolved. Caitchen stated that he and his wife had been destroyed by these false accusations and Lilias Peebles ought to be fined twenty pounds, with fifty pounds expenses.

Alexander Caitchen appeared on 20 July 1789 to give his statement, which detailed that he had served with Mr Kennedy for about twelve years. About eight years previously Lilias Peebles had come to serve that family for around twelve months, but about six months after that, she had left to serve the Minister of Newlands. Whilst she was there, Caitchen had certainly kept company with her, but had *"never had enjoyment of her person and never courted her in marriage."* This case lasted for several months and various statements were given by both parties. On 22 October 1789 Caitchen had further explained that he had been married to a virtuous woman for several years and that she had already borne him one child and was expecting a second. He was working for the Hamilton family as a ploughman at

Newlands, but he was furious that his minister had stopped all church privileges due to the allegations being made by Lilias Peebles. He wanted to know why she had waited so long to make her accusations, when she had known he was living openly as the husband of Jean Noble, daughter of William Noble of Langstrutherburn. If he and Peebles had been married and had been living apart for four years, she could have claimed divorce on the grounds of desertion, for instance.

What was the outcome of this case? On 5 February 1790 at Edinburgh, having considered the libel of declaratory of marriage at the instance of Lilias Peebles against Alexander Caitchen, and whole complaint, the Commissary Court found the libel not proven, and Caitchen was therefore dismissed from the action. Lilias could no longer persist in these accusations and Caitchen could be accepted back to church privileges.

National Archives of Scotland reference CC8/6/834

THOMAS WILSON, ALEXANDER HARVIE AND DANIEL/DONALD CAMERON

ESCAPE FROM LINLITHGOW PRISON (WESTER JAIL) 6 JANUARY 1820

It was during the night of Thursday, 6 January, or the early morning of Friday, 7 January 1820, at the *"Wester Jail"* of Linlithgow when the break out occurred, with three prisoners escaping. William Handyside was one of the Town Officers and a Keeper of the Jail of the Burgh of Linlithgow. As far as his records were concerned, the three prisoners had been incarcerated from the date of their commitment until the date in question, ie Thomas Wilson, a canal labourer from Broxburn, who had been imprisoned from 16 August 1819 for stealing five pounds from a chest belonging to Erskine Gray of Broxburn; Alexander Harvie, shoemaker in Linlithgow, who had been imprisoned from 21 September 1819 for throwing a stone at William Hastie to the danger of his life; and Daniel or Donald Cameron who had been imprisoned from 4 October 1819 for stealing a considerable amount of money from Robert Halliday in Queensferry. They had certainly been there when Mr Handyside locked them up for the night, which was between three and four o'clock on the afternoon of the 6th. After securing the prison, he had taken the keys along to Mr Peter Clark's house – he being one of the baillies of Linlithgow – and given them over to one of his maid servants. When the prison was locked, William Gardener, Town Treasurer, John Devine, Town Drummer, and Ann Hastie, wife of James Halliday – one of the keepers of the prison – were present.

Handyside had subsequently gone to Baillie Clark's house on the morning of the 7th around nine o'clock to collect the keys from Jenny Meikle, maid servant, as he was due to give the prisoners their breakfasts. The outer door of the prison was found to be securely locked, but when he had gone inside, the three prisoners were nowhere to be seen. They had escaped! It appeared that they had taken the bed frame, placed it up against the east wall of the cell, and stood on it to reach the wooden ceiling. They had then taken a hot iron bar from the fireplace and burnt a square hole in the ceiling which led into the Council Chambers under the Council table. They had afterwards opened the window and made their escape into the street by sliding down the front pillars of the square. On making this unfortunate discovery, Handyside had immediately informed the Town Treasurer.

Ann Hastie (wife of James Halliday) lived with her family in the same building where the common prison, Town House and Sheriff Court Room were contained. Due to her husband being nearly blind, she and her eighteen year old son, George Halliday, had been present when the three prisoners had been given their rations and locked up again for the night by William Handyside. She confirmed that the prison door had been securely locked and said that she had heard nothing to indicate that an escape had being made during the night.

John Devine, Town Drummer and one of the Town Officers, concurred with Ann Hastie's description of events. The escape having been discovered, he had gone with Andrew McKay, head constable of police, searching through the town of Linlithgow for the prisoners, to no avail. Harvie's mother had apparently only learnt of the escape a short while before he arrived.

A slightly embarrassed James Rae Esq. wrote a letter to Hugh Warrender, Crown Agent at Edinburgh, on 7 January in which he stated that he was sorry to advise him of the escape of the three prisoners. He said that a constable had been despatched to Broxburn, and he was to proceed to Edinburgh in order to establish intelligence relating to the prisoners' whereabouts. Also, the Magistrates of the Burgh were to advertise details of the escaped prisoners and offer a reward for their capture.

Fortunately, the subsequent letter he wrote on 9 January indicated that the search had produced some positive results. Mr Rae was then able to state that the officer who had been despatched had returned on the evening of 8 January and brought the escaped prisoners, Wilson and Harvie, back with him. They had been arrested at the Grassmarket in Edinburgh and were now safely lodged in the Jail "*in a more secure place*"! Measures had also been taken to find Cameron, who had unfortunately been more difficult to locate.

Note: A report from the Select Committee on the state of prisons in Scotland (7 April 1826) mentions for Linlithgow that in consequence of some misconduct of the woman who carried out the principal duty as jailer for her husband who was blind, and most probably because of the improper arrangement having been brought into public notice, Halliday and his wife had been dismissed and another person taken on trial.

In the same report it was noted that Linlithgow Jail was capable of containing 22-25 prisoners. There were two apartments of cells for the worst criminals – without fireplaces – and they could take two prisoners each. These cells were said to be "*sufficiently strong*", cased with stone and well secured with strong doors. The Wester Prison had been adapted for prisoners not confined for "*atrocious*" crimes and this could take six or seven prisoners. The Easter Prison was reserved for females and could take four or five. The Debtors' Prison (one room measuring approximately eighteen by fifteen feet) could take around seven prisoners. The cells other than those for the worst criminals were described thus. "*These apartments, although not very strong, may be considered pretty secure.*" (This was clearly not the case when the event occurred on 6 January 1820!)

In the year 1825 there had been forty three male criminals, five females and nineteen debtors - eighteen male and one female.

National Records of Scotland reference AD14/20/258

DAVID MORRISON AND ALEXANDER WARDLAW

RIOT IN THE STREETS OF LINLITHGOW 19 APRIL 1823

It was the evening of Saturday, 19 April 1823 at Linlithgow. John Law from Girvan in Ayrshire had been arrested for stealing a one pound bank note and was being escorted along the High Street by James Armour, Sheriff Officer, and Andrew McKay, head constable of police, to the tollbooth of Linlithgow to be incarcerated there for further examination. Law had been apprehended on a charge of stealing the money from John Gordon's house at Magdalene's and had appeared before James Rae, Sheriff Substitute of Linlithgow. John Gordon was Charles Grant Esquire's gardener and Law had gone to his house at about one o'clock in the afternoon of the day in question to visit John and his wife, Jean, and had remained there until about three o'clock. He had then left with the Dundee Union Bank note, having stolen it from a wooden box in the house during the temporary absence of Jean Gordon.

Escorting Law along the High Street should have been a straightforward enough affair. However, David Morrison and Alexander Wardlaw – both shoemakers in Linlithgow – had maliciously incited a mob, causing a massive riot in the town. Near to the Cross a crowd of approximately two hundred people had assembled, which was attributed to the fact that Morrison had wickedly shouted out that Law had, in fact, stolen a child for the purpose of giving it over to the doctors for dissection - a statement which was utterly false.

Bearing in mind that this was around the time that body snatching was reaching new heights and the medical schools in Edinburgh were constantly seeking corpses for dissection, this was a very sensitive subject and one which had obviously inflamed the crowd to become extremely violent and disorderly. (It was not until 1827 that Burke and Hare would smother seventeen people over a period of a year. That way, the bodies would be undamaged and a better price would be obtained when sold to Dr. Knox, the local surgeon. Fortunately by 1832 this practice would be outlawed due to the introduction of the Anatomy Act, which allowed the unclaimed bodies of those who had died in prisons and workhouses to be used for dissection.)

The malicious pair - Morrison and Wardlaw - had persisted with these false accusations by every means in their power, working the mob to a pitch of fury. They had also used the most threatening language to Armour, McKay and Law, assaulting them with sticks and other offensive weapons. They had thrown blows at the officers, striking them repeatedly on the head and body and had knocked down poor John Law, beating him whilst he was prostrate on the ground. The officers did everything in their power to try to assure the crowd that these accusations against Law were totally untrue, and Law's cries had become so loud that they had reached the ears of Bailie Clark and other good people in the town of Linlithgow. These kind citizens eventually came to the aid of the officers and the unfortunate John Law was ultimately carried off to the jail.

Linlithgow Cross

David Morrison gave a statement on 21 April saying that he had certainly been on the streets of Linlithgow on the evening when the event had taken place. He had seen James Armour and Andrew McKay conveying a man to the prison, and a huge crowd gathering. He was adamant that he did not, however, see anyone striking the officers or that prisoner, although they were being pushed and jostled about and obstructed by the crowd. There was pandemonium, with a great deal of screaming and uproar from the crowd, but Morrison said that he had certainly not struck anyone - to the best of his recollection.

Alexander Wardlaw also gave a statement confirming that he had been on the streets of Linlithgow on the Saturday night in question. He concurred with David Morrison's statement generally in that he had not seen anyone hitting the prisoner or officers. He had heard the prisoner cry out, *"murder!"*, however, but could add nothing further. They had obviously thought the better of these statements later, however, and told the whole truth.

What happened to Wardlaw and Morrison after being tried on 2 June 1823 at the High Court in Edinburgh for the crime of assault, mobbing and rioting? Alexander Wardlaw was found guilty in terms of his own confession. He was imprisoned for eight months, with hard labour. Likewise, Morrison was found guilty in terms of his own confession and given the same sentence. Morrison would offend again!

National Records of Scotland reference AD14/23/233; JC26/448

CHARLES MACEWAN FROM IRELAND ASSAULTS HUGH ROBINSON, BITING OFF HIS NOSE

SOUTH BRIDGE STREET, BATHGATE 22 MAY 1824

It was Saturday, 22 May 1824 at South Bridge Street, Bathgate.

According to **his** version of events, Charles MacEwan, a travelling wire worker and bell hanger from Ireland, had travelled from West Calder to Bathgate the day before looking for work, staying overnight at William Gray's lodging house at South Bridge Street, Bathgate. Lodging at the same house were two brothers named Robinson – Hugh and John. Apparently, in the morning, whilst MacEwan was at his breakfast, Hugh Robinson had brought a bottle of whisky into the room and "*insisted*" that MacEwan take a glass of it with him. He also insisted that MacEwan should spend the day with him in Bathgate and that if he wanted the loan of a few shillings, then Robinson would be happy to oblige. MacEwan had declined the offer of money, but had joined him in the whisky drinking. He had then taken his box of tools, left the house and continued on his journey looking for work.

According to MacEwan, Robinson and his wife had followed him on his way and asked him to go into a public house with them in Bathgate, where Hugh Robinson had ordered up some strong ale and whisky and then proceeded to share it with MacEwan. A lively afternoon had ensued and both men had become extremely intoxicated during the course of several hours. In due course, as is often the way with such drinking sessions, a serious quarrel had developed, following which Robinson had struck MacEwan on the eye with his fist and knocked him down – with the help of his brother, John Robinson. The two brothers had subsequently pinioned his arms down by his side while he was down on the ground and struck him again. They had then thrown MacEwan's box of tools on the fire and torn his hat to pieces. All he could do was use his teeth to liberate himself, having no hands free at the time. This was certainly MacEwan's version of the events which took place on that day.

However, MacEwan was indicted for a serious crime in that he did "*wickedly and feloniously attack and assault Hugh Robinson, travelling jeweller and merchant from Longtown, Cumberland, England*", who had fallen to the ground in a state of intoxication. MacEwan was accused of leaping upon Mr Robinson as he lay defenceless, grasping his throat and then biting off a considerable part of his nose, resulting in a huge amount of blood springing several feet away.

Several statements were given by witnesses at the scene.

William Steven of Bathgate (who went on to become a Sheriff Officer) said that at about six o'clock that evening he had been informed that a disturbance had taken place on the streets of Bathgate, when a man had bitten off the nose of another individual during a fracas. Steven had gone along to the house in South Bridge Street and witnessed Hugh Robinson sitting on a chair there, with a young medical student,

John Dickson, who was trying to attach the piece of nose onto Robinson's face by binding it with bandages. It was certainly a grizzly sight to see! Whilst talking to others in the room, Steven heard that Robinson had lost a considerable quantity of blood during the incident. Following the treatment by young John Dickson, Robinson had been put to bed, being in a most dangerous state of health. Steven and James Johnston, Sheriff Officer in Bathgate, took the responsibility of apprehending MacEwan and Mr Steven was subsequently directed by Mr Corbet, one of the Justices of the Peace, to take MacEwan to Linlithgow.

John Dickson, student of medicine, confirmed that on the evening in question he was called to the assistance of Robinson at William Gray's lodging house. When he arrived he had seen the poor victim sitting on a chair by the fireside with his head hanging down. After examining Robinson, he was found to have had the point of his nose bitten off, with the inner cartilage of the nose completely torn away. Mr Dickson had asked all those who were present to search for the missing part, which, when found, was cleaned and bandaged onto what remained of his nose. Although he had done all he could and the man's general health had since improved, it would never be known if the nose would ever heal satisfactorily. During the examination, Mr Robinson was also found to have a swollen and bruised knee.

James Weir, a surgeon Bathgate, confirmed that he had also visited Mr Robinson afterwards and that he approved of John Dickson's treatment and agreed that Robinson's condition was much improved.

Other locals gave their version of events as to what had taken place.

William Martin, a Bathgate weaver, said he had been looking out of the window of his house at around five o'clock that evening, when he had seen two men and two women walking along the street – obviously in a drunken state - following which they had gone into William Gray's lodging house. These individuals were quarrelling and fighting on the streets and that quarrel continued after they went into the house. Mr Martin looked through the window and witnessed the men stripping for a fight. Not only that, but they were asking for knives, so he certainly did not venture there himself for fear of injury. Afterwards, he had seen one of the men coming out of the house, so he had gone in, whereupon he had been met with the sight of Robinson with the end of his nose missing, and blood gushing in amazing torrents from the wound. He actually assisted the doctor to dress the wound half an hour after the injury was sustained.

Another weaver in Bathgate – fifteen year old Robert Glen of North Bridge Street - confirmed that he knew Hugh Robinson by sight. He had seen him going into William Gray's house in the company of two women. He had looked in a window of the house to see one of the women, who he understood to be MacEwan's wife, upbraiding Robinson. She had asked him if he would strike a woman, but Glen had not seen Robinson strike her at all, rather he had tripped up her heels with his feet.

Robinson, being drunk, had fallen onto the ground with her. Glen had then seen MacEwan falling down on top of Robinson, seizing him by the throat and horrifyingly taking Robinson's nose in his mouth, worrying at him like a dog. After biting off the nose, he had then seen the man getting up and trying to leave. Robert Glen had seen the ghastly sight of blood springing about a yard in height, at which point he was so traumatised that he fled the scene instantly!

South Bridge Street, Bathgate

Peter Gardner, another weaver in Bathgate who lived with his father, Henry Gardner, a tailor, gave his version of events. He had seen Hugh Robinson and another man (who he heard was Irish and had subsequently been taken to Linlithgow Prison) fighting on the streets of Bathgate on the night in question. He had followed the fighting men to William Gray's house, when he saw the Irishman's wife making a fool of Robinson, challenging him that he would surely not strike a woman. The drunken Robinson had then tripped up the woman, making her fall to the ground, with him falling backwards with her. The Irishman, sitting on a chair, had immediately jumped on Robinson, grabbing him by the throat, taking his nose in his mouth, which he bit and worried for the space of about five minutes. Robinson had been unable to move during the attack, but he had shouted and begged MacEwan's pardon for the incident which had occurred. When Peter Gardner first saw the amount of blood caused by the assault, he had been convinced that Robinson's throat was cut as well.

William Gray's wife, Ann, concurred with Peter Gardener's story as to what had taken place between MacEwan, the Irishman, and Hugh Robinson. She confirmed that she thought MacEwan to have been more like "*a dog on a mouser*" than a man and that it had been impossible for her to prevent what had taken place at her house. She further stated that Hugh Robinson's brother, John - a boy about seventeen years old – had endeavoured to pull the Irishman off his brother. When MacEwan had risen up, he had then tried to do the same to him. As it was, the younger Robinson had the marks of MacEwan's bloody mouth on his shoulder, but fortunately MacEwan had been prevented from doing him any serious injury.

Archibald Cameron, another weaver, confirmed that he had seen the scuffle in Mr Gray's house. He had seen one man give a woman a push, the woman falling on the floor, the man then falling backwards, with the accused person getting up from a chair, falling onto the first man and attacking him. He had seen MacEwan lying on Robinson for the space of three or four minutes and, on rising again, Cameron had seen Robinson with his nose bitten off and bleeding dreadfully.

James Walker, a weaver, had seen a great riot taking place on the streets of Bathgate on the afternoon in question. He had seen Robinson and an Irishman named MacEwan wanting to fight, but Walker and some other men had tried to prevent them. MacEwan had followed Robinson, wishing to fight, and Robinson had said that he would fight him if he would fight a fair battle. This did not happen, however, as Robinson's brother had interfered and prevented it. MacEwan had then followed Robinson, struck him with an iron rod which he used in his trade as a tinker, but Robinson had evaded this blow. The men had gone into William Gray's house and a short time afterwards Walker had been informed that one of the men had cut the other's nose off. Walker had called for assistance and had gone into Gray's house, whereupon he had seen Robinson bleeding profusely.

Hugh Robinson's sixteen year old brother, John Robinson, confirmed that he lived with his brother and father at Longtown in Cumberland. They travelled the countryside with a horse and cart, selling their goods as they went along. He recalled how they had been staying in Bathgate for a few days and had fallen in with Charles MacEwan, an Irishman. A scuffle had broken out between his brother, Hugh, and the Irishman, which had evolved into a real fight in William Gray's lodging house. Whilst John had gone out for a moment, MacEwan had gotten on top of Hugh and when John returned he had tried unsuccessfully to drag MacEwan off his brother. MacEwan had then struck John and tried to bite him, but he had successfully escaped the mad Irishman's clutches. John described the awful state of his brother's nose and how ill he had been following the assault.

But what of Hugh Robinson? He was a licensed hawker in the hardware and jewellery line, living most of the time at Longtown, Cumberland. According to him, he had arrived in Bathgate on Friday 21 May and met MacEwan, a travelling bell hanger who said he was "*a Freemason in distress*". As Hugh Robinson was also a Freemason, he had given MacEwan five shillings and they had shared some drink that afternoon. When they were walking along a street in Bathgate, however, they had become quarrelsome and MacEwan had struck at him with an iron instrument. Robinson had evaded the blow and had gone back to his lodgings at William Gray's in South Bridge Street. MacEwan, however, would not leave him alone, and followed him there. MacEwan's wife also came to the house and so did Hugh's wife and brother. All of them were rather tipsy and MacEwan's wife had got up, struck Robinson's face, whilst taunting him and asking him if he would fight. Robinson admitted that he had pushed her back, whereupon she had fallen down on the floor. Robinson had also fallen backwards on the floor, striking his head against a tub. He had become quite insensible and upon regaining consciousness and trying to get up, he had discovered that there was an excruciating pain in his nose and part of the point of it had been bitten off.

What was the outcome of such a horrific assault by this insane Irishman? At the High Court in Edinburgh on 13 July 1824 Charles MacEwan was found guilty of the crime of assaulting, maiming and mutilating and was sentenced to a whipping at Glasgow, following which he was imprisoned for 12 months with hard labour. Hugh Robinson did not venture back to Bathgate!

National Records of Scotland reference AD14/24/35; JC26/458

JOHN TODD OF MAUCHLINE

CULPABLE HOMICIDE OUTSIDE BROXBURN – ON THE HIGH ROAD FROM EDINBURGH BETWEEN KILPUNT AND EAST MAINS FARMS ON 15 MARCH 1825

It was Tuesday, 15 March 1825. John Todd of Mauchline travelled the country in a two wheeled cart selling china and stoneware. According to his account, he had left Prestonpans on the day in question and was passing along by Colt Bridge (in the Roseburn area of Edinburgh) when he overtook George Halliday there. Todd had known Halliday for some time, as they dealt in the same line of wares and they had always been very friendly. They travelled along the road together until they arrived at Corstorphine, where they stopped to water their horses and take some refreshments. They then proceeded on their way to Glasgow, via Uphall. At the Golf Hall public house they stopped to take more refreshments and their wives went ahead of them while they sat and became somewhat intoxicated. Todd and Halliday's brothers were also at this establishment, as well as Halliday's fifteen year old son and his brother's thirteen year old son. Due to their intoxicated state, Todd and Halliday started acting foolishly and began to run races on the road, and although this had begun as a childish game, it resulted in Halliday becoming rather over-competitive. He decided that if Todd could beat him at racing, then he could beat Todd at fighting and so struck him down to the ground. Apparently the two young Halliday boys had joined the affray and started to throw stones at Todd, who had run for his life.

Afterwards, John Todd had encountered George Potter further along the road, informing him of events that had taken place between him and the Hallidays. The brothers of both men had gone on ahead to Broxburn, but whilst John Todd was talking to Potter, George Halliday had come running along with his son, continuing the quarrel. Todd told Halliday that he thought he and his son had been extremely nasty to him, to which Halliday retorted that he could be even nastier! Todd didn't want to quarrel any further, so had tried to fob off Halliday by saying he would fight with him the following day for a prize of five pounds. However Halliday was adamant that the fight should continue at this time for the prize of a bottle of whisky. He then threw off his coat, as did Todd, and they fought together in the middle of the main road. Todd told James Rae, Sheriff Substitute of Linlithgow, on 19 March that near the end of that fight he had struck Halliday on his body with his left hand, resulting in the latter falling into a ditch. He had then made a sort of run towards Halliday with his foot, but did not actually kick him. Matthew Todd, John's brother, had come back along the road towards them, along with William Halliday, George's brother, and they had raised him up in a sitting position, following which they had returned to Broxburn. Todd had later found out that George Halliday had been taken to Broxburn on a cart and died shortly afterwards, whereupon Todd had gone to see Halliday's widow, giving her five pounds towards the funeral costs. Halliday was subsequently buried in the churchyard of Uphall on 17 March.

Matthew Todd, when questioned, stated that he also lived at Mauchline with his brother, John, and described himself as an *"itinerant vendor of English china and stoneware"*. He and John travelled the country together and he concurred with John's story in that they had all met up at Colt Bridge, together with their wives and children. The Todds and Hallidays had always got on very well together and this event was out of character for both. He agreed that they had stopped at the Golf Hall public house about four miles outside Edinburgh and the men had taken some drink, whilst the women had gone on together with the carts. Apparently George Halliday and John Todd had taken rather too much liquor and had become very intoxicated, acting very foolishly by running races, but had subsequently quarrelled. Matthew had tried to stop them fighting, but had been hit himself in trying to do so. He had then gone on ahead quickly with Todd's brother, William, thinking that this would induce the two intoxicated individuals to follow them and forget their quarrel. It was just past Newbridge when he had passed by George Potter. Matthew had asked Potter to wait for his brother and bring him along to Broxburn with him, and rode further along the road, but he had subsequently heard a cry of *"murder"* from George Halliday's son behind him. George Halliday seemed to be sitting on his bottom by the side of the road, supported by his son. William Halliday carried his brother to the other side of the road to get some water and Matthew washed the man's face. George Halliday was alive at this time, but seemed incapable of speech. His breathing was very laboured and he was making a snoring noise. Matthew carried his brother on his back some way along the road towards Broxburn and was met by his sister in law, who was driving a cart. They had laid the unconscious victim on the cart and taken him along to Hugh Potter's house in Broxburn. Matthew heard that George Halliday had died at around eleven o'clock that evening. He confirmed that it had been dark when he had seen George Halliday by the side of the road in such a sorry condition. He also confirmed that he had attended the funeral on Thursday, 17 March at Uphall Churchyard.

When William Halliday, who lived in Hawick, gave his statement he confirmed that he was a travelling stoneware dealer and was often away from home for three to five weeks at a time. He concurred with the statement of Matthew Todd, saying that they were both sober on the afternoon in question, although George Halliday was somewhat intoxicated and John Todd was even more so.

George Halliday, son of the deceased, who lived in Lockerby or the parish of Dyfffsdale, Dumfriesshire, confirmed that he was fifteen years old on 22 January last. He concurred with the statements of Matthew Todd and William Halliday. He was perfectly sober on the day in question. He had seen John Todd strike his father on the side as he fell into a ditch and while his father was lying there Todd had thrown a blow or kicked his father's head, but he could not be absolutely certain what had actually happened. George had helped his father to sit up, upon which Todd had come at them, striking his father with his foot. He had also struck George Halliday junior on the shoulder, although he thought this blow had actually been aimed at his father's head. He had then shouted out "*murder!*" His uncle and Matthew Todd had come back to the spot where the fight had occurred and helped him. George Halliday had been to the churchyard of Uphall and seen the grave where his father had been interred, but the corpse had later been removed and taken into the church for identification. George completed his statement by saying that after the scuffle had broken out at Golf Hall, John Todd had kicked him twice, following which George had thrown a stone at him, striking him on the face.

George Potter was a sawyer in Broxburn, following his employment wherever he could get it. He had been employed at Kirkliston over the last six to eight months, but his family lived at Broxburn. He had left his work at Kirkliston at around six o'clock on the evening in question, having travelled about six miles along the high road from Edinburgh to Glasgow by Uphall and Airdrie. He had seen two men looking for another two who were coming up behind them. One of these men had asked him if he had seen anyone on the road, but as he had just come off a small country lane, he replied in the negative. He recognised one of these men as a china and stoneware seller that he had seen around the area and he had since learned that his name was Matthew Todd. Todd had asked Potter if he would take care of his inebriated brother, who had now made his appearance about one hundred yards away. Potter did not want to become involved, particularly if the other man was in a quarrelsome mood, but these two men had subsequently gone off in the direction of Broxburn. The brother who had been identified had then overtaken him and he seemed very drunk, his face being covered in blood. Another man appeared with his son and a fight ensued between the two men, which was apparently being carried out for the prize of a bottle of whisky. It was dark by this time and Potter had tried in vain to stop this drunken fighting, although John Todd's son did the opposite, goading his father and even instructing him which way to best aim his blows at Halliday. He witnessed George Halliday falling in the ditch and saw John Todd aim his foot towards him, although he could not confirm if it had actually struck him. The son of the man who had fallen went to his assistance, but before he could do so, Todd had flown towards Halliday again and seemed to kick him in the head. Potter did then try to prevent any further mischief occurring and was assisted by the first two men who had gone on the road to Broxburn. They told Potter to go to Broxburn to fetch the wives of the two fighting men, which he did.

Potter confirmed the exact location of the fight as being on the high road from Edinburgh, between the farms of Kilpunt on the south and East Mains of Broxburn on the north. The man who had fallen in the ditch was still alive when Potter had left the scene, although he had been unable to speak and was breathing with great difficulty. George Potter had then gone to the house of Hugh Potter in Broxburn that evening, about a half an hour after the injured man had been brought along in the cart. The victim had been in quite an insensible state, with his eyes shut and his mouth open, but it was not easy to see if he was actually breathing at this time. He had then heard that the man had died and he was asked to go along with Joseph Thomson and John Hardie to an ante room in the parish church of Uphall where he had identified the body as being the man who had fallen in the fight. Potter confirmed that John Todd had visited him in his own house on the Wednesday evening and had enquired very anxiously about the victim.

Joseph Thomson was a surgeon in Broxburn and he described that on the evening in question he had been sent for by Hugh Potter, requesting him to assist a person in his house who had suffered injury due to an earlier scuffle. He had been directed to this house by three men who were waiting for him. He had visited Potter's house at around eleven o'clock that evening and found a man lying in bed, with some women sitting round a fire in the same room. When he had examined the man, however, Mr Thomson found that he was quite dead and had been for about half an hour. The women were astounded to find out that the man had died and were naturally quite agitated and anxious. After examining the body, there were no external injuries to be found other than a slight mark on his nose, but his head was covered in mud. Following this, Thomson was asked to go to a room in the Church at Uphall to examine the body, which was now lying in a coffin. Also present at that time was George Potter and another man who knew the deceased. Thomson recalled that after the death of the victim, he had been visited by a man who had complained of headache and an injury which had apparently been inflicted by the deceased during a fight. He also confirmed that he could hardly remember the incident, due to the fact that he had been very drunk indeed. He had asked what would be done regarding the body of the deceased and said that if nothing more was said about the matter by Thomson, then he would be willing to pay for all expenses incurred, but if any further action was taken then he would be forced to go east to see Mr Jeffrey, advocate.

George Dick, Kirk Officer and grave digger of the parish of Uphall, confirmed that on Thursday, 17 March, the body of a man had been buried in the parish churchyard of Uphall. The deceased, he gathered, had been killed in a fight the day before, but Dick did not know his name. The Sheriff Substitute and Procurator Fiscal had later asked him to open the grave and the body (inside the coffin) was subsequently placed in a room in the church in order that they could see his face. The room was locked when they left. John Nimmo, a labourer in Uphall, concurred with this statement and said he had assisted in opening the grave, raising the coffin and unscrewing the lid. He had witnessed surgeons and others removing a cloth from the deceased's face and, as darkness approached, George Dick had been told to lock the room. John Hardie, clerk to Thomas Liston, Sheriff Clerk in Linlithgow, confirmed that he had also been present when the coffin was opened. James Boyd Fleming, surgeon at Linlithgow, had met the others in the church and witnessed the lid being taken off the coffin. He had not able to examine the body until it was identified. He and Mr Laing were unable to carry out the examination under candlelight, however, and this was postponed until next day. He confirmed that the lid had been put back, every person had been instructed to leave, and the coffin and body were left there, the door having been locked by the sexton. They had examined it next morning and found that death had been caused by suffusion of blood on the brain, which had been produced by a blow on the head or a fall on it. John Laing, surgeon in Linlithgow concurred completely.

What happened to John Todd? At his trial at Edinburgh High Court on 20 June 1825 he was found guilty of the crime of culpable homicide in terms of his own confession. He was carried from the bar to the Tolbooth of Edinburgh, subsequently transmitted to the tollbooth of Linlithgow and detained there for 3 months. He was then set free, but the Hallidays and Todds would always have that event to marr their friendship.

National Records of Scotland reference AD14/25/43; JC26/1825/256

JAMES BARTHOLOMEW, WILLIAM SOMMERVILLE, JOHN MEIKLE AND JAMES WATSON

FURIOUS DRIVING OF CARTS ALONG THE KING'S HIGHWAY TO THE TERROR OF THE SERVANTS OF JOHN MOWBRAY ESQ OF HARTWOOD, WEST CALDER 14 JULY 1825

It was on Thursday, 14 July 1825 when the incident of the furious driving of carts along the King's highway occurred on the Edinburgh to Glasgow (by Mid Calder) road, at the Addiston or Kiershill Toll Bar, near Ratho.

Several carters, some from West Lothian, were accused of this crime to the danger of others, who were driving peaceably. They were James Bartholomew who lived with his father, Thomas Bartholomew, farmer at Leyden, Kirknewton, William Sommerville in the employment of George Ford, farmer at Uphall, lately living at Milkhouses, Uphall, John Meikle living at the house of James Millar, milk dealer and cow feeder, Livingston Mill, Livingston, and James Watson, servant to Robert Cross, farmer at Corston, Kirknewton.

William Finlay was a farm servant employed by John Mobray Esq, Writer to the Signet, whose country house was Hartwood Lodge in West Calder. Finlay had been instructed by Mr Mowbray to go to his Edinburgh residence to collect some furniture and bring it back to Hartwood. He had left Edinburgh in a horse drawn cart at around eleven o'clock on the morning in question and behind him was another horse and a cart containing the furniture and upon which rode three of the Mowbray female servants. The rearmost cart was loose, in that the horse's halter was not tied to the first cart. Both of these horses were quiet and docile beasts, according to William's statement. The servants passed a peaceful and enjoyable journey until they arrived at Kiershill Toll, where nine horses and carts were standing by the toll bar. There were empty milk containers on the carts, but nobody was present. According to William, when he was about two hundred to three hundred yards past the toll, some of these carts had ridden up to his. As his attention was fixed on the horse and cart behind him, however, he was unable to specify exactly how many carts there were. The horses were galloping; the carters – some of whom were standing on the carts– were cracking their whips and creating a deafening noise. One of the carts had passed his, closely followed by others, and before he knew what was happening, the rearmost cart was overturned to the near side among a pile of stones. He was actually knocked down, either by the horse or the cart, and when he got up he had seen the carters galloping ahead. About a hundred yards up the road some of them had stopped and rode back, seeing that an accident had occurred.

Ann Knight, one of the servant girls, was found underneath the cart and the other two women were lying at the side of the road, having been thrown off. William was bruised on his legs and thighs, his face was cut, his breeches torn and his pocket watch broken. Elizabeth Brown had a broken leg and she had to be carried to a neighbouring house for treatment. Barbara and Ann Knight were also bruised, due to luggage falling on them. Much of the furniture was broken and the cart itself was wrecked. The poor mare was cut on the haunch and knee. When eight carters were shown to him, William was only able to identify three of them, namely William Henderson, John Meikle and William Sommerville – and these were the carters who had galloped up the road. They had appeared a little intoxicated, whilst William confirmed that he himself had only drunk a tumbler full of porter prior to leaving Edinburgh.

Hartwood House

Barbara Knight concurred generally with William's statement, although she was able to confirm that there were actually four horses and carts which had ridden up to them at full gallop. The noise they had made was thunderous, not only due to the cracking whips, but because the empty milk containers had been rattling about madly. The road was covered in dust and the Mowbray horses had taken fright at the noise. Finlay had tried to get hold of the horse behind when the carts were opposite to his in the road, but the rearmost cart had been quickly overturned, coming against a pile of stones at the side of the road. Barbara said that all the girls had been thrown out of the cart and her sister was very much injured. She had been so afraid and so taken up with helping her sister that she was unable to identify those responsible. A crowd had gathered and helped with the overturned cart and William Bryce, a weaver at Brucehill, was in one of the four carts which came abreast of theirs. He did, at least, come out of his cart to help them all after the incident had occurred.

Ann Knight concurred with Barbara's statement. She had been seated at the fore part of the cart at the off side, with her face towards the horse. Her sister had been next to her with her back to the horse and Elizabeth had been sitting on the near side facing the horse. When they were passing the six mile stone from Edinburgh, she had heard the sound of galloping horses. One cart had passed them and another three had come up abreast of them in a race. The lads were using their whips and one of the carts had actually struck theirs, causing it to overturn. The poor horses had been terrified. She had ended up under the cart, the three carts with drivers having galloped ahead. She was assisted by a man named Bryce, but she was still bruised and had been confined to bed because of her injuries. The incident had happened so quickly that she was unable to identify the perpetrators of the crime.

James Erskine, tacksman of Kiershill Toll Bar, stated that he had seen two carts loaded with furniture bound for Mr Mowbray's residence on the day in question. Three women had been on the rear cart. At this time around eight or nine carters had been in the Toll Bar with a lad named Bryce and they had been drinking porter and whisky. He could recognise them again, but did not know their names. They had all left together shortly after the Mowbray carts had passed by, but he had not seen what had happened. He had heard later that one of Mr Mowbray's carts had been overturned about a quarter of a mile from the Toll bar so had gone along to help. Some of the carters had been heard to say that the accident had been caused by Mr Mowbray's cart running off the road when the others were passing.

William Bryce confirmed that he lived at Brucehill, West Calder. He had left Edinburgh at around eleven o'clock on the morning of 14 July and a little way past the town he had met up with three or more carts containing empty milk barrels. He had asked for a lift and David Nisbet, a carter, took him and they had all gone onto Kiershill, where they had drunk porter and whisky at the toll bar. They had seen the two carts going past with the furniture. He had gone into Nisbet's cart again and they had apparently *walked* past the two Mowbray carts. However, minutes later three other carts had come galloping along at full speed. He had heard the noise and seen the Mowbray cart being overturned and the women being thrown out. Chaos ensued, with furniture falling and women screaming. He was unable to say, however, exactly what had made the cart overturn.

Archibald Gibb, a carter living at the Latch, Kirknewton, stated that he had been in Edinburgh on Thursday, 14 July with his horse and cart, selling milk. He had left at around eleven o'clock in the morning with his empty casks and he had joined another seven carters on the road. He named the others as James Watson, James Bartholomew, William Sommerville, David Nisbet and William Henderson. They had been sober at the time and had ridden along steadily until they came to Addiston Toll, where they had drunk four bolls of porter and half a mutchkin of whisky. He confirmed that Sommerville, Meikle, Wardlaw and Nisbet had gone away first, but he could not have said if they walked their horses or trotted. When he rode along behind them he had seen the overturned cart and heard a woman crying that her leg had been hurt. A crowd had gathered at the scene, some of whom had assisted.

Gibb's version of events was that the man in charge of the first cart had not blamed any of the carters for the accident and thought that a wheel had struck a pile of stones by the road, making it overturn. He said that he had not witnessed any of the carters cracking their whips at all.

David Nisbet, who worked for his father, Alexander Nisbet, a farmer at Norton of Kirknewton, made a statement saying that it was actually James Watson and James Bartholomew who had galloped past the Mowbray carts. The Mowbray horses had taken fright and he had then galloped off in his cart. He had lost sight of them at a turn in the road, but had heard a mighty commotion and had returned to see the overturned cart and the women and horse lying on the road. He had not witnessed any of the carts coming up against the Mowbray carts, but thought it was merely the noise of the galloping horses which had frightened their horses. He had also seen the track of a cartwheel beside the heap of stones and suspected that to be the cause of the accident.

Peter Wardlaw, servant of William Boag, farmer at Livingston Broom, confirmed that he had gone to Addiston Toll bar and drunk with the others. He said that they were, however, perfectly sober. He could only say that he himself was trotting his horse, although Nisbet had been galloping. He did not see any carts touching Mowbray's, but thought that the wheel may have come up against the cairn of stones on the road, causing the accident.

William Henderson said that he thought it improbable for a cart with empty barrels to overturn a loaded cart such as the one in question. He also said that he had found a lynch pin about five yards to the west of the place where the cart was upset and he had left the pin with James Houston, a wheelwright, who he afterwards understood had then given it to Bartholomew.

Mid Calder born James Bartholomew, carter at Leyden in Kirknewton, stated that he had driven his empty milk cart from Edinburgh at about half past ten in the morning of the day in question. James Watson was with him driving his own cart and they went on to Addiston Toll Bar where they had taken a drink. There were some other milk carters there including John Meikle, William Sommerville, David Nisbet, Archibald Gibb and William Henderson and they all had drunk a half mutchkin of whisky and four bottles porter, but were supposedly quite sober. Sommerville had driven off first, followed by some others, but none of the carts were driving abreast. They were driving very quietly, according to him, when they passed the other two carts with the women and furniture on them, but he stated that his own horse was a young one, prone to taking fright when passing highly loaded carts. Needless to say the horse had taken fright, gone off at a hard pace and he had unsuccessfully tried to rein him in. He did not witness any of the other carts going at a pace and could not say what had caused the accident. He had reached Burn Wynd and noticed the lynch pin was missing from the fore wheel of his cart. It was brought to him subsequently by William Henderson, who informed him that it had been found near the place where the cart had been upset.

William Sommerville of West Calder worked for George Ford of Uphall and he had left early from Milkhouses with milk for the Leith Market on the 14th. He had sold all of his milk and returned home on his cart at a walking pace, with twelve empty milk barrels, via Broughton and along Princes Street, then out by the old Glasgow Road till he came to Addiston Toll Bar. He intimated that he may have taken a glass of ale at his master's brother's house at Leith, but although he had met the others in the Toll House, he had nothing to drink there with them. He said that he had merely trotted past the two Mowbray carts, because it was *"against the rules"* for two carts to drive abreast. Behind him were James Bartholomew and James Watson. The noise from behind had made his horse go at a trot and although he had tried to rein him in, the rein actually gave way and the horse had set off at a gallop. He did not see any others galloping, but noticed that the second Mowbray horse was not tied to the first cart. His denied that his cart had touched either of these.

John Meikle of Linlithgow lived at Livingston Mill with James Meikle, the miller, there. He said that had driven his milk cart to Edinburgh and returned to Kiershill at around ten o'clock in the morning. He fell in with the other carters at the Toll House and they had shared around four or five bottles of porter and half a mutchkin of whisky – but they were nevertheless sober. He confirmed that Bryce had gone into Nisbet's cart and then his horse had gone at a hard trot after the other three carts had galloped off. He denied that any were abreast, however, or that any carters had been standing in their carts. He had seen the overturned cart and the woman with the broken leg being conveyed to Mr Stewart, the surgeon, but he had not actually seen the cart being overthrown. As far as he had heard, Mowbray's horse in the rearmost cart was easily frightened and often ran away. He had been of the opinion that the carts passing may have startled the beast, with the cart being overturned by the pile of stones. He would never be persuaded that an empty cart could overturn a full one.

Finally James Watson, farm servant to Robert Cross, farmer at Corston, Kirknewton, said that he had sold all of his barrels of milk in Edinburgh and returned home via the Toll House. His version of events was basically the same as Meikle's.

A report from the Royal Infirmary in Edinburgh dated 18 August 1825 stated that twenty six year old Elizabeth Brown was admitted as a patient on 14 July. Her father was described as being the deceased David Brown, servant to a gentleman in Perthshire. The incident leading to her injuries was described in detail, following which she had been taken to Mr Mowbray's house in Edinburgh and then onto the Infirmary. She had been bled in Mr Stewart's house and her leg tied up. She named William Sommerville as the carter whose cart came up against Mr Mowbray's cart. She believed that a Peter Wardlaw had driven the first cart. On the day the report was written she had stated that she felt slightly better. She had received a simple fracture of the left fibula a little below the middle, which had produced swelling of the soft parts of the leg. She had also sustained a contusion in the dorsal vertebrae. The injuries were considered to be severe. After a few days of her being admitted there had been such an inflammation of the soft part surrounding the fracture that it had been suspected it might become gangrenous. It was reported that the patient, after discharge, would *"enjoy as much use of her limb as previous to the accident"* and this was signed by G A Gordon.

The items which were listed as being badly damaged were the stand of a piano, a small bed, a writing desk, three washing tubs, a small trunk, a water pail, two bottles of blacking, three bandboxes, two bonnets and a shawl, a hay cart, ropes, a cart saddle and blinders, a pair of pantaloons and a silver watch. Also, the mare was said to be cut on its head, haunch and knee.

William Finlay wrote a letter to John Mowbray from Hartwood on 15 November 1825. He advised that Saturday, 5 November had been a wet day and he had gone to the coals with three carts. When coming home somebody had fired a gun on the same side of the road and a woman had come past with an umbrella, both of which had startled the colt. He had galloped past the other two carts and the coals had fallen out. This incident had occurred west of Longford and the colt had been stopped by James Douglas and two other men. Finlay had been quick to point out that this was the colt **- not one of the horses which had been in Edinburgh in the summer** when the family had come out. He was writing to tell Mr Mowbray that two businessmen had been out to Hartwood that day enquiring anxiously what had occurred on the day the cart was overturned and wanting to know which particular horse had gone forward. He clarified to Mr Mowbray that it was the four year old colt which had bolted in November, but in July it had been the two mares which had been pulling the furniture, the grey mare being the one leading the cart which had overturned. He advised that none of the *"delinquent*s" had been fined yet and one had absconded.

What was the outcome of this incident?

The trial took place at the High Court Edinburgh on 21 November 1825. James Bartholomew, William Sommerville and James Watson were found guilty, sentenced to 12 months imprisonment and put on probation for 5 years, with a £30 penalty. John Meikle, although named in the indictment, had no case brought against him.

National Records of Scotland reference JC26/1825/271; AD14/25/36

JOHN RUSSELL

POACHING AT MOSS PLANTING, TORPHICHEN 10 JANUARY 1827

It was Wednesday, 10 January 1827 at the Wallhouse Estate, Torphichen. Alexander Kirkpatrick was a gardener to William Downe Gillon Esq of Wallhouse and he lived at the gate of the estate, near to Collieside farm steading at Torphichen. Having become suspicious that game was being poached by someone connected with the Westfield Wool Mill on the west extremity of Wallhouse, he had gone out to the fields in that direction with David Lin, Mr Gillon's gamekeeper, on the evening in question at about ten o'clock. On arriving at the mill, a man's footprints and pawmark's of a dog were immediately visible in the snow. Kirkpatrick and Lin had followed the track towards the Kenning Hills, but they had subsequently lost sight of the footsteps. Continuing along the Armadale Road, Kirkpatrick had gone into the corner of the Moss Planting where he had caught sight of a man who was crossing the adjoining field towards the Moss, by way of a dry stone dyke separating Crawhill from Westfield, carrying a gun. Having noticed Kirkpatrick, however, this individual had quickly changed course and walked north to the side of the Moss Planting, whereupon he had been lost to sight.

Determined to identify the culprit, Kirkpatrick and Lin had hidden under a whin bush about two hundred yards from the house at the mill. After waiting there patiently for about an hour in the freezing cold, the same person had appeared from Crawhill direction. Kirkpatrick had rushed to the front of the mill house and Lin to the back, so that the man could not gain entry, but he had eluded them by running into an outhouse and bolting the door behind him. Then two women had appeared at the door of the house, asking what Kirkpatrick and Lin were doing there and on being advised of the reason, the women had said that it was impossible for a man to be in that outhouse, as the door had been locked fast earlier. They had then vehemently refused to give the men either a key or a light in order to examine the premises fully. Kirkpatrick had left Lin guarding the outhouse, and had hurried immediately to Thomas Anderson's house at Westfield. Anderson and another two men had returned to the mill house with him and this was around midnight. Once again the key for the outhouse had been requested, but the women continued to refuse, so that Lin had had no alternative but to ram the door in with his foot. Without a light, however, it had been quite impossible to see inside. One of the Westfield men had subsequently obtained a lighted candle and a thorough search could then be undertaken, the result of which was that the culprit had been located hiding amongst some peats in a small loft.

This person – John Russell, a workman at Westfield Wool Mill - had admitted that he had been the man in the field, and that he had thrown his gun into another old outbuilding prior to hiding in the barn. Russell was taken off to Wallhouse after being apprehended and Kirkpatrick had gone home to fetch his constable's baton. On returning to Wallhouse, however, he had found three men, one of whom was

William Liddell, Russell's master – who had previously been described as being away from home. Why these three men were there and what their intentions were was never discovered. They had no sticks with them, however, and they did not appear to be intent on any mischief.

David Lin – who lived at the south east gate of Wallhouse, on the west side of the road leading from Torphichen to Bathgate, a little south of the farm steading of Slackend - concurred with Kirkpatrick's statement, other than that on separating from Kirkpatrick at the Kenning Hills he had not seen the man in question until he arrived at Westfield Mill. He had, however, witnessed him throwing his gun into an outhouse near the mill. Also, he had not seen the three men who had arrived at Wallhouse later, as he was guarding Russell in another room, but he *had* heard their various voices.

Andrew Stewart, who was a farm servant to Thomas Anderson, tenant at Westfield, said that Alexander Kirkpatrick had come to his master's house on the night in question at about half past eleven in the evening and wakened him and Alexander Down from their beds. Kirkpatrick had asked them to come with him to William Liddell's wool mill to assist him in apprehending an armed man who had been out on the Wallhouse estate. Whilst David Lin was guarding the byre, Stewart and Down had gone to the mill house requesting the key and a light, but they had been refused. Down had then gone all the way back to his master's house at Westfield and returned with the lighted candle. He had seen Lin kicking open the byre door where John Russell, who admitted that he had "*gotten into a sad scrape*", was found. On the way to Wallhouse Russell had admitted that he owned the gun. Alexander Down concurred fully with Stewart's statement.

When John Russell made his statement on 11 January 1827 he confirmed that he had worked at the Westfield Mill for two years. The previous evening his master had been away from home, so he had decided to go out at about nine o'clock to "**take a shot**". He had walked through the Wallhouse estate towards what were known as the Kenning Hills. At this location, however, he had seen a man coming towards him, which had induced him to quickly change direction and go to the Moss Planting, where he had lain down and hidden for about an hour. Taking an indirect route to avoid detection, he had gone home by Crawhill. About thirty yards from the mill he had seen two men in hot pursuit of him. Throwing his gun into an outhouse, he had hidden in an old byre, locking the door fast behind him. Lin and some other men had discovered him after kicking the door open, however, and he had been taken back to Wallhouse. He *did* admit that he had gone out to kill "***any beast he could find***" that night, although he was fully aware that this was illegal, and said that he was now very sorry for what had occurred. (*It was against the law for a person to be found between the hours of six pm and seven am armed with a gun, cross bow, firearm, bludgeon or other offensive weapon and the sentence for those convicted of such a crime could be as serious as being transported for seven years!*)

What happened to John Russell? Fortunately his sentence was not too severe. He was found guilty of the crime of poaching in terms of his own confession and imprisoned in the Tolbooth of Linlithgow for two months.

National Records of Scotland reference AD14/27/70

Note: William Downe Gillon Esquire of Wallhouse and Hurstmonceaux, Sussex, was a landed and West India proprietor. Born on 31 August 1801 - the only son of Lieutenant Colonel Andrew Gillon and Mary Ann Hall (daughter of William Hall of Dorsetshire), he subsequently married Miss Ellen-Eliza Scott in 1820, by whom he had two sons and three daughters.

The Wallhouse estate in Torphichen had been owned by his ancestors for several centuries.

WILLIAM AND JOHN BRAIDWOOD

PASSING COUNTERFEIT MONEY AT BATHGATE
31 DECEMBER 1829 – 13 JANUARY 1830

It was around midnight on 13 January 1830 when James Johnston and David Alexander, officers of the Burgh Court of Bathgate, had gone to apprehend two individuals who were suspected of passing over counterfeit silver sixpences to shop owners in Bathgate. On that evening John and William Braidwood were found and arrested in William Alexander's lodging house at Mid Street. A considerable quantity of counterfeit coins, some of which were in an unfinished state, and some of which were ready for circulation, were also located.

The Braidwoods were accused of trying to pass these coins over on 31 December 1829 at Alexander Arthur's grocery shop at Main Street, Bathgate for a mutchkin of whisky, on 6 January 1830 to Margaret Russell or Arthur for the same thing, on 13 January 1830 at Margaret Brock's shop at Jarvey Street for a penny roll (receiving five pence in change) and on 10 January 1830 at Archibald Marshall's house for a dram of whisky.

Thomas Walker, butcher in Bathgate, had accompanied the officers along with William Roberts and had seen them apprehending the suspects and taking the counterfeit money which was lying by the mantelpiece in their room. The suspects had actually admitted that they had made these coins themselves. William Roberts, also a butcher in Bathgate, concurred with Walker's statement. He also said that he had been in Archibald Marshall's shop on the evening of 10 January when he had seen the two men, with the one of the fairer complexion (William) offering a sixpence to Mr Marshall for whisky, after which he had been challenged.

On the evening of the arrest, James Johnston, Sheriff Officer, had been given a spoon with some fused ore on it, appearing as though it had been in the fire, by Mrs Alexander, who had found it under the bed. On searching the Braidwoods, Mr Johnston had found two tin boxes, a whetstone, a leather purse, a small quantity of tin, three shillings four pence of good copper money and two pieces of sandpaper – suspicious, to say the least!

John Braidwood was a twenty three year old mole catcher, formerly a weaver, born at Carstairs, but brought up in Lanark. He had been in the mole catching profession for the past three years, as had his twenty one year old brother, William. According to John, he had come to Bathgate a few days before to see some friends and they had lodged with Widow Clark. They had then moved on to William Alexander's house. Before they left Lanarkshire for Bathgate, however, they had been at Rosebank, east of Hamilton, where they had fallen into company with an individual named O'Neil in a public house on the Lanark Road there. The three had *"blethered"* (chatted) amicably and eventually O'Neil had taken out a silver sixpence, asking them if they thought it was "*good*". They were unsure as to its origins, but O'Neil had been persuasive when he had told them that if they were able to change it for coppers, he would give them half the money. They were successful with that transaction, and another coin had been changed and the proceeds shared again. It was not too long afterwards when O'Neil had showed them a pile of these sixpences, which were rough round the edges and still in an unfinished state, saying that he would make a bargain for them. A deal was struck, after which they had apparently never seen O'Neil again and they had left, bound for Bathgate. William Braidwood confirmed everything his brother related, but also described that O'Neil had instructed them on how to file down the edges of the coins to make them appear "*good*".

On the evening of 31 December – Hogmany – a customer had come into the shop of Alexander Arthur, a grocer and spirit dealer in Main Street, Bathgate, and he had asked for a half mutchkin of whisky. When Mr Arthur had given him this in a bottle, the young man had thrown down a silver sixpence in payment, but it had been immediately obvious that this was not a "*good*" one. This fair complexioned man – William Braidwood – had tried in vain to satisfy the grocer that it was indeed a legitimate coin, but Arthur had refused it and the whisky had been taken back. Arthur recalled that on the morning of Wednesday, 6 January he had been getting dressed at the top of the stairs when another young man had come to the door asking for the same thing (half mutchkin of whisky) from his wife. She had not looked particularly closely at the sixpence when it had been handed over, however, but the young man had rushed as fast as he could out of the shop – taking the whisky with him. Mr Arthur had sprinted around several streets trying to find him, but had been unsuccessful in his search. However, he did identify him at the Tolbooth of Linlithgow as being the darker complexioned of the two brothers – John.

Margaret Russell, Alexander Arthur's wife, concurred with her husband's statement, saying that she had not had enough time to "*challenge the buck*", as it was market day and the shop was very "*throng*" (busy). The coin had been put amongst other change in the till.

William Alexander, a weaver and lodging house keeper in Bathgate, identified the Braidwoods as being the two young men who had stayed at his house at the rate of two shillings per week until they were apprehended by the officers. He said that they had told him that they were mole catchers who could not work until the frosts melted and they were quiet and regular individuals, who caused him no trouble at all.

Margaret Brock of Jarvey Street recalled that a young man had come into the shop on the evening of Wednesday, 13 January, asking for a penny loaf. He had kept himself slightly hidden by the door, as though afraid that he might be seen properly and when he had passed over a sixpence for the bread, she had enquired if it was a good one. Having assured her it was, she had given him change in five copper pennies.

She could not identify his face, but his size and general appearance corresponded with that of William Braidwood.

Archibald Marshall, a weaver and public house keeper, stated that on Sunday, 10 January two young men had come in to his establishment asking for a dram (of whisky) and he had taken them upstairs and given them a gill. They had sat there for around a half an hour and had come back downstairs with the candle and a sixpence. He had challenged them about it and was given five copper pennies instead for payment of the whisky. He was able to identify William Braidwood.

Alexander Bryson, a grocer and spirit dealer, confirmed that the prisoners had been in his shop several times, but not together, and they had generally bought half an ounce of tobacco, paying for it with a sixpence, and getting change of fourpence and a halfpenny in copper. He had not even noticed that the coins were counterfeit. His daughter, Katherine, could recall the Braidwoods being in her father's shop over the space of a fortnight, when they had purchased tobacco, but she could not say how they had paid for it.

What happened to the Braidwoods when they were tried at the High Court, Edinburgh on 15 March 1830? They were found guilty of uttering base coin and sentenced to transportation for seven years, setting off for New South Wales on 3 September 1830.

National Records of Scotland reference AD14/30/290; JC26/1830/381

JAMES BROWN

ASSAULT AT BARGABER BRIDGE, EAST WHITBURN 16 APRIL 1831

It was Saturday, 16 April 1831. There are different stories as to what actually happened up on the high road leading from East Whitburn to Bathgate, about three quarters of a mile to the north of East Whitburn. However, James Brown was taken prisoner at Linlithgow Tolbooth and subsequently appeared at the High Court in Edinburgh on 15 July 1831 after being accused of attacking and assaulting Peter Love, a crockery ware dealer, and robbing him of a silver watch, two pounds twelve shillings and one or more stoneware basins.

James Brown was a twenty four year old journeyman blacksmith, son of William Brown, weaver in Whitburn. According to Brown's story, and his first statement on 18 April, at around ten o'clock on the morning in question he was at West Whitburn where he met Peter Love. Love was always referred to as the "*pig man*", the old term for someone who sold pottery ware around the local towns. Apparently, according to Brown, Peter Love had mistaken him for another individual by the name of Leishman and they had started chatting. Mr Love had subsequently asked Brown to go along to a pub with him and take a dram there. After about twenty minutes Brown had left and met up with two of his friends – Peter Espie and James Steel - who were moulders at Shotts Iron Works, where Brown had worked at one time. Brown had ambled along with them for a couple of miles to the north of Bathgate and later admitted that they had taken a good deal of liquor there together. On returning home, Brown described how he had encountered Peter Love again, as the latter was going along with his donkey and cart, with three little boys running alongside it. Love had appeared tipsy and requested that Brown – apparently by now his "*old friend*" – come along the road and have another dram with him.

The pair had then gone on to Mr Forsyth's kitchen at East Whitburn, where they had partaken of yet more alcohol, but Mrs Forsyth had told Brown to take the very tipsy Love out of her house, as he was getting quite bothersome. This he did, and he had helped him along the road about a mile, past Torbane's house, near to what was commonly known as the Bargaber Bridge, outside East Whitburn. Brown said that he had subsequently left Love at about half past seven, returning to West Whitburn where his brother, David, lived. James Brown was in the habit of sleeping at his brother's house, but took his meals at his father's house, which was further along the road. He said he had been alone at the time and he had no quarrel with Love and certainly did not attack him.

On 25 April James Brown made some modifications to his previous statement. He mentioned that when he was going along to Bargaber Bridge with Love he had, because he was a bit tipsy himself, taken one of the earthenware basins from Love's cart, stuck it on his head, and walked along the road like that just in fun. He had put it back into Love's cart afterwards. He had forgotten to say that before going back to his brother's house he had visited Janet Ayton at West Whitburn. Dusk was beginning to fall and his visit lasted about an hour. During that time Mrs Ayton's daughter, Margaret Thorn, was there, as were Agnes and Helen Wood. He had been shown an earthenware basin when giving his statement, but denied that he had left this at Mrs Ayton's house or had given it to her or to her daughter. He recalled that he had met a man by the name of Bishop, who was an apprentice to Robert Taylor, a baker in West Whitburn, when he left Mrs Ayton's house, as Bishop was going north to water his horse.

He made yet another statement on 2 May, however, in which he expanded the story further by saying he had drunk the first dram with Peter Love at Alexander Addie's pub in West Whitburn. He had the second lot of liquor with Peter Espie and James Steel at a pub in Bathgate kept by a man called Arthur, a weaver. He reiterated that he had only arrived at Mrs Ayton's house half an hour after leaving Love on the road. He remembered that he had accompanied Janet Ayton's daughter and the two Wood girls to the well and, when he got back to Mrs Ayton's, two of his friends – Robert Dickson and Robert White – were there at the time. He did not remember mentioning to any of them that he had been with Peter Love earlier.

What was Peter Love's story? He was a crockery ware dealer who had lived at Torphichen for the past three years. He travelled the country selling his wares, although he did not actually have a licence to do so. He had met up with James Brown at Forsyth's pub in West Whitburn and had only drunk a couple of drams with him there. In fact, he had only drunk three drams in the whole day, as far as he remembered. When he was having a drink with James Brown, the latter had told him his name was George Leishman and that he was a weaver at Condorrat. Not only that, but he was related to Mr Love's wife in a distant way. He was friendly and talkative and Brown thought he was a very pleasant young fellow. He said that afterwards, when going along the road to Bathgate with Brown, a man had passed by them without speaking. Then two other men – who he had later indentified and who were known to the constable in the neighbourhood – had jumped out from behind a wall and together with Brown had attacked him and robbed him of money and a watch at about seven or eight o'clock on the evening in question. He did not know the manufacturer of his watch, but said that it did have an easily identifiable mark on it. He also said that he would be able to identify the other two men if requested to do so. One of them was tall, about twenty five or twenty six years old, with a black patch on his left cheek under his eye and the other man had a terrible stutter.

Apparently Brown had struck Love on the temple after seizing him by the breast. A terrified Love had then protested, asking him what on earth he was doing. Love had struck him back, but this was when the other two individuals had appeared and he had known a moment of hope, thinking that they were about to come to his assistance. The opposite was the case, however, and one of them actually took a weapon like a small dirk out of his pocket, telling him to be quiet, but his accomplice had cautioned him and told him not to use this knife on Love. The man with the knife proceeded to cut the poor donkey with the weapon. The tall man grabbed Love by the cravat and nearly choked him, threw him to the ground and kicked him. Brown then seized Love by the waistband of his pantaloons, pulled him up by the ears and, with the assistance of the others, threw the poor man into the cart. They had stripped off his braces so that when he tried to get up he fell back down again, which is when he noticed that his watch and money had been stolen.

He had then headed southwards crying *"murder and robbery"*, whereupon the three came back and attacked him again until he was almost unconscious. He was able to get to Wood's farm, however, and the farmer took him to the constable's house. He had been informed that one of the men was David Brown and the other one was Thomas White. The bowl which had been on James Brown's head was quite broken now and apparently Brown had taken another patterned one away with him.

There were, of course, others who were able to give their side of events. What, for instance, did David Brown and Thomas White have to say about the matter?

David Brown was, of course, the brother of James Brown. He was a weaver to trade, but he related that on the day in question he was working to clear a piece of land at Townhead for potato planting along with his father. They completed the work at about seven o'clock that evening and had come down from the loan from the south of West Whitburn about fifteen minutes later. They had been carrying out that work for Mr Nokes, the innkeeper, using his own wheelbarrow. David left the barrow in Mr Nokes' yard and went to his father's house for supper. He saw Thomas White in passing, and conversed with him for a couple of minutes. It was gloaming when he returned to his own home – at around eight o'clock in the evening– and sometime later he went to the public house kept by John Wilson in Whitburn. He met William Martin, Robert Dickson and Robert White there and only sat ten minutes with them, having only a small amount of liquor, before proceeding to Alex Addie's public house, where he had taken a gill. When he left Addie's, he went home and found Thomas White sitting there chatting to his wife, along with Jean Martin and Christian Walker. It was quarter past nine by this time. David stated that he saw his brother, James, about breakfast time on that day when he was shaving. He then heard him coming in later on Saturday night after he had gone to bed and on asking him what the time was, was told it was eleven o'clock. It would have been impossible for him to say whether James was sober at the time, since he was almost asleep when he heard his brother coming in.

Thomas White was also a weaver and he lived with his mother, Jean Russell, widow of Thomas White senior, weaver in West Whitburn. On the day in question he had been working at his loom and had stopped at around half past one in the afternoon. He had subsequently gone walking with a friend and workmate, William Bell, until late. He then returned to his mother's house and after he had gone to bed his brother, Robert, came home. He confirmed that he had seen David Brown in the street at about seven o'clock in the evening and then later at David's house at around quarter to nine. William Bell was there at the time, as well as two girls named Martin and Walker. After he had gone into David Brown's house, James Brown came in about ten minutes later. White stayed there until quarter to eleven, as did the girls, and William Bell left about an hour before that. He confirmed that he had seen James Brown at breakfast time on the day, but did not see him afterwards. He said he had never drunk at all that evening and was quite sober. He also stated that he had been afflicted with a **terrible stutter in his speech** since he was an infant, and this always got worse when he was agitated.

Other people had their versions of events. Kenneth Sutherland, a weaver who lived with his mother, Elizabeth Robertson, widow, in East Whitburn, was going to Bathgate on the evening in question at about eight o'clock - just as the light was beginning to fade. He passed James Brown and Peter Love walking along the road together behind Love's donkey and cart. They appeared to be rather tipsy. Brown was holding Love by the breast and Love held Brown by the arm and they seemed to be in excellent humour. In fact, Brown had one of the earthenware basins belonging to Love on his head and was jumping about foolishly. Love, however, seemed anxious to get the basin back on his cart. Sutherland could not hear the exact words which were being said, as he was a bit dull of hearing. When he was returning from Bathgate at about ten o'clock that evening he noticed the broken pieces of the basin lying on the road beside Bargaber Bridge, but saw no sign of either of the two individuals. He did hear the next morning that the pair had met Robert Aikman of East Whitburn on the road and that Love had been robbed at some point.

What of the time spent at the public houses by Love and Brown? Jean Forsyth, who was the wife of Thomas Forsyth, the innkeeper at East Whitburn, said that James Brown came into the public house at about six o'clock that evening in the company of a man who had been selling his crockery ware around the village. They proceeded to drink two gills of whisky, but Mrs Forsyth advised her girls – Jane, Margaret and Elizabeth - to give them no more. On going outside to see the coaches which were changing horses, however, one of the girls had stupidly given them a third gill. Brown did not seem to be in the least affected by the drink, but the other man seemed a bit tipsy, although not inebriated at this stage. They requested a fourth drink, but at this point Mrs Forsyth thought it best to advise the pig man to go home to his lodgings, and to take away his horse and cart which had been standing at her door for far too long! The two men had left her house at around seven o'clock and they seemed to be on friendly enough terms. Her girls had advised her that Love seemed to have plenty of money with him and had paid for the drinks, whereas Brown had paid nothing. Love had also bought a pound of meal for his donkey and this had been fed to it in some cold water.

James Watt was a mason and he was also one of the Justices of Peace constables in the district. He had returned from work and seen the pig man's donkey and cart at the front of the door of the vintner, Thomas Forsyth, at around eight o'clock that evening. He also saw James Brown and Peter Love walking to the west of the village. He was curious to see what was going on, which induced him to go outside. He then saw them turning north by the public house leading to Bathgate and he had remarked to his sister that the pig man was not in very good company. (The villainous Brown was notorious all over the countryside.) It was getting dark and he went to bed at around ten o'clock.

A knock came to the door and it was Love himself who stood there saying that he had been robbed by James Brown - assisted by two of his friends - about a mile north of Whitburn. He mentioned that one of these friends had a black patch under the left eye and the other had a speech impediment in the form of a stutter. He related how the man with the patch had drawn a dirk and was going to stab him, but the man with the stutter had stopped him. The pig man's mouth was bleeding, his clothes were dirty, his watch fob had been torn away and buttons from his trousers had also been ripped off. He was in a very agitated condition, all the while crying because of the loss of his money.

Mr Watt went to Robert Calder's house, as he was the other constable in Whitburn and they proceeded to Bathgate to inform Mr Smith, the writer there, what had happened. At this point Love related his story again, saying that he had left Forsyth's at approximately eight o'clock in the evening, leading his donkey by the hand. He had been drinking, but was not inebriated. Love had told Brown, who had been extremely friendly to him, where he had put his money.

There were so many versions of events that it was obviously very difficult for a jury to decide on the outcome.

What eventually happened to James Brown? After all the evidence was heard at this trial at the High Court in Edinburgh on 15 July 1831, it was found that the case was not proven. Who knows if the *"pig man"* ever came back that way again?

National Records of Scotland reference AD14/31/337; JC25/563-587; JC26/1831/310

DAVID MILLIKEN SCOTT - ALIAS DAVID MILLICAN or MILLIGAN
RETURNING FROM TRANSPORTATION – LINLITHGOW BRIDGE DECEMBER 1831

It was 4 May 1827 at Glasgow Circuit Court of Justiciary when David Milliken Scott, alias David Millican, was indicted for cattle stealing and, having been convicted of that crime, was sentenced to transportation for seven years. According to an act passed in the fifth year of the reign of Majesty King George the Fourth, Chapter 84 entitled "**An act for the transportation of offenders from Great Britain**", however, if he had been found at large within any part of his Majesty's dominions *afterwards*, without some lawful cause, before the expiration of the term of his transportation, he could have suffered death as a felon.

William Hart, clerk of George Salmond, writer in Glasgow, had been present when David Millican was convicted of cattle stealing in 1827 and he was now able to identify him as the same David Millican or David Milliken Scott. Millican had, however, escaped from the jail about month after his sentence was pronounced and Hart had seen him again in Stirling Jail about the beginning of April 1832. Hart described Milliken Scott as being a native of Whitburn, who was thirty eight years old, five feet four inches tall and stoutly built. He had grey eyes, dark brown hair, a round face with a pock-pitted, fresh complexion, and he had the scar of a burn on his right hand.

John Macdonald, Sherriff clerk depute of Lanarkshire, concurred with this statement. Angus McPherson, turnkey in the Jail of Glasgow, remembered Millican or Scott being imprisoned in that jail after receiving the sentence of transportation that May and that Millican had made his escape on 3 June 1827.

Richard Sowness, Sherriff Officer at Linlithgow, stated that around 23 December 1831 there had been strong reasons to suspect that David Milliken Scott, a labourer living at Linlithgow Bridge, had been stealing sheep at Stirling. Sowness had, therefore, gone to the market at Linlithgow Bridge to apprehend him. Scott had been committed to Linlithgow Jail until further details had been ascertained and then transmitted to Stirling. James Armour, Sheriff Officer at Linlithgow, had been present at the Market Cross at Linlithgow when Milliken Scott had been taken into custody and also when he had been taken to Stirling. He had subsequently heard about the jail being broken out of, with a number of prisoners escaping. Armour had been sent to Scott's former residence to search for him and had eventually found him hiding at the back court behind the house of Edward Hogg, a publican at Linlithgow Bridge.

James McArthur, a blacksmith who lived at Linlithgow, stated that his mother, Mrs Margaret McArthur, rented some houses at Linlithgow Bridge. After the harvest in

1830 – maybe October – David Milliken Scott, labourer, and a woman named Elizabeth Paterson had come to Mrs McArthur asking if they could rent one of her residences. The couple had started living there as man and wife a month later and then, around Christmas time that year, they had been arrested for sheep stealing and were incarcerated at Linlithgow Jail. The poor woman, it was understood, had then committed suicide, and the man had been sent to Stirling Jail. However, around three weeks later, Milliken Scott had apparently returned to Linlithgow Bridge. Mrs McArthur concurred fully with her son's statement, further explaining that she had seen neither of the two prisoners prior to them renting her house.

On 19 December 1831 sixty year old William Boyd said that he had bought a sheepskin for fourteen pence from a woman who said she originated from Uphall district. Robert Fergie, a butcher at Causeway End, Linlithgow, had passed by Boyd's house about five minutes later and instantly recognised the sheepskin there as one of his own by the tar mark on it. This particular sheep had apparently gone missing from Manuel Haugh, which was situated to the west of Linlithgow and near to Muiravonside. On the following Friday, the same woman had come to him, offering another sheepskin for sale, and Boyd had paid her two shillings for it. The first skin had been rather raggedy, with a piece missing around the neck and other parts and it was obvious that it had not been cut by a skinner, flesher or tradesman. Boyd had immediately gone to the market and advised Fergie about the matter, but Fergie could not identify this sheepskin as being his.

Robert Fergie, a butcher living at Causwayend near Muiravonside, said that around December 1831 he had about fifty *"wedders"* (*castrated male sheep*) and ewes grazing at Manuel Haugh, Muiravonside and during that month two wedders and one ewe had been stolen from there. The wedders had all been marked on the top of the shoulder with tar, but he was unsure about the ewes. He had called in on William Boyd one Monday during the month of December, when returning from Borrowstouness, and had casually asked him if he had bought any sheepskins from strangers lately. Strangely enough, he was told, Boyd had actually bought one only a half hour before from a stranger woman. On Fergie confirming it as one of his own, Boyd had left the house immediately and tried to find the woman. The following Friday, Fergie had been at the market place of Linlithgow selling butcher meat, when Boyd had told him that the same woman had been at his house with *yet another* sheepskin. However, because all of his sheep were black-faced and this was a white-faced skin, he had realised that it was not from his flock.

James and John Fram, butchers in Linlithgow, when requested, had identified the carcase of a sheep and two sheepskins, one of which was from a white-faced sheep and the other a black-faced sheep. The carcase weighed fifty eight imperial pounds. They confirmed that the sheep had not been skinned by a professional skinner or flesher.

Malcolm Adam, candlemaker at Linlithgow, stated that a man calling himself a cadger or hawker, who lived four miles from Linlithgow, had come to his shop at about nine o'clock on the Friday morning, 23 December 1831, offering some sheep tallow for sale and he had purchased it for five pence per pound, amounting to one shilling and ten pence halfpenny. This tallow appeared to be from a recently killed sheep.

In his statement of 26 December 1831, David Milliken Scott said that he had called himself David Millican for about six years. He and Elizabeth Scott Paterson had lived together as husband and wife for about three or four years, although they had never officially been married. The house at Linlithgow Bridge had been taken by Elizabeth around the September and he had not actually lived there very much, having worked at various locations. He did not know, or declined to answer, when asked about the origins of a skinned carcase of a sheep lying underneath the bed in the house at Linlithgow Bridge. Neither had he anything to say about the mutton hams, some tallow and two sheep's bladders which had been found under the bed! He had never seen Elizabeth with any sheepskins in her possession. He had sold some tallow, which he had found about a mile or two from Linlithgow, to a candlemaker there on Friday 23 December for twenty pence.

In his next statement given on 4 February 1832, he said that he was born at Shotts, but at the age of six had gone to live at Gallowayshire with his parents. He had lived there until he was sixteen. He had worked at Kelso and Jedburgh for a time, following which he had worked for Mr Russell at Meadowhead. He had then worked at Bangour, which he had left on the Whitsunday, and from that time to Martinmas he had been heaving stones on the Whitburn Road. About the time of raising the potatoes the previous harvest, he had gone to Linlithgow Bridge and worked in the vicinity, when he had lived with Elizabeth Scott Paterson, who had previously lived at Bangour and other places. He stated that he had never seen a sheep in her house and had no idea how she had been in possession of nine pounds in money. He certainly had not stolen a sheep and did not know of a place named Manuel Haugh at Muiravonside. He had definitely found the tallow wrapped up in a piece of cloth at the side of the road, about three miles south of Linlithgow, and a dog had been tearing at it. Apparently a ten year old boy had been there at the time and had taken just as much of the tallow as he had! He did not know the boy's name, only that he lived about four miles south east of Linlithgow where there was an old castle.

On 17 May 1832 David Milliken Scott, when interrogated, stated that he was forty four years old and had been a ploughman at Whitburn. He confirmed that he had been tried at the Glasgow Spring Circuit Court of Justiciary in May 1827 for theft of sheep, receiving the sentence of transportation for seven years. About a month later, whilst in the Glasgow Jail, some of his fellow prisoners had broken out and he had taken his chance to escape with them. He had then gone to work for Russell, a farmer at Meadowhead, five miles outside Edinburgh on the Bathgate Road, and he had been there for approximately nine months. He had then worked for three and a half years with David Neil, farmer at Wester Bangour, in the parish of Inch Machan, Linlithgowshire (*Ecclesmachan*) and lastly at Whitburn. Whilst at Whitburn, he had occasionally spent a Saturday and Sunday with Elizabeth Scott Paterson – who "*washed his linens*" - at Linlithgow Bridge. He confirmed that he had been arrested at the east end of Linlithgow about two weeks before New Year's Day in 1831. He completely denied saying to a man that he was a cadger who lived four miles south of Linlithgow.

What happened to David Milliken Scott, alias David Millican, when he was tried at the High Court in Edinburgh on 9 July 1832? He was found guilty in terms of his own confession and sentenced to fourteen years transportation.

National Records of Scotland reference AD14/32/434 JC26/1832/222

DAVID DOBBIE

THEFT AT BATHGATE 8 DECEMBER 1832

It was Saturday, 8 December 1832 in the town of Bathgate. David Dobbie was the fourteen year old son of Sarah Dobbie or Murrell, widow of James Dobbie, a painter, and they lived at North Street, Bathgate. Although just a young lad, David was already known as a criminal in the neighbourhood. David Alexander, the sheriff officer of Bathgate, remembered that a year and half previously young David had been caught stealing a metal grating off a common sewer, and had appeared before the magistrate where he confessed, expressed his contrition and was dismissed. In June of 1832 David and some acquaintances had cut a pane of glass from the window of the baker shop in Bathgate belonging to William and James Bowie and, although he and his companions had at first denied this, he subsequently admitted that he had committed this crime and stolen some bread and pies that were in the window. On that occasion he promised to recompense the Bowies for any damage. He was, in effect, *a thief by habit and repute*.

On the evening in question Isabella Hamilton, widow of the late William Young, grocer and spirit dealer, was in her house in Main Street, Bathgate. Her husband had only died about three weeks prior to this, but she was adamant that she would carry on the business. There was a stable behind her house – which was at Livery Street – and this had formerly been used as a small brewery. The house consisted of a flat with a loft above and this was joined by a trap to the stable. Two doors opened onto Livery Street and another door was by her kitchen. The doors were always locked with iron bolts from the inside. The under flat was used as a cellar for storing the wine and spirits.

Isabella had mentioned to her sister, Elizabeth, who looked after the cellar and ensured that the doors were properly locked, that she had a feeling that the London porter was disappearing faster than it should, but could not account for this, as it could only happen if someone was able to enter the property.

Elizabeth Hamilton, Mrs Young's sister, had taken charge of the cellar since William Young had died, ensuring that the doors were secured every night. At about eight o'clock that evening she noticed that the doors opening onto Livery Street were bolted. Just before ten o'clock, however, she found that someone had drawn the bolts of the large door opening onto Livery Street, and thought perhaps children were the culprits, so she once again locked the door securely.

At around nine o'clock in the evening Mary Cameron, who was living with her mother, Elizabeth Downie Cameron, in the High Street of Bathgate, was helping to serve customers for her uncle Thomas Crawford, a publican in Main Street. His wife was feeling unwell and Mary had been asked to step in to help. David Dobbie came into Crawford's with Andrew Fleming and James Thomson and they remained there until about ten o'clock that evening. During that time they had drunk roughly four gills of whisky. Dobbie and Fleming left and Thomson – rather the worse for the drink – remained slightly longer. Dobbie didn't seem to be particularly drunk. She knew what sort of reputation he had in the neighbourhood, as he had been charged with theft and had appeared before the magistrates of Bathgate on more than one occasion.

Elizabeth Bowie's brother was James Bowie, baker and publican in Bathgate. Elizabeth recollected that between eight and nine o'clock in the evening David Dobbie had come into her brother's house with two bottles of liquor, offering them to her for sale. She had asked him about their origins and he had replied that his mother had been away in the countryside and had got them there. He said he would sell them at the common rate, which was thrupence half penny a bottle, and she gave him thrupence for the two of them. She didn't see exactly what kind of liquor was in the bottles and he had certainly not been in the habit of selling these at her brother's premises. She agreed that Dobbie was a known criminal, which had induced her to ask him how he came by these bottles.

At around ten or eleven o'clock that evening, Mary Scott, who was the servant of Mr John Johnston, the merchant and bank agent in Jarvey Street, Bathgate, came to the house for a few bottles of porter, so Isabella had gone down to the cellar to fetch them. Imagine her surprise, however, when she found David Dobbie crouching in a large device (called an underback) in which she kept the bottles. He had a bottle of the porter in each trouser pocket, as well as another two beside him ready to be taken. He seemed sober enough to her, although extremely shocked to have been found, and she made him come upstairs immediately. On reaching the parlour, he had immediately vomited a good deal. Elizabeth, her sister, had then noticed on going down to the cellar that the spirit cask had also been opened and it appeared that David had been drinking the whisky from there as well, no doubt causing his bout of sickness!

Mary Scott, the servant, remembered the incident very well and how she had been sent for the porter and how David Dobbie had been discovered in the cellar. She remembered that he had struggled madly and tried to get away when he had been caught. She also remembered that the doors were *well and truly locked fast*.

On the following Monday, Isabella was looking up at the loft when she noticed that three tiles were missing from the roof, but she could not understand how someone who was drunk could possibly get down from there without falling or injuring himself in the process.

When David was questioned and made his statement on 10 December he said that he was, as far as he knew, fifteen years old and his parents were James and Sarah Dobbie. His deceased father had been a painter to trade. He said that he had met up with Andrew Fleming, weaver, and James Thomson, labourer, in the Main Street of

Bathgate at about half past nine in the evening. It was Fleming who had devised the plan to go to the old brewery house at Livery Street owned by Isabella Young to get a few bottles of porter, which he knew she kept there. Dobbie had apparently refused, left him and gone home. He then said that Fleming had come to his mother's house and once again encouraged him to go to the Young's cellar, but Dobbie had refused a second time. Fleming had then told Dobbie that if he would accompany him to the house of Thomas Crawford, the publican in Bathgate, he would buy him a drink there. They, along with James Thomson, had proceeded to drink about five gills of whisky over the space of about half an hour and Thomson was already pretty drunk by that time.

Fleming, if it was true that he had devised the plan initially, must have finally persuaded the drunken Dobbie to carry out the crime. They had left Thomson behind, he being the worse for wear and refusing to be involved, and proceeded to Livery Street at about a quarter past ten. Dobbie had climbed on a dung hill, with Fleming's assistance, and crept onto the roof of the house. He lay on top of the tiles and was followed by Fleming, who had lifted two of the tiles from the roof. With that opening having been made, Dobbie had dropped down on top of a copper boiler, followed by Fleming. They had gone down to the cellar where Dobbie had put some bottles in his pocket, following which he had gone over to a whisky cask and helped himself to some of that. On hearing a noise, Fleming had drawn the bolt of the door into Livery Street and made a quick escape, but Dobbie was not quick enough. He had known the layout of the cellar, he said, because he had helped Mrs Young to carry some coal in there on a previous occasion.

David Dobbie's case was heard at the High Court in Edinburgh on 4 March 1833. He was found guilty of theft aggravated by it having been committed by means of house breaking. He was sentenced to 12 month's hard labour in the Bridewell – the House of Correction. (The Bridewell in Regent Street, Edinburgh was situated to the west of the jail. It was erected in 1791 and designed by Robert Adam. It had five floors with 134 cells, each containing a bed and a bible. It was not a pleasant place.)

What happened to David Dobbie after his time in jail? He was back living at Cochrane Street, Bathgate by 1851, where he was once again working as a weaver. He died unmarried on 6 September 1857 at Engine Street, Bathgate at the age of 42 years of chronic nephritis and is buried in the Old Churchyard of Bathgate.

National Records of Scotland reference AD14/33/482; JC26/1833/553

Death record for Bathgate 662-105

JOHN FLEMING AND JAMES MITCHELL

THEFT BY HOUSEBREAKING AT POLBETH 9 APRIL 1833

It was a Tuesday evening, 9 April 1833, at James McLeod's farm at Polbeth, West Calder, when twenty four year old John Fleming and thirty one year old James Mitchell, both of Broxburn, had apparently stolen ten bolls of oats from a loft at this property, together with a boll of oats, three bags and a calf from a barn there. The barn, which contained a threshing mill, had four doors, which were never locked. There were also some small openings in the walls to let in light, but these were not large enough for a person to squeeze through. A ladder was set near to the trap door into the loft and this was the only access to that part of the building.

James Gray, Mr McLeod's servant, had secured the iron bolt to the loft above the cart shade at around eight o'clock on the evening in question and Alexander Stewart, another servant, was with him when he did so. It was a complicated locking system and James had taken the key home to Hermand. James stated that there had been about fifty bolls of oats in the loft that evening, as well as some empty bags, seven of which were boll bags. When he had returned the following morning at around five o'clock to fetch some corn for the horse, however, he had discovered that the bolt had been tampered with and the door to the loft had been forced open. He had discovered that a considerable amount of oats had been stolen and he and Mr McLeod estimated the loss to be around ten bolls. A bag containing a boll of oats, together with two empty bags, had also been stolen from the barn. The bags could have had either the names "*Gibson and Walker*" or "*McLeod and Bruce*" written on them. When Gray and Mr McLeod had gone outside to examine the road running through the farm, the wheel marks of a cart could be seen about one hundred yards from the loft and it looked as though a cart had come from the south, turned and gone back again. No footprints could be found, however. The oats – called white seed oats - which had been taken from the loft were completely cleaned, but the others were not.

Thirteen year old Alexander Stewart, who was Agnes Stewart's son, had been working for Mr McLeod for several weeks and slept in the stable at Polbeth. He confirmed that he had seen James Gray securing the loft. He had been in the barn at around eleven o'clock that evening and there were four calves there. When he and Margaret Bryce, another servant, had gone in to the barn at around seven o'clock next morning, however, they had discovered that one of these calves, which was brown with white spots and around two weeks old, was missing.

James McLeod confirmed that he had not been in the loft for several days prior to the theft, so could not confirm the exact quantity of oats which had been stored there. He saw that the "*bing*" (pile) of oats was not in the condition it had been, however, and some were scattered around the floor, as if others had been taken away quickly in a careless manner. He also confirmed James Gray's description of markings on the road.

Peter Dunlop was a carter at Broxburn and he knew Fleming and Mitchell. On the Tuesday evening in question, Dunlop had seen both of them at the east end of the Old Bridge at Broxburn. They were heading west with Fleming's cart and Mitchell's horse. Dunlop had enquired where they were headed for and Fleming had told him that he was going to help Mitchell to load some items, but did not specify exactly where this was to take place. They were, strangely enough, *on the road to Polbeth*.

Thomas Morrison was a butcher from the Grassmarket in Edinburgh and he confirmed that on the Wednesday, 10 April, at around five o'clock in the morning he had been at Long Hermiston and had seen the two prisoners, who were strangers to him, passing along with a horse and cart. A brown and white calf was lying in a bag with his head protruding, on top of some other filled bags. He had enquired if the calf was for sale and Mitchell had said that he would sell it to him for eight shillings. The deal was struck and the three individuals had gone into a public house to seal the transaction with a dram. During their conversation Morrison had asked where the calf had come from and Mitchell, who had taken the money for it, said that it had come from around Biggar. Morrison had remarked that this was not the road from Biggar, but was informed that the pair had some business dealings in the Hermiston area. The calf was subsequently taken to Edinburgh by Morrison and his colleague, Robert Gray, had sold it at the Grassmarket for him. Apparently Mitchell had appeared perfectly sober, whereas Fleming had been quite intoxicated.

Elizabeth Forsyth of Long Hermiston, Currie, confirmed that Morrison, Mitchell and Fleming had come to her house at around four or five o'clock in the morning and taken a dram. She had overheard Mitchell and the butcher bargaining, although she had observed that Fleming had not taken much interest in the proceedings. Mitchell, she confirmed, had paid for the dram and he had described that the young brown and white calf, which was outside in the cart, had come from Peebles.

Andrew McArthur was a boat contractor who lived at Fountainbridge in Edinburgh. James Mitchell, an acquaintance of his, and John Fleming had come to him at approximately seven o'clock in the morning on Wednesday the 10th. Mitchell had told him that he had a cart load of oats which he could sell cheaply, but as McArthur had no money at the time he referred Mitchell to his friends - Russell and Dickson. During the time McArthur had a quick dram with Mitchell and Fleming, Mitchell described that the eight or nine bags of oats actually belonged to Fleming and had been grown on a bit of ground north of Bangour. The money for the oats, however, was to be paid to Mitchell, as Fleming owed him some money for a horse.

They had all gone to see Thomas Russell, a baker and victual dealer in Edinburgh, and he confirmed that they had been there at around seven in the morning on that Wednesday, 10 April. Apparently he had also been asked if he wanted to buy some oats which were on a loaded cart outside his door. On taking out a sample to examine it, he had also been advised that they were Fleming's oats. Mitchell had informed him that they had come twenty two miles from the west that morning and that there were roughly ten bolls of oats on the cart, but Russell thought that it was more like seven and the bags had not been measured properly. A price could not be agreed upon and both Mitchell and Fleming (who had been intoxicated) had gone on to their next stop.

The next place they had visited was Alexander Dickson's victual dealer's shop at St. Anthony's Place, Edinburgh and this was at around ten o'clock in the morning. Dickson confirmed that they had come with McArthur with some oats that they were apparently taking to the market. He was asked if he wanted to buy some and at fourteen shillings a boll, he told them that he could have bought them cheaper at the market! Eventually, however, a price of eleven shillings and sixpence was agreed upon and he purchased four bolls and two bushels of these coarse oats. Mitchell had taken the lead in the transaction and Fleming had seemed totally disinterested in the proceedings. Subsequently, however, Dickson had been visited by James McLeod, who told him that these oats had actually been stolen from his own farm.

Joseph Bruce was a canal boatman who lived at Fountainbridge. He confirmed that he had known Mitchell for around two years and Fleming by sight only. He had seen them at around nine or ten o'clock in the morning of the 10th at Mr Dickson's shop with a cart full of oats. He had witnessed Mr Dickson buying some of these from Mitchell and had assisted in carrying them into Mr Dickson's shop. Mitchell had said that the oats belonged to Fleming and that Fleming owed him money for a horse. By this time the inebriated Fleming had been fast asleep on the premises.

The last witness was John Meikle, who was overseer on the Eastern District of the Union Canal, and who lived at Ratho. He confirmed that James Mitchell had been employed by him since May 1831 and, as far as he was concerned, was an honest man. He confirmed that a few days prior to his arrest James Mitchell had been sent the sum of two pounds twelve shillings and sixpence, which was the sum due to him as wages.

What of John Fleming? He was a twenty four year old carter born at Linlithgow, but resident at Broxburn. He admitted that he knew Mitchell. His version of events was that he had gone to bed at around nine o'clock on the evening of Tuesday 9th, rising again at about four o'clock next morning. He had gone to Edinburgh alone, but met Mitchell by accident at around seven o'clock at the canal basin, as he was going to take some bags from Broxburn to Bathgate. He had been quite surprised to see that Mitchell had a half a dozen bags of oats, which apparently had been purchased from a man outside the town, in his cart. Mitchell had told him that he was going to sell the oats and they had gone to get a drink before Fleming assisted him in unloading them at a meal dealer's premises beside the canal basin. A slightly intoxicated Fleming had fallen asleep in this establishment and was obliged to walk home, as

Mitchell had driven away without him. On being questioned, Fleming said that he had no idea that these oats had been stolen. He knew nothing of a stolen calf and did not know where either Polbeth or Long Hermiston was situated. He was acquainted with Mr McPherson, the tacksman at Binnie quarry, but he did not remember seeing him on either the Tuesday or Wednesday in question. He did not remember seeing Peter Dunlop, the carter, on the Tuesday evening either.

What did thirty one year old James Mitchell have to say for himself? He was born at Houston, but lived with his mother, Marion Gilchrist or Mitchell, at Broxburn. He admitted that he was acquainted with John Fleming. According to him, Mitchell and Fleming had made a plan to go to Prestonpans for some plants, which they could sell on for profit. They had left Broxburn at around nine or ten that evening of Tuesday, 9 April, with Mitchell's horse and Fleming's cart, making their way to Hatton on the Mid Calder road, where they had discovered that they could get plants, thus shortening their journey. They had overtaken a man with a horse and cart and bought six bags of oats from him for three pounds ten shillings, and the man had decanted them into the bags they had for the plants. They had then made their way to Edinburgh and sold four bolls of these to a victual dealer named Dickson at the canal basin for eleven shillings the boll, with Fleming taking the rest home. Mitchell denied going near West Calder either on the Tuesday or Wednesday and had not known anything about the oats being stolen. John Meikle, overseer at the canal who lived at Ratho, had given him two pounds twelve shillings some days before and he had that money with him when he left home on the Tuesday. He had kept all of the money from Dickson (who had not asked where the oats had come from) apart from four shillings, which he had given to Fleming. He also remembered that he and Fleming had taken a dram together in Douglas' house at East Calder and they had taken another drink at the Tyne Castle Toll.

What happened to James Mitchell and John Fleming when they were tried at the High Court of Edinburgh on 24 June 1833? Both were found guilty and sentenced to transportation for seven years.

National Records of Scotland reference AD14/33/484; JC26/1833/613

JOSEPH AULD BORN IRELAND

THEFT AT BATHGATE 17 SEPTEMBER 1834

It was 17 September 1834 at North Bridge Street in Bathgate.

Joseph Auld was a labourer who had come to Bathgate looking for work a couple of weeks previously. According to the description given by his victim, he was a stoutly built Irishman, around thirty years old, five feet eight inches in height, with a smooth, dark, round face, fair hair and short whiskers.

When Joseph Auld had arrived at Bathgate he had found it difficult to find any lodgings. He had appeared at the house of Agnes Shaw, a widow who supported herself by keeping lodgers. Her house had been full at the time, but one of her lodgers, thirty four year old Terry Herring, had agreed to let him have a share of his bed and room to help him out. (This was a common enough occurrence in those times and beds were often shared by individuals who were not related.) Mr Herring had kindly asked his employer, Thomas Logan in Bathgate, if he had any work for Auld and soon Auld was working at the same place as him. The arrangement had seemed to be working well enough until the day in question.

Terry Herring kept a chest in his room, which was always kept locked and he had been in the habit of secreting the key underneath the chest after locking it. It appeared, however, that Auld had seen him doing this on one occasion. At around five o'clock in the morning Herring had got up and left the house before Mrs Shaw was up. By seven o'clock that same morning a very worried Mrs Shaw had arrived at his workplace, telling him that Auld had disappeared with a pair of stockings belonging to Herring, which she had washed for him the day before, as well as his hat. Terry Herring had then returned to Mrs Shaw's house and, on going into his room and lifting his chest, it was found to have been much lighter in weight than it should have been. The key was not in the place where he had put it. He had then obtained another key and, on opening the chest, had discovered that several items had been stolen.

The missing items could be described in great detail. One item was a double breasted, dark blue cloth coat with short broad tails, which was lined with white twilled flannel, the sleeves lined with white twilled calico, and having plain gilt buttons and pockets on the outside at the lap holes. There were two single breasted waistcoats with a plain neck, one of them in red plush with a small black spot on it, the other yellow and white striped, with the stripes running vertically. The latter was described as being rather straight and Herring had inserted another piece of fabric into the back of it himself, which had been clumsily sewn and it was lined with white cotton. The plush one had a moleskin back and was wholly lined with white plaiding and both of the waistcoats had small yellow buttons. Also missing was a linen shirt which Herring had purchased some time ago from an individual who had lodged at

Mrs Shaw's house, whose name was on it, but he could not recall what that name was. This shirt was worn at one of the shoulders and a piece of cotton had been put on the place to hide the flaw, but the sewing had not been quite finished. Missing also was a black silk neck cloth - a little stained in the middle. The hat which had been stolen was a black one and the stockings were a pair of blue or grey worsted ones.

As well as these valued clothes, there was around a shilling in coppers which had been removed from the chest. Terry Herring had been informed that a girl named Jess Glen (Janet Stewart Glen, daughter of Alexander Glen, the weaver) had seen Auld leaving the house at a very early hour with a bundle under his arm, and that he had then been seen in the evening within four or five miles of Edinburgh. Auld had come to Mrs Shaw's house with nothing, and it was obvious that whatever had been taken in the bundle did not belong to him.

Joseph Auld's citation could not be delivered to him, as he had already absconded. It did state, however, that he was guilty of opening a locked chest with a key which he had taken and stealing a blue cloth coat, a plush waistcoat, a striped waistcoat, a linen shirt a black silk neck cloth, a shilling or thereabouts in copper, the lawful possession of Terry Herring, lodger at Agnes Shaw's house. He had also stolen a black hat and a pair of worsted stockings, also the property of Terry Herring, and he had absconded and fled from justice.

Mr James Watson, Fiscal of Court for the public interest, wrote a letter from Linlithgow on 31 October 1834, which stated that the accused had been seen in the neighbourhood of Edinburgh on the evening of the day of the theft and it was understood he was making his way to Lauder. He intimated that he had immediately written to Mr Scott in Edinburgh and the Procurator Fiscal of Berwickshire with a description of Auld and of the stolen articles, but no discovery had yet been made.

Joseph Auld, who had failed to appear at Court on 26 January 1835, was outlawed and put to the horn.

Note: The expression "outlawed and put to the horn" means that the individual was denounced as a rebel, or pronounced as an outlaw because he did not answer a summons. Originally the King's messenger had to give three blasts of his horn and the relevant individual would be understood to be proclaimed as a rebel to the king for contempt of his authority.

National Records of Scotland reference AD14/35/365; JC26/1835/483

WILLIAM ADDIE AND WILLIAM HAMILTON

ATTACK AT UPHALL 22 JUNE 1835

It was 22 June 1835 when 42 year old David McCulloch, a labourer living in Bathgate, had been sent to Edinburgh by Mr Durham, his employer, to sell a mare for him. He was returning homewards at about six or seven o'clock in the evening, quite sober, and had come to the entry to Caputhall Farm Steading, occupied by Mr William Fairley, the farmer. On arriving there, he had come across three young men - William Addie junior, James Martin, and William Hamilton - all weavers from Bathgate. They appeared to be very intoxicated and one of them had spoken to David McCulloch and asked where he had been. David told him and asked where they were all going, and they replied that they were going to Edinburgh to enlist in the army. He said that a townsman by the name of George Fleming, who had enlisted a short time earlier, had told him he was to be in Bathgate that night, so perhaps they had better go homewards and speak to him on the subject. Being the worse for drink, however, James Martin had *"squared up"* to McCulloch at this point and attempted to strike him, but McCulloch had successfully warded off his blows. Hamilton, sensing a fight, had urged Martin to keep at McCulloch, but McCulloch had threatened to report them to a magistrate if they didn't stop. Addie, who was obviously the ringleader, had then thrown off his coat, saying he would give him something to report and had immediately struck him several severe blows, one of which caused him to stagger and fall down. This was followed by a kick from Hamilton. McCulloch had a bridle in his hand when he was attacked and he had dropped this on the ground. James Martin had then taken hold of the bridle, but McCulloch had told him to give it back to him – which he did.

Addie had then come towards him and, taking hold of McCulloch, said that he had not been at Edinburgh without getting money (for the horse), whereupon he had put his hand into McCulloch's waistcoat pockets and taken out a shilling and a halfpenny, which was all the money he had. Hamilton was also holding him and, before letting him go, they both made him promise not tell the Sheriff anything that had taken place there. Not wanting to anger them further, McCulloch said nothing more and the three drunkards had left the scene. McCulloch had heard afterwards that Addie had absconded and Hamilton and Martin had enlisted in the army.

In his statement, 18 year old James Martin said that he had met up with William Addie and William Hamilton on the high road leading from Uphall to Bathgate, near the road to Caputhall Farm Steading. James was actually on his way to Edinburgh to enlist as a private in her Majesty's 18th Regiment. He had met up with the other two individuals on the road and they had said that they would walk with him part of the way. They had stopped at Glen's public house at Uphall and had a few gills of whisky there. Being somewhat the worse for drink, they had come upon David McCulloch, who they knew from sight as living in Bathgate. Martin agreed that a scuffle had taken place, but in his statement he denied that Addie had taken any money from

McCulloch. He remembered seeing two men, one of whom had a pair of horses, passing by to the east and thought one of them was called Buchanan, who lived at Westercraigs Inn. McCulloch had called out to these men to come off their horses and help him, but the men had paid no attention. He seemed to remember that Hamilton had taken hold of the horse which Buchanan led, but had let it go again. His story differed from McCulloch's in that on parting McCulloch had shaken hands with Addie in good humour and told the lads where they would meet a man called Fleming, who had enlisted a short time before. Martin stated that the three of them had gone to Uphall and met Fleming with a corporal and Martin had enlisted there and then.

One of the men passing the scene was Archibald Buchanan, who was forty five years old and servant of Mrs Jane McKay, widow and innkeeper at Westercraigs Inn, Torphichen. He was returning home with a pair of horses from Uphall Inn at about seven o'clock on the evening in question. He had seen David McCulloch near the place where the road branches off to Caputhall and three men beside him. He knew one of them as William Addie, weaver in Bathgate, but did not know the names of the others and was not sure he could identify them if requested to do so. The men were pestering McCulloch and he saw Addie strike him with his fist. He also noticed one of the men taking the bridle from McCulloch, but that he had let it go again. He saw that Addie's coat was off, but as he was trying to take care of the horses at the time, he did not see everything that had passed during the scuffle. He went about a hundred yards along the road with a groom of Sir Archibald Campbell of Succoth. When he turned to look back, he saw that the three men were still standing around McCulloch. He could see that McCulloch was sober, but the others were extremely intoxicated. He also noticed that McCulloch had not tried to strike anyone, but when Buchanan rode by he had said, *"Gentlemen, I take you to witness"*.

John Cossar was the other individual who was passing by when this incident occurred. He was a thirty five year old groom in the service of Sir Archibald Campbell of Succoth, Baronet. John lived with his master at Garscube, East Kilpatrick, although his wife and family lived at 20 Downie Place, Edinburgh. He had left Edinburgh on the day in question with a pair of horses which he was taking to Garscube, but about six miles from Edinburgh - on the Glasgow road by Uphall - he had encountered a man who was walking and carrying a bridle. He had started talking to McCulloch and learned that he had been in Edinburgh delivering a horse which had been sold, and that he was returning to his home in Bathgate. The man – who he remembered vividly - was dressed in a drab frock coat and looked to be about forty years old. They had walked along together for about a quarter of a mile. Cossar had fed his horses at Uphall, where he stayed for about an hour and a half. He had left Uphall at about six o'clock in the evening in the company of a post boy who worked for Mrs McKay of Wester Craigs and travelled along the road with him. He had seen McCulloch, who was by now surrounded by three other men. The tallest of these three had struck McCulloch two or three times, whereupon his victim had fallen down and his hat had come off. McCulloch had then been hit by another one of the three. Cossar had shouted to them, telling them that it was shameful to strike the man like this, and they seemed to stop. However, he had then seen one of them take McCulloch by the collar, but he did not actually see them stealing the money from him, as he was occupied with his horses. He had even said to the post boy that it was disgraceful, but the boy had only remarked that the three of them were known to be criminal characters. It was not, he said, advisable to get involved, as it would be dangerous and they themselves could get into a scuffle. About fifty yards further along the road he had seen them strike the man again, although the man had made no resistance and seemed to be in a bit of a daze, but not because of alcohol.

Elizabeth Millar or Glen, who was the wife of David Glen, publican at Uphall, also gave a statement and described how James Martin, accompanied by two other men - strangers to her - and by George Fleming and a soldier, had come into her house between six and seven o'clock on the night in question. They had called for some drink and she had served them with it. She had heard them talking about someone enlisting, but not about anything else. They didn't talk about meeting a man on the road or having had a scuffle. They had asked for half a mutchkin, which they paid for in a sixpence and four pennies, but she did not see who put the money down. That was all she had to say on the subject.

What was the outcome of the trial which took place at the High Court of Edinburgh on 9 November 1835? William Addie junior and William Hamilton could not be found, despite being searched for. Consequently they were outlawed and put to the horn.

National Records of Scotland reference AD14/35/457; JC26/1835/584

JAMES BELL

CULPABLE HOMICIDE AT SELMS FARM, KIRKNEWTON 20 JULY 1836

It was Wednesday, 20 July 1836 at Selms Farm, Kirknewton, which is situated near to East Calder. Robert Ferrier farmed Selms, employing several servants to assist him, and on the day in question there were at least four of them who witnessed the incident at the Langgreen field, where they were thinning turnips. Alexander Knowles, who slept in the stables at the farm steading, had assisted with this in the morning. He had gone to the farmhouse for dinner and returned later to carry on with the thinning. According to him, John Kerr had joined in this work after dinner. Seventeen year old James Bell had already been working with some women in a particular row in the field and he had returned to it after dinner – at around three o'clock – to complete the job. Kerr, however, had come over to Bell's row and insisted in working it. This had caused a scuffle, with Bell telling Kerr to keep to his own row, shoving him with his elbow, and Kerr shoving him back, which had riled Bell to strike Kerr with the iron part of his hoe on the forehead.

This must have been a fairly harsh "clout" (smack), because Kerr had fallen flat and had to be assisted to his feet by Knowles, whereupon he had fallen again. Knowles could see that Kerr's forehead had been cut severely and was bleeding profusely, so he had immediately ran for Mr Ferrier, who was in another field nearby. By this time, a slightly stupefied Kerr had stood up again, with Bell crying his eyes out with remorse nearby. Kerr had vomited, but had seemed to rally, and after Mr Ferrier had bound up his wound, had thinned another two or three rows. However, the poor boy was clearly very unwell and his employer had insisted on taking him back to the farmhouse and putting him to bed. By six o'clock that evening Kerr was quite unable to speak and Dr Thomson, who had been called, had arrived at around eight o'clock to examine him. Knowles and some others had been instructed to take the injured lad to the Infirmary in Edinburgh and they had set off in the cart. He had spoken very little on the way and seemed quite stupefied.

When Knowles was questioned further, he said that when Kerr had been in bed at Selms, Knowles had heard him telling Bell not to "*greet*" (cry), as it had all been as much *his* fault as Bell's. Apparently, prior to the pushing and shoving, Kerr had annoyed Bell by calling him "*Carrotty*" – a nickname he had been given due to the fact that he had been stepping out with a woman with red hair. Knowles had not thought this was the reason for the fracas getting out of hand, however, but it seemed to relate more to Kerr having taken the easier row to work on. He had not seen the pair quarrelling on any other occasion particularly, but he did admit that Bell could be a little fiery when antagonised – although his general nature was good.

Archibald Fairlie was another one of the farm servants and he slept in one of the stables. He confirmed that on the day in question Kerr had already come to the turnip fields to work after dinner. But when Bell came along, he had begun working at a row which had been partly thinned. Kerr had then stood before him at this row and Bell had told him to go away to another row. He would *not*, however, and Bell had shoved Kerr with his hand, Kerr had pushed him back and the blow on Kerr's forehead had then been struck by Bell with the iron part of his hoe. After Kerr had fallen, according to Fairlie, it was Bell who had lifted him up again, with Fairlie running for Mr Ferrier. He confirmed that Mr Ferrier had bandaged up Kerr's head and the boy had started to work again, but had been taken back home due to the condition he was in.

James Bell had been inconsolable, sobbing all the while. Kerr had been taken to the Infirmary and Fairlie had visited him there later. When questioned, Fairlie's opinion was that Kerr had had no right to work on Bell's row. He had heard Kerr calling "*Carrotty*" to Bell, but he did not think that this was the reason for the dispute developing. On being interrogated, Fairley stated that he was quite sure that the "*drill*" (row) in question had not actually been worked on until Bell arrived after dinner. He was of the opinion that it was Bell's privilege to take that row and that Kerr had no right to interfere by leaving his own row and coming to Bell's. Because of the inclement weather nobody had worked the turnips for a few days beforehand and, as far as he could recall, only Kerr, Knowles, Isabella Stewart and he had been working in that field before dinner.

Marion Macara was Mr Ferrier's servant and one of those thinning turnips on that day. She confirmed that she had seen Kerr working the field after dinner and that Bell had not arrived until after three o'clock. She had witnessed that Kerr had come to Bell's row, saying he would take it, and that Bell had retorted, but she was unable to confirm what had been said. She had not been paying much attention, being engrossed in her work, but she had definitely seen Bell striking Kerr on the forehead with the hoe, knocking him down. He had stood up again eventually, trying to work, but he had been taken away by Mr Ferrier shortly afterwards, being very ill. She thought that Kerr had no right to take Bell's drill, but the lads had generally been friendly with one another in the past twelve months that she had known them. On being questioned, she did say that she recalled Kerr calling Bell "*Carrotty*" but that had been a good while prior to the fracas developing. She had said to Bell, "*Oh, Jamie Bell, what is that you have done?*" and he had replied that he would rather pay £100 than this having taken place, whilst crying freely. She confirmed that Bell had gone to Selms Farm to see Kerr when he was in bed. She herself had seen Kerr in bed that evening, but he had been very ill indeed and she had not spoken to him prior to his being taken away in the cart to the Infirmary. The following day Bell had been extremely quiet, hardly speaking a word, and all of the other servants had avoided questioning him to avoid hurting his feelings.

Isabella Stewart, another servant employed in thinning the turnips on that day, lived with her mother Isabella Paul, a widow in Mid Calder. As far as she was concerned, she said that she had returned to the field, where she had been working with Knowles, Fairley and Kerr, after dinner. She had gone to the unfinished drill that had been worked on that morning and she had seen Bell coming along at around four o'clock in the afternoon, working on the drill that he had been on already. She said that it was not the correct way of working for Kerr to interfere with Bell's row. She was some distance away, however, when the assault took place.

Robert Ferrier, the farmer at Selms, confirmed that James Bell had been his servant for twelve months, and John Kerr since January last, although he had carried out some occasional work on the farm before that. Mr Ferrier had heard a woman screaming in the field named Langgreen at around four o'clock on the afternoon in question, and on running over there he had heard one of the men calling out that Bell had *killed* Kerr. On arriving at the scene of the crime, he had seen Kerr standing with a hoe in his hand, although he had a very deep wound on his forehead which was bleeding heavily. Ferrier had bound this up with his handkerchief and sent for Dr Thomson. Kerr had tried to carry on working, but Mr Ferrier had stopped him and taken him home to bed. Bell, at this time, was crying a great deal and obviously in distress, but would not tell his employer why he had struck Kerr. The workers had told him what had happened, however. On taking Kerr home, Bell had come along and had been crying in the kitchen where Kerr was lying. Mr Ferrier had distinctly heard Kerr saying to Bell that he should not cry so much, as what had taken place was *as much his fault as Bell's*.

The farmer had returned to the fields, leaving Bell and Kerr in the kitchen, but Bell had come running to him saying that Kerr had taken some sort of fit. He asked Bell again why he had struck Kerr and the latter replied that his temper had been so inflamed that he did not know what he was doing, but on realising what he had done, he had immediately regretted it bitterly. The row had commenced because Kerr had taken Bell's row of turnips from him. Kerr had been taken to the Infirmary after Dr Thomson's visit and his employer had not seen him since. As far as the two lads were concerned, Mr Ferrier thought they were well enough behaved, but both were rather fiery tempered. Previous to the fight, he had always seen them being friendly towards one another and, in fact, they slept in the same place, with Bell often helping Kerr with work. Kerr had been unable to say much on the matter at all.

When interrogated, Robert Ferrier explained that no work had been carried out in the turnip fields between the Friday and Saturday preceding the incident on the Wednesday. He understood, after making enquiries, that the drill in question was one of several which had been left unfinished the previous Saturday and nobody had touched it until Bell had worked it after dinner that day. Kerr, who had been working at a completely different row, had gone over to Bell's, saying he would take it over. If this was the case, then it was clearly the wrong thing to do.

David Kerr, a mason who lived at East Calder, was John Kerr's father and he confirmed that he had seen his son injured at around seven o'clock that evening at Selms Farm and that he had subsequently accompanied him to the Infirmary on the cart. He had not asked his son about the events which had led to this severe injury, as he seemed extremely ill at the time, and Doctor Thomson had recommended that his son be kept very quiet on the journey. Mr Kerr had heard the particulars from the others working at Selms. The only thing his son *had* said was that Bell "*had done for him*"! Even although he had visited his son in the Infirmary several times, he had asked him no further questions.

Dr Thomson's medical report dated 23 July indicated that John Kerr had received a wound measuring about one and a half inches on the frontal bone an inch above the centre of his eyebrow and a portion of the frontal bone had bent inwards on the brain, due to the violence of the blow. The surgeon attending Kerr at the Royal Infirmary in Edinburgh was John Lizars. His report stated that Mr John Kerr had been brought to hospital on the morning of 21 July, having sustained a compound depressed fracture of the cranium, which was caused by a blow from a hoe. The severity of the injury implied considerable danger.

John Kerr died in the Royal Infirmary Edinburgh on the evening of 27 July in consequence of the severe injuries inflicted on him by the blow by James Bell.

In his first statement of 22 July seventeen year old James Bell, who was born in Fife, confirmed that he worked for Mr Robert Ferrier, a farmer at Selms, Kirknewton and slept at one of the stables there. He said that John Kerr, another servant, had been thinning and "*yarring*" turnips on Wednesday, 20 July in the Langgreen field. Kerr and he had been working on different rows and there had been two rows of turnips between them. Kerr had come to *his* row and annoyed him, saying that Bell had had relations with a certain female with red hair, who he named, which was totally untrue. According to Bell, Kerr had pushed him back three times and on the third push Bell had lost his temper and struck him on the front of his head with the metal part of his hoe. Kerr had immediately fallen down and it was obvious that the blow had produced a very deep cut. Kerr had tried to work again, but had been bandaged up by Mr Ferrier, who had come to the field hearing the screams coming from that direction. Kerr had been taken to Selms and put to bed and Bell had followed later, when he had heard him admit to Mr and Mrs Ferrier that *he* was to blame for the incident. Kerr had also said to a sobbing Bell that he was worse (behaved) than Bell and that Bell was to stop his weeping. Bell had seen Dr Thomson arriving and Kerr being taken to the Infirmary in a cart, after which he had never seen him again. He had had no quarrels with Kerr up to that point and he was extremely sorry for what had happened. He said that Alexander Knowles and Archibald Fairlie could vouch for what had transpired, in that Kerr had insulted Bell and pushed him a few times before Bell had struck him.

He made a second declaration on 29 July after he had been informed that John Kerr had died and that he would therefore be accused of murder or culpable homicide. He once again adhered to his first statement, saying that he was extremely remorseful that Kerr had died.

What was the verdict when James Bell was tried at the High Court in Edinburgh on 14 November 1836? He was found guilty of culpable homicide in terms of his own confession and his sentence was transportation for 7 years.

National Records of Scotland reference AD14/36/165; JC26/1836/524

ROBERT FAIRFOWL

ASSAULT OF HELEN ALEXANDER, WIFE OF WILLIAM ALLAN AT BROXBURN 16 MAY 1837

It was 16 May 1837 in a house occupied by William Allan, a labourer in Broxburn, when Robert Fairfowl, a collier, assaulted Helen Alexander or Allan, William's wife. He had struck her two blows on the head with his clenched fist, after which he had pursued her as she was trying to escape, and near the door of the house continued to strike her several severe blows on the face, neck shoulders and other parts of the body, by which she was seriously injured. He had then absconded from justice.

When fifty year old Helen Allan was questioned, she described that at between six and seven o'clock on the evening of the Tuesday in question she had been sitting alone at her fireside when Fairfowl had come into the house, accusing her of telling the church minister that he had struck David, her sister's son. She denied this, saying she hadn't even seen the minister, but went on stupidly to say that if she *had* told him, it would have been nothing but the truth! Fairfowl had persisted with his accusations, however, declaring further that he would send her and her sons *"to Hell in five minutes"*. He had then struck her on the crown of her head with his fist. She had lifted up the poker, questioning that he would strike her in her own house, and had run towards the door. However, he had struck her a second blow whilst she tried to escape and followed her outside, attacking her again and again on the body. She had not fallen, but was stooped over and was becoming dizzy and confused due to the attack. Fortunately her neighbour, Mrs Fairne, dragged Fairfowl off the poor woman and brought her some water.

Helen stated that she had not offered any resistance to him or used the poker, which she had only been holding because she was stoking the fire at the time he had come in. Doctor Thomson had been sent for immediately, but had not arrived until Wednesday morning, whereupon he had bled her, visited her another four times that day, followed by two visits the following day, and three the day after that. On the third day, another young medical gentleman – by the name of Simpson, she believed, had accompanied Dr Thomson and examined her also. She had severe pain in her neck and shoulders due to the frenzied attack, and was still suffering from violent attacks of vomiting.

James Ritchie, a carpenter in Broxburn, gave evidence to the fact that at around six o'clock on the evening in question he had been on the street near the house of his neighbour, Mrs Allan, when he had witnessed Robert Fairfowl running out of her house and striking her with his fists. He was hitting her on the shoulders and head and she was crying out for help, but not resisting in any way. As he had rushed to assist her, Mrs Fairne had reached Helen first and stepped between her and her attacker. Ritchie had dragged Fairfowl – a powerfully built man and a known criminal – away from the frail woman.

Mary McKinlay, wife of George Fairne, miller in Broxburn, concurred with Ritchie's evidence. She also described that Mrs Allan had been holding a poker when she and the drunken Fairfowl had come out of the house, and they were having some kind of heated argument.

A letter had been written to David Cleghorn at the Crown Office, Linlithgow dated 20 October 1837, in which it was stated that officers had been on the lookout for the offender, but to date he had not been found. Recently, however, he was reported to have been seen working at a colliery at Gilmerton, Edinburgh, but on sending a superintendent there, no such person was ever found and nobody matching his description had ever been employed there.

There were two medical reports in respect of this attack. Joseph Thomson, surgeon at Broxburn, had attended Helen Allan and his report of 19 May certified that he had been called out on 17 May to attend her. She had such a considerable swelling of the left eye and cheek that she could not see properly. She had a slight scratch on back of neck and complained of severe pain of head, neck and breast and had been in a feverish and vicarious state since the incident had occurred.

The other report was written by **James Young Simpson, Fellow of the Royal College of Physicians of Edinburgh** who wrote that Helen Alexander/Allan's left cheek and eye bore the marks of a recent severe blow and the area was covered with severe bruising. She complained of pain in her head and chest, had thirst, a quick pulse, and the symptoms of fever.

Robert Fairfowl was never apprehended. Although he was lawfully cited and called at the High Court of Edinburgh on 18 December 1837, he failed to appear. He was therefore outlawed and put to the horn.

Note: On 9 February 1857 44 year old Robert Fairfowl, born Old Liston, who had lived most of his life in Linlithgow, but was presently living at Bathgate was incarcerated at Linlithgow Jail for one calendar month for theft of a large plaid cloth.

National Archives of Scotland reference AD14/37/515; JC26/1837/611

CHARLES CREASE FROM EDINBURGH

ASSAULT OF DAVID PURVES WITH INTENT TO ROB AT BATHGATE 26 JUNE 1837

It was Monday, 26 June 1837. Twenty year old David Purvis, a carpenter who lived with his mother, Rachel Ramage or Purvis, widow, was walking from Edinburgh to his home at Torphichen. Purvis worked for James Linn, carpenter in Whitburn. On the preceding Friday he had gone to Glasgow to attend his brother's wedding and had left on the Monday morning, taking the steam train to Airdrie. On arriving there, however, and realising that he had missed the coach, he had been forced to make his way home on foot.

About five miles to the east, a lad had joined him and told him that he came from Edinburgh, but had just got back from Paisley where he was looking for work. Being unsuccessful there, he had thought that he would now try Linlithgow. The pair had walked along, chatting in a friendly manner and Purvis had told the boy that he lived near Linlithgow, so the stranger had replied that he would accompany him, as he had an uncle who kept a Toll Bar to the west of that place.

About one hundred yards to the north of the road leading off to Wheatlockbrae, Bathgate, however, and without saying a word or giving the slightest warning, the stranger had struck Purvis on the head with a thorn-studded stick he had picked up on the way. Blood poured down Purvis' head and the stranger had attempted yet another blow, but was foiled by Purvis wrenching the stick from him. The stranger had then thrown Purvis, who was by now shouting out for help, down on the ground and had tried to choke him by twisting his scarf round his neck and violently assaulting him. He had forced his hands into Purvis' trouser pockets, trying to rob him, but due to the struggle taking place he was unsuccessful in getting anything.

Fortunately for Purvis, Thomas Gowans, cattle dealer at Adam Brae Mill, had heard the shouting, managed to pull the stranger off his victim and had immediately taken him into custody. Shortly afterwards Mr Auld, surgeon, had arrived at the location where the attack had taken place and had subsequently accompanied Purvis to Armadale, where the wound was dressed. Purvis had brought along the stick, with which he had been attacked, to be used in evidence.

In his statement, Purvis confirmed that he had never seen this lad before and they had been quite friendly until the assault took place. The only way the stranger could have known that Purvis had a watch in his pocket was due to the fact that he had asked about the time when they were on the road. He had also been aware that Purvis was carrying money (two shillings and sixpence) for the coach which he had missed on arriving at Airdrie.

Thomas Gowans, who was a farmer and cattle dealer at Adam Brae Mill, Mid Calder, said that at about seven o'clock on the evening in question he had been riding along the road from Torphichen to Armadale. One hundred yards from Wheatlockbrae, he had seen a man lying on the root of a low hedge by an earthen bank and when he realised that someone was actually lying beneath him and crying out *"murder"*, he had demanded to know what was on earth was happening. Gowans had jumped down off his horse and pulled the man off the other. The stranger lad had tried to explain that they were merely wrestling, but Purvis had denied this vehemently, saying that the former had told him he was a watchmaker and wanted to see his watch. He had then violently struck Purvis with the offending stick – which was now marked with blood – and tried to rob him. The blood was flowing profusely down Purvis' head and he was weak and faint by this time. When Mr Gowans saw the pair, they were holding each other by their neckcloths, but he had not witnessed the stranger putting his hands in Purvis' pockets beforehand. After apprehending him, he had immediately taken the stranger to the constables at Armadale.

The medical report from Doctor Robert Auld – Bathgate 30 June 1837 – was given in evidence. Dr Auld confirmed that on the evening of 26 June 1837 at half past six he had found David Purvis of Torphichen between Collinshields and Armadale with a contused and lacerated wound of his scalp, which was three inches in length and bleeding freely, and which he subsequently dressed.

Charles Crease, in his statement given on 27 June, said he was aged twenty three and an optician and mathematical instrument maker to trade. He generally lived in lodging houses in Edinburgh and the last one had been kept by Mrs Margaret Wilson at Low Calton. He confirmed that he had left to go to Glasgow, then Paisley, looking for work. He had left there on 26 June, making his way back to Edinburgh, but at around three or four o'clock that afternoon, about four miles east of Airdrie, he had overtaken David Purvis. As they were going in the same direction they had walked together, conversing all the way. Crease had told Purvis about his uncle at the Toll House and instead of going on to Edinburgh he had said that he would go to visit *him* instead. They had turned off the road leading from Linlithgow and Crease confessed that he had struck Purvis a blow on the head with a thorned stick about a quarter of a mile along there. He admitted that he had then pushed Purves down on the ground. Both had grappled with each other, whilst holding on to the other's neckcloth. A man had then ridden along and stopped the attack. Crease said that they had both been sober and friendly up to the point when the attack took place.

Crease had previous convictions for assaulting, stabbing and wounding on 7 June 1828 at Edinburgh Sheriff Court and for assault before the High Court of Justiciary of Edinburgh on 21 March 1836. His age given in the trial in 1836 was twenty one and he was described as being an army pensioner living at Buckrain's Land, Moray Street, Pilrig, Leith at the time. For that crime he had been sentenced to fifteen months imprisonment with hard labour.

What happened to Charles Crease? Having been found guilty in terms of his own confession at the High Court of Justiciary on 7 November 1837, he was transported to New South Wales for 7 years.

National Records of Scotland reference AD14/36/354; AD14/37/489; JC26/1836/442; JC26/1837/559

WILLIAM TROTTER

EMBEZZLEMENT AND BREACH OF TRUST AT MID CALDER 4 NOVEMBER 1837 – JANUARY 1838

It was mostly during the months of November and December 1837 and January 1838 when William Trotter embezzled money and was found to be in breach of trust, when he was working for Robert Borthwick, the baker in Mid Calder. He had also embezzled at other times during 1837, however. Robert Borthwick was a well respected and busily employed baker and he had taken on Trotter as his apprentice for the last two years. Part of the job was to deliver bread and take payments on delivery or on account, as some preferred to pay fortnightly. If the payment was to be on account, Trotter was obliged to inform his employer each day in order to keep him appraised of the current position regarding his customers. Mr Borthwick would personally go round to visit his customers once a month and, when he had done so at the beginning of December 1837, he had discovered to his horror that some of the customers had made payments, but these had not been accounted for by Trotter.

On challenging his young apprentice, Trotter had admitted that he had been very foolish, but would make reparation by getting the money from his mother to pay back his employer. He excused his crime by explaining that some bread had been stolen from the cart when he was on his delivery run. This was a very disappointing situation as far as Mr Borthwick was concerned, as he had always thought Trotter to be a sober and likeable lad and had only seen him twice at the most being slightly the worse for liquor. He had no idea what on earth his apprentice could have done with the sum which was deficient in the accounts, however, as this amounted to around thirty pounds!

Some of the money missing was from:

Adam Forrest, the farmer at Howdenhall, Mid Calder (or his wife, Jean Carmichael) who received bread three times a week – five shillings and sixpence;

William Paris, a spirit dealer at Bellsquarry (or his wife Jean Bryce) – twenty seven shillings;

John Paris, spirit dealer at Bellsquarry, who had bread delivered every Thursday – twelve shillings sixpence;

Thomas Chalmers, tacksman at Long Livingston Toll Bar (or Margaret Smith, his wife) who had bread delivered every Monday, Wednesday and Saturday - thirty shillings;

John McKay, tacksman at Whitburn Toll Bar (or Martha Douglas, his wife) who had bread delivered twice a week - twelve shillings;

William Watt, weaver at East Whitburn (or Jean Forrest, his wife) - one pound;

Robert Calder, weaver at Whitburn (or Margaret Roberts, his wife) who received bread about three times a week - fifteen shillings;

Alexander Millar, spirit dealer at Whitburn – seventeen shillings;

Alexander Martin, weaver at Whitburn (or his wife, Elizabeth Finlay), who was supplied with bread three times a week – twenty five shillings seven pence;

Margaret Russell at Whitburn who received bread three times a week – five pounds eighteen shillings eight pence;

Christian Main or Waterston, widow at Blackburn, who received bread three times a week – one pound two shillings;

James Thom, teacher at Whitburn (or his wife, Janet Waterston) who had bread delivered three times a week – one pound fourteen shillings;

Robert Binnie, spirit dealer at Harthill – one pound nine shillings;

John White, spirit dealer at Harthill - one pound.

Some of these customers were quite rightly furious about the matter and they explained that they owed nothing at all, mostly having paid for their bread on the day that it had been delivered.

What did eighteen year old William Trotter have to say about the matter? When questioned, he confirmed that it was part of his duties to take payments and account for them daily to his employer, Mr Borthwick. He explained that the only money he had kept was one pound twelve shillings, which he had spent on clothes over the past year, fifteen shillings which he had spent on a dog to guard his cart, as he had often had bread stolen from it, and about six shillings a week over the year, which he had spent on drink in different public houses. He had excused the drinking by saying he had done so to increase potential sales!

He went on to say that over the course of around fourteen months a quantity of bread had been stolen from the cart and he had been embarrassed to inform his employer about it, as the thefts had occurred when he had been in the pubs drinking with his friends. He had devised a rather complicated method of accounting, pretending that those customers who had credit facilities had not paid immediately, borrowing from some of the other payments to provide himself with ready cash, and generally successfully keeping Mr Borthwick in the dark as regards the financial position. He seemed to know to whom he owed money and exactly how he could repay it.

What happened to William Trotter at the trial which took place at the High Court in Edinburgh on Saturday 17 March 1838? He was found guilty for the crime of breach of trust and embezzlement and sentenced to imprisonment in the Bridewell of

Edinburgh for twelve months, with hard labour, subject to the rules and regulations of that establishment.

What happened to Mr Borthwick, the baker? By the time the 1841 census was taken at Mid Calder he had two new apprentices – and no doubt they would be supervised with more care.

National Records of Scotland reference AD14/38/471; JC26/721; JC26/1838/485

GEORGE YORKSTON (with David Morrison and George Wardrop)

THEFT AT HIGH STREET, LINLITHGOW 9 DECEMBER 1837

It was on Saturday evening, 9 December 1837 or in the early morning of the Sunday at Linlithgow when the theft occurred. Mrs Jean Johnston or Gibb lived on the south side of the High Street, opposite the post office. There was a stable forming part of her property, situated just behind the house, where she kept several fowls. George Yorkston was indicted for theft in that he broke into the south gable of the loft of that stable by removing several pieces of wood securing a window, entering the window and stealing a cockerel and a hen. This was aggravated by the fact that he was *"by habit and repute a thief"* and had previously been convicted of theft. During the course of the investigation into this crime, two of George's friends – David Morrison and George Wardrop – were also found to have been involved.

Henrietta Rule lived with her grandmother, Jean Gibb. She explained that the stable was in the garden - south of her grandmother's house. At around three o'clock in the afternoon of the Saturday in question, Henrietta had gone into the stable to ensure that her grandmother's seven fowls were on the roost and she had locked the door behind her when she came out. The window in the loft was about three or four feet from the ground and was secured by a piece of wood from an old cart, which was laid loosely in front of it on the outside. It was an old window opening, without either a frame or glass. The next morning, at around nine o'clock, however, her uncle John Campbell had gone to the stable to let the fowls out. He had been somewhat surprised to find that the door was open and only five of the seven fowls were there – a black cockerel and a white hen were missing.

The following day, Henrietta had heard in the town that a black cockerel and white hen had been sold to Captain Charles Grant at Greenpark, Linlithgow, and after discussing the matter with the procurator fiscal, she had proceeded there with her uncle the next day. On enquiring about the birds, Helen McGregor, Captain Grant's housekeeper, had brought them out and they had immediately been identified as those belonging to Henrietta's grandmother. The fowls had then been taken home to their rightful owner. Henrietta also explained that the garden ground at the back of her grandmother's house was raised to around three or four feet on the south of the gable of the stable and one could easily have gained access by pushing the piece of old cart and going down the stable hack, which was open at one end. Her thoughts were that thieves had gained entry this way, coming back out by the stable door which had been opened from the inside. She had noticed no signs of forced entry on the door or its lock.

John Campbell, Jean Gibb's son in law, was a clerk to Adam and Dawson Distillers in Linlithgow. He concurred with Henrietta's statement and said that there had been no obvious sign of a break in, but he could see that a number of bricks had been removed from a window in the adjoining cellar, which would have left a large enough opening for a thief to gain entry. At midday on the Monday, John had been speaking to Robert Meikle, foreman at Saint Magdalene's Distillery, who had informed him that he had just seen David Morrison, George Yorkston and another lad going east along the canal bank and they were carrying a bag with something in it. He had later discovered that they had sold a cockerel and hen to Captain Grant at Greenpark and he and Henrietta had subsequently gone to retrieve the stolen birds there.

Helen McGregor – Captain Charles Grant's housekeeper – stated that on the Monday a young lad had come to the kitchen door at Greenpark at about one o'clock in the afternoon. He had been dressed in a light coloured moleskin jacket and trousers, with a harm apron over the top of the trousers, but she had not particularly looked at his face. He had carried a black cockerel and white hen in a dirty canvas bag and had told her she could have them both for three shillings. She had offered him two shillings, which he had accepted readily, and then he had left. She confirmed that the fowls had then been taken away again to Mrs Gibb by Henrietta and her uncle.

Robert Anderson, servant to Captain Charles Grant, had been cutting the hedge round a field at Greenpark, on the south side of the Edinburgh Road, opposite the house, that Monday. At around one o'clock that afternoon he had seen three lads walking eastwards on the bank of the canal - two of them dressed in light garments and one in dark dress (Morrison). When these lads had been passing along the canal bank, he had heard them talking, saying that one of them had sold hens at the Marches Day. Robert had seen two of the lads coming along eastwards along the Edinburgh Road, but neither of them was carrying anything, whilst the other lad, who was wearing a harm apron, had gone by a small gate towards Captain Grant's house. David Morrison had gone west near to the Toll House and a few minutes later the lad wearing the harm apron had come out by the gate, with a bag in his hand, and called out to Morrison, who had returned to join him. Unfortunately, Robert was only able to identify Morrison, but not the others. The third lad had come to join them on the canal bank. After Mrs McGregor had bought the fowls, John Campbell had arrived, claiming the two fowls as being the property of his mother in law, Mrs Gibb.

When questioned, Robert Meikle stated that he had seen Morrison, Yorkston and another lad at the canal bank near to the Distillery on the Monday around noon. The lad who he did not know was dressed in a light moleskin jacket, dark trousers with harm apron over, and a bonnet and he had gone eastwards along the bank. The three lads were walking briskly. The lad with the harm apron had been carrying a little canvas bag, which obviously contained something live, as this was moving around a good deal and sounded like a bird! He'd heard from John Campbell about the theft at his mother in law's premises and had immediately informed him about these lads. They had returned along the Edinburgh Road, after the young lad with the now empty bag had made a signal to the others. He did not know that lad's name, but he had seen him around the town frequently and he lived not far from his own house.

Ann McIntosh, wife of James Russell, shoemaker, had been in Morrison's house one Monday morning in December. According to her, Morrison, Yorkston, Wardrop, and Elizabeth Yorkston, were there when she had arrived. She had only remained there for a few minutes, but she had seen Yorkston going to the foot of Morrison's bed, lifting out a cockerel and hen and placing them into a bag. The three lads had left and gone up the Lion Well Wynd, with Yorkston carrying the bag. Nothing had been said which led her to suspect that the fowls had been stolen, and she had not seen Yorkston or Wardrop for some months afterwards.

William Jamieson was one of the officers of the Burgh of Linlithgow. He received a petition and warrant on 12 December from the Procurator Fiscal against Yorkston and Morrison for the theft of the cockerel and hen. He had immediately gone to Morrison's house and apprehended him, but Yorkston had run off. He had received the other warrant in respect of George Wardrop the following day, but could not find him. He made several searches over the course of three months, but could find neither Yorkston nor Wardrop and believed that they had absconded. James Nicholl, messenger at arms from Linlithgow, confirmed that he had known Yorkston and Morrison for around seven years and knew them to be common thieves. He could not say the same, however, of George Wardrop. William Hendrie, Sheriff Officer at Linlithgow, concurred with this.

Who was George Wardrop? He was an eighteen year old shoemaker and son of Daniel Wardrop. When apprehended, his version of events was that on the evening in question he had gone to David Morrison's house at about seven o'clock and had sent for a gill of whisky. George Yorkston had arrived and they had all drunk at least four gills of whisky in total. After the first two gills, Yorkston had left and Morrison and Wardrop had gone looking for him at around eleven o'clock. They had found him in *"Jocks"* - John Balcanquhar's house. The three of them had returned to Morrison's house and had a third gill. Wardrop and Yorkston had left again about midnight, and Wardrop had returned first, with Yorkston twenty minutes later. Yorkston had disappeared *yet again* for three quarters of an hour, after which he had returned with a cockerel and hen stuck inside his clothes. On being questioned by the others, Yorkston had said that he had *"got"* them in the town – not that he had stolen them – but did not mention from where. At around one o'clock on the Sunday morning Wardrop had left Morrison's house, but Yorkston had remained, and Wardrop had met up with the others later on that day.

On the Monday Wardrop was at Morrison's again with Yorkston, when the latter had said he might send his sister, Jean, to try to sell the two fowls. Morrison's wife had noticed a hole in the bottom of Morrison's bag, so they had asked for the loan of Wardrop's sack, which contained some leather for making shoes. Wardrop had emptied his bag, with Morrison's wife and another woman holding it open and Yorkston had put the fowls into it. The three of them had then left, going up the Lion Well Wynd to the canal basin, continuing by the back path of the canal to the aqueduct bridge over the Edinburgh Road at St Magdalene's Brewery. They had gone near to Captain Grant's house, with Yorkston stopping there and Morrison and Wardrop walking on. Wardrop had gone to Captain Grant's house to sell the birds, and it was *his* idea to ask for three shillings for the fowls, if not then half a crown, if not then two shillings, if not then anything he could get! He had sold them for two shillings to Captain Grant's housekeeper, giving the cash to Yorkston, who had treated him and Morrison to a gill of whisky at John Sherman's public house. Yorkston had used some of the money to repay a debt to Mr David Henderson, a cloth merchant in Linlithgow, and when the three arrived back at Morrison's house, Yorkston had treated the two of them to yet another gill. Yorkston had kept the rest of the money and Wardrop had returned home afterwards. Yorkston had returned that night, telling him that the town officer had been looking for him, as he had actually stolen the fowls from Mrs Gibb's byre, with the door having been left open, but that he had escaped. Wardrop confirmed that he had not been with Yorkston when he had stolen the birds and had not known they were stolen when he sold them.

There were four letters in respect of Wardrop's good character and these were from his previous employers:

Letter dated 1 October 1838 from Rob Eagan stating, *"George Wardrop while in my service, which was three several times, was honest and faithful to his trust so far as I know and I always considered him as a well behaved young man."*

Letter dated 2 October 1838 from Will Henderson stating, *"This is to certify that George Wardrop was some time in my employment and that he conducted himself in a regular manner."*

Letter dated 3 October 1838 from Alex Law stating, *"I hereby certify that George Wardrop shoemaker was sometime in my employment and that he conducted himself in a regular manner."*

Letter dated 3 October 1838 from Alex Murray, foreman to Mr Edward Spence stating, *"This is to certify that George Wardrop which under My Master's employ behaved himself in every respect that nothing can't be said to him in any respect."*

Another letter from John Wilson, Linlithgow dated 5 October 1838 stated, *"The prisoner George Wardrop's father has applied to me with the view of getting him out on bail, as his health is suffering much from the confinement. Will you have the goodness to inform me whether I shall consent to the liberation of Wardrop on bail and to what amount the bail shall be taken? Seems to be his first offence. Also Yorkton says he committed the crime on his own."*

Who was George Yorkston? He was a twenty year old shoemaker and son of Alexander Yorkston, labourer. According to his statement, on a Saturday evening at the beginning of December he had been in company with George Wardrop and David

Morrison in the latter's house. They had drunk some whisky, but Yorkston had left at about ten o'clock, to seek his wages from Mr Henderson, his master. He had returned about half an hour later, finding Morrison and his wife (Yorkston's sister) and Wardrop there. They had drunk some more whisky and Yorkston had left alone around eleven o'clock, following which he had gone to the foot of the Lion Well Wynd and bought a bottle of whisky from a person named Mathieson.

Elizabeth Yorkston lived with David Morrison, although she was not married to him. According to her, on Saturday evening 9 December, Wardrop had been in Morrison's house and had left with him, looking for Yorkston. They had all returned shortly afterwards, after which the other two had left and she and Morrison had gone to bed. Apparently, Yorkston had kept a red cockerel at Morrison's from the Friday till the Monday, but she had never seen either a black cockerel or white hen. Morrison and Yorkston worked together in Morrison's house and on the Monday morning Wardrop had appeared with a bag rolled up in his hand, asking Morrison to take a walk, but she had begged him not to go. All three of them had then gone up the Lion Well Wynd, returning to Morrison's in the afternoon.

On their return, none of the three had carried a bag. On the Monday afternoon Wardrop had been dressed in a fusham jacket and light trousers and had on a cap or bonnet, but she had not observed whether he had worn an apron. Yorkston had been dressed in a dark coat and light fusham trousers, with a leather bonnet and apron. At no time on the Saturday night had Wardrop and Yorkston left and returned with a cockerel and hen in their hands. After their return from their walk on Monday afternoon she had heard Wardrop and Yorkston talking together about selling a cockerel and hen, but Morrison had been smoking his pipe by the fire!

Forty two year old David Morrison made his first statement on 20 November, saying that when he had left his house with Yorkston and Wardrop to take a walk on the Monday morning there had been nobody in the house except Elizabeth Yorkston, but on his return in the afternoon Elizabeth's mother was also there. Wardrop had emptied his bag of some leather in the morning, but he had put it back into the bag later, carrying it away with him. Morrison had heard nothing of anyone having sold fowls that day and he had certainly not received a share of any money got by either Yorkston or Wardrop. In his next statement of 12 December, Morrison stated that at about eight o'clock on Saturday evening Wardrop had come looking for Yorkston, who they had eventually found in the house of John Balcanquhar at about eleven o'clock, and they had all returned to Morrison's house. Having drunk some whisky, Wardrop and Yorkston had left, with Wardrop returning first and Yorkston about half an hour thereafter, which was at around half past twelve. Neither Wardrop nor Yorkston had had anything of a suspicious nature in their possession and shortly afterwards, Morrison had gone to bed, leaving his friends sitting by the fire, but having fallen asleep, he was unable to confirm when they had actually left the house. He had seen Yorkston the next day and on the Monday morning he had been with him and Wardrop. They had walked along the canal bank as far as the Magdalene Aqueduct, returning home by the Edinburgh Road at around one o'clock in the afternoon. Before leaving Morrison's house, Yorkston had got an empty bag from Wardrop and had gone away with it. Morrison had gone out to the head of the Wynd and he had been joined by the other two five minutes later, with Yorkston carrying a bag which seemed to contain something, although he could not say what it was.

On coming opposite the Magdalene Distillery, Yorkston had transferred the bag with its contents to Wardrop, who had carried it till they reached house of Captain Charles Grant of Greenpark. Yorkston and Wardrop had stopped there, but Morrison had gone on further. On looking back, he had seen Yorkston standing on the road and Wardrop coming out from the entry, having received two shillings for the two fowls. The three of them had gone to John Sliman's public house, where they had drunk some whisky - paid for by Yorkston – and returned to Morrison's house. Morrison reiterated that he had not gone into the stable occupied by Mrs Gibb on the Saturday night or any time in Sunday morning, nor had either of the others.

What was the outcome of the case of the stolen fowls? At the High Court in Edinburgh on 27 December 1838 George Yorkston was found guilty of the crime of theft by housebreaking, habit and repute, and previous conviction in terms of his own confession and sentenced to transportation for 7 years. His friends, it appeared, were not found guilty of any crime.

Note: According to an appearance at Linlithgow Sheriff Court on 13 May 1845 a George Yorkston appeared for the theft of a quantity of wearing apparel. He was described as being aged twenty five, born and residing at Linlithgow, having a ruddy complexion, brown hair and grey eyes. He was said to be of clean and sober appearance, a shoemaker to trade and having already appeared once before the Sheriff. For this crime he was sentenced to imprisonment for one month. He appeared again on 4 September 1847 before the Magistrates for theft of breaking into a garden, for which he was sentenced to imprisonment for 3 months.

Note: On 18 August 1858 David Wardrop or Morrison, shoemaker and son of David Morrison and Elizabeth Yorkston, was incarcerated in Linlithgow Jail for 7 days when he was eighteen years old for theft of pears.

National Records of Scotland reference AD14/38/569; JC26/1838/635; H421/18/1

ROBERT FERRIER AND MARY PORTEOUS

THEFT BY HOUSEBREAKING AT HOWDEN PARK, MID CALDER 29 MARCH 1844

It was on Tuesday, 12 March 1844 at Howden Park farm, Mid Calder (*not to be confused with Howden Park House in Livingston*) and the snow was melting on the ground. William Auld, who lived there, had no family and the only people living with him at the house were his maid servant, Grace Wood, and manservant, James Murray. James Murray slept in the stable, but kept a chest containing his clothes inside in the milk house at the back of the main house. On the day in question Mr Auld had left during the day to go to the Mid Calder Fair, leaving the servants, who would follow later, behind. As far as Auld was concerned, the windows were secured (usually by means of a nail), his sword was in the kitchen and Murray's chest was in the milk house. Grace had passed him the house key when she had arrived at the Fair later, so he had returned home that evening at around five o'clock to an empty house. What had met him on his return, however, was the sight of the under part of the milk house window being out altogether, lying outside beside the wall, with the glass completely broken – the opening left being large enough to let a thief enter. Murray's chest was standing outside the window and, being unlocked, it was obvious that a great many of his clothes had been stolen. Mr Auld had not seen anybody lurking by the house, either when he left or on returning, and he confirmed that the nearest house to his was about one hundred and seventy yards away.

James Murray, his servant, had quite a few clothes in the chest and he could describe them all. He had left Howden Park at around eleven o'clock that morning to go to the Fair. He confirmed that his master had already left, but Grace Wood was still there attending to her chores. On his way out, he had met a middle aged woman, who was going to the kitchen asking for charity, and then as he passed the threshing mill he had seen an "*oldish*" man dressed in a drab coloured great coat, blue bonnet (with night cap underneath) and corduroy trousers. Feeling sorry for the man, he had given him a piece of bread and cheese, which he had been carrying, and had then gone on his way. This man had already been to Howden Park about a month before asking for charity, so Murray had told him that if he was to go along to the kitchen he might be lucky enough to get something there from the servant, the master having left the house.

Murray returned from the Fair about midnight and he had had to "*rap Grace up*" (knock on the door for Grace) to get the key to the stable, whereupon he had been informed that his chest had been opened and all of his clothes stolen. When he had arrived at the milk house the shutters were closed, but on opening them, the undersash of the window was found to be missing completely. He had closed the shutters and gone to bed. The chest was unlocked, because he had lost the key to it a fortnight before. The lock had been taken off, therefore, and a new key was being made for it. In the morning, Murray had noticed a footprint in the snow outside the window, which appeared to have been made by a well-worn shoe, with tackets and heel and two piece. The clothes which were missing were two black cloth coats, a black cloth waistcoat, a pair of black cloth trousers, a pair of drab coloured cassimere (all-wool woven fabric) trousers, a drab coloured great coat, a shepherd's tartan plaid in white and black, two white cotton shirts (one with linen breast) two pairs of worsted stockings, a flannel shirt and a green and white cotton handkerchief. A lilac striped cotton shirt and a red cotton handkerchief had been hanging on a nail on the wall and they had also disappeared, as well as two drab coloured waistcoats with sleeves, a drab coloured cassimere waistcoat with sleeves and a tartan waistcoat. The list of missing items had been given to the constable at Mid Calder the following day and after the prisoners had been apprehended and the articles retrieved, Murray had been able to identify all of them, although the lilac striped shirt was not his and the shepherd's plaid, although similar to his, could not be identified accurately. Murray said that he was sure that Ferrier was the man who had been at the house, but he was unable to identify Porteous.

Angus Falconer, an Edinburgh constable who lived at Mid Calder, verified that James Murray had come to him that evening at around seven o'clock to inform him of the break-in. He had accompanied Murray to inspect the premises and he had seen the broken and missing window pane, as well as the footprints in the snow. As to the man's description which was given to him, he knew that it *completely* matched that of Robert Ferrier of Queensferry.

Grace Wood, Mr Auld's servant, said that she had left Howden Park at around noon for the Mid Calder Fair. Prior to this, the Porteous woman had come to the kitchen asking for charity and Grace had kindly given her a bowl of broth, which Porteous had taken outside to share with her "*husband*" (who was nowhere to be seen). Mary had left about half an hour afterwards, checking the windows beforehand. She had seen James Murray's great coat, three or four waistcoats and striped shirt hanging on the wall and had seen her master's sword in the kitchen a few days before, but was unsure if she had seen it on the day in question. After locking the door, she had noticed footprints of a worn shoe in the snow, but had thought nothing more of it. She had passed the house key to Mr Auld at the Fair and returned after a good day out, at around eight o'clock that evening. Her master had immediately informed her of the break-in and indicated the missing window. She had also observed that Murray's clothes were no longer on the nail, the lid of his trunk was off, and all his clothes were missing. Her master's sword had also been taken.

There were several people who had seen Ferrier and Porteous that day. William Wyllie, son of James Wyllie, a farmer at Craigs, Mid Calder, had seen Ferrier sitting on the dyke round his father's field, which was about three hundred yards from Howden Park. The man had remarked that it was a stormy day, but although there had been a woman further away, Wyllie could not have identified her.

John Thomas, servant of John Law, farmer at the Holygate, Uphall, had met the two accused at about two o'clock that afternoon on the road just outside Broxburn, when driving the turnips home. (He explained that this was about three miles away from Howden Park and on the road from Mid Calder to Queensferry.) Ferrier and Porteous had been carrying bundles at the time - the former's wrapped in a tartan plaid - and Ferrier had been shouting for Porteous to hurry up.

It appeared that Ferrier and Porteous were well known thieves! George Miles, a Linlithgow Sheriff Officer who lived at South Queensferry, had been with John Kerr on the road from South Queensferry to Kirkliston at about five o'clock on the evening in question and he had seen both of the accused. Both were wearing tartan shepherds' plaids, but Ferrier's looked quite new, and both were carrying bundles, with Ferrier's being the largest. However, on Saturday 23rd Kerr and Agnes Falconer had come to Miles' house to inform him of the housebreaking, describing the stolen articles. They had all gone to Porteous' house, where Ferrier was lying in his bed. The stolen articles were located, as was Porteous, who was standing out in the street. She completely denied any involvement in the theft, of course, but Miles had already known of a previous conviction dated 26 September 1843 and that she had been a thief *"by habit and repute"* over the last three years!

Angus Falconer had also been there when the prisoners were arrested, when Ferrier had told him that he had bought the shepherd's plaid at Gallawater. Falconer had scolded Ferrier in no uncertain terms that he should be absolutely ashamed to have stolen from those who had been so charitable to him, but Ferrier had only retorted that he had thought the clothes belonged to the Laird. To confirm matters further, a pair of shoes had been found in Porteous' house which completely matched the footprints in the snow.

And what of the two accused? Robert Ferrier was a sixty year old labourer born at Corstorphine, Edinburgh, who said that he lived with his brother, Alexander, at Currie, unless he was working away. When questioned, he denied ever having seen any of the stolen articles until the 23rd when they had been discovered in a chest belonging to Mary Porteous. The striped shirt was his. He went on to say that he lodged with her when he had work in her area and slept with her, although they definitely were not married. His story was that he had been at the house of a man called Cochrane at Broxburn on the day in question and had gone on to the Mid Calder Fair later. He had accidentally encountered Mary Porteous en route. They had both then passed by Howden, where Mary had gone to the door *"to ask for a piece"* (piece of bread and butter) and proceeded to Letham Farm. Apparently Mary had sought food at various locations at Broxburn later. He had lost sight of her at New Liston and proceeded to Queensferry on his own, where he had arrived after sunset. When asked if he had eaten any broth, Ferrier confirmed that Mary had shared some with him at Howden Park and this had been at around ten o'clock. Apparently Mary had been carrying a bundle when he first met up with her. Ferrier stated that he had gone to widow Brown's about half an hour after arriving at South Queensferry – her house being in a close opposite the distillery - but had gone to bed when he got back to Mary Porteous' house.

Widow Brown (Janet Jamieson or Brown) confirmed that he had, indeed, come to look for Mary Porteous at around eight o'clock in the evening. Ferrier had told her that he was getting his clothes ready to go down to the south country.

Irish Mary Porteous, aged thirty, confirmed that she lived at South Queensferry and that Ferrier had lived with her off and on for about four years. They had stayed at a farm house near Broxburn on 11 March and slept in the byre. The following day they had gone to another farm where they were given some broth and after she had taken the bowl back to the servant, Ferrier had disappeared. Her version of events was that he had returned to her house a few hours later *"about gloaming"* (about dusk), carrying a bundle wrapped in a shepherd's plaid, but he had not had this when they were together. He had put the bundle into the chest in her room, but she had not enquired as to what it contained.

Mary Porteous had previously been imprisoned for theft one week after appearing at the Linlithgow Sheriff Court on 26 September 1843.

Robert Ferrier (alias George Gray) had a previous conviction at the High Court Ayr dated 30 April 1822 for cattle stealing, for which the sentence had been 7 years transportation.

What was the outcome of this crime? Both Robert Ferrier and Mary Porteous were found guilty of theft by housebreaking, habit and repute at the High Court in Edinburgh on 10 June 1844. They were both imprisoned for 15 months.

National Records of Scotland reference AD14/44/295; JC26/1844/417

DUNDAS McCRINER

CULPABLE HOMICIDE AT MOUNTEERIE, BATHGATE 19 MAY 1844

It was a Sunday afternoon, 19 May 1844 up at Mounteerie, near to Cathlaw, Bathgate, which is about two miles from Ballencrieff Tollhouse. Marion Wardrop, the daughter of Thomas Wardrop, handloom weaver in Livery Street, Bathgate and Mary Anderson, had married Dundas McCriner on 29 September 1838 and the banns were called at Torphichen, where he lived, and at Bathgate, where she was born. She had moved up there to Mounteerie with Dundas in the January of 1844. She had borne four children to him, but only one of them, four year old Isabella, was alive by that year. Two of their sons had been named Robert, after their paternal grandfather, but one son, Robert "*Macriner*", died of apoplexy in September 1840 when he was aged three years, and the other son, Robert "*McGrainer*", as it was spelt in the Old Parish Registers, had died of fever only months before , in January 1844, when he was an infant. There was nothing suspicious about this, with the rate of infant mortality being so high then.

The McCriners' neighbour was Janet Kerr, widow of James Kerr, quarryman, and daughter of John Tripney, lime burner, and Agnes Aikman. She had lived in that cottage for well nigh twenty five years and had been very happy there. The wall between the two cottages was very thin and when her neighbours spoke quietly she could hear only faint voices, but not what was actually being said. If the voices were raised, however, she could hear every word. She had heard a commotion next door one evening about six weeks previously, with Dundas McCriner shouting and swearing and even apparently beating his wife. This had gone on all night long, with occasional outbursts of singing on his part, as he had been clearly quite inebriated.

Mrs McCriner had come to her door the following morning after this incident when Janet was getting ready for church and her face had been badly bruised. Mrs Kerr had told her that she had heard all that had passed that night and could not stay there any longer to hear such goings on – even if Marion paid her. Marion had replied that it would never happen again and apologised. Later, when Mrs Kerr was returning from church, she had seen Marion's parents going up the road to visit the McCriners and had told them it would be better if they didn't, since her daughter and husband had been somewhat the worse for liquor. They proceeded, however, and on being told that the family had not eaten any breakfast, had taken a walk for half an hour to let them do so. Mr and Mrs Wardrop had subsequently put both of them to bed, having taken the child, Isabella, to John Bain, the McCriner's neighbour. They hoped that after a good sleep they would be somewhat reconciled! Apparently Dundas had struck his wife with a poker on that occasion, after which he had felt very vexed and ashamed, *according to his wife*.

Dundas was an agricultural labourer and Marion was a tambourer (an embroiderer), helping to augment the family income with her work at home. It was a pleasant enough day in May and Marion's sister, Julian, who was at that time living at the home of her uncle, William Anderson, also a weaver in Bathgate, decided to go up to visit the McCriners. She went along with her sister, Mary, who was usually working at Dullator as a servant, and her brother David, as well as Robert Davidson, Julian's sweetheart. They had left Bathgate at around three in the afternoon and it was a good hour's walk up there, so they had eventually arrived at around four o'clock. They had taken some whisky with them for the visit, as drink was cheap enough, but Marion had asked David to go to the Ballencrieff Tollhouse for another three gill, which they had drunk whilst talking and socialising. Time was getting on, so Marion and Dundas had walked the visiting party homewards, but they had all decided to call into the Ballencrieff Tollhouse, which was kept by Matthew Wilson, for another mutchkin of whisky, chased down with a bottle of strong ale, which was bought by Robert Davidson. The visitors had left the McCriners at the road leading to Sunnyside, thinking that the little family (Marion had young Isabella with her) would then return homewards. They seemed to be in fine fettle, on good terms and nothing was amiss.

Perhaps it *would* have been better if they had gone home at that point.

Ballencrieff Toll

What kind of man was Dundas McCriner? He was born on 24 February 1818 to Robert McCriner and Isabel Wilson at Ratho, but had moved to West Lothian with his family some time afterwards, settling for a while at Torphichen. He had brothers – Peter, George and Robert. It was common knowledge in Bathgate, where the couple had lived for a while, that he could be cruel to his wife if he had been drinking, although Marion's sisters said that they had never actually witnessed any physical cruelty, but had heard high words being shouted on a few occasions. Marion's eighteen-year old brother, David, had also witnessed Dundas threaten to take off her jacket and thrash her! In other words, he already had a reputation in the neighbourhood as someone who mistreated his wife.

Robert Davidson, who was stepping out with Julian Wardrop, was a nineteen-year old farm servant working along at Ballencrieff Mill for John Chapman, the miller, there. In his evidence he described that the visiting party had taken a small parish road to the east of Bathgate on the way to Mounteerie. His story differed from Julian's in that it had been Dundas McCriner who had gone down to the Tollhouse originally to buy the whisky. He had also confirmed that it was well known that McCriner was abusive to his wife, although in the three years he had known him, he had witnessed nothing himself. He said that on the way down by Ballencrieff, the visiting ladies had stopped by the house of Mrs Marshall at Sunnyside.

Instead of going home, Dundas, Marion and the child – Isabella - had gone back to the Tollhouse where two servants - David Nicol and Thomas Hill - and another – William Stewart from the Kipps Colliery - had arrived there. At about eight o'clock that evening McCriner and Marion, with Scott's men and Stewart, had gone up the hill to Ballencrieff Mains, but once again Dundas had required yet another drink to sustain him. Thomas Baillie, a Bathgate weaver, and Robert Fleming – an engineer in Blackburn – had socialised with the McCriners at the Tollhouse and gave statements to this effect. There still seemed to be nothing amiss, but with time going on and with Marion having the child with her, she had mentioned to her husband that they should be getting home. Now, whether it was this last statement which had angered him or something else, it will never be known.

A violent death, however, awaited poor Marion McCriner. Despite various witness statements to the effect that Marion herself was not overly intoxicated, she was found in the early hours of the next morning, wet and mortally injured, lying near to the gate at Sunnyside.

The story which Dundas McCriner told was that his wife, with the child, had returned homewards, and gone into Mrs Marshall's house at Sunnyside en route. (That was Margaret Boyd, wife of Robert Marshall, the miller.) The Marshalls were actually in bed, but Margaret had quickly put a coat on over her nightdress and walked up part of the road with them, carrying the child herself. Dundas had explained that this was because his wife was very intoxicated and could have fallen. They had walked as far as the gate, which was two hundred and fifty yards from the Marshall's house, and

Margaret had gone home again. This was at around ten o'clock. Apparently, as far as Dundas was concerned, what happened next was that when they had arrived home he had "*joked*" with his wife about appearing drunk in front of her friends and she had subsequently gone outside for a walk, shutting the door behind her. He had then fallen asleep with the child on his knee, waking up three hours later. He had gone out searching for her and found her lying in the middle of the road, quite cold and wet and covered with blood, with almost all of her clothes torn and hanging about her. There was a small run of water which was damned up near to the gate next to Mrs Marshall's, which was the only place she could have gotten wet apparently. He had tried to lift her, but couldn't do so alone, so he had run to Mrs Marshall's for help. She and her son had dressed themselves, ran to the spot and David Marshall had carried Marion on his back to the McCriner's cottage, with Dundas carrying her legs. When she had been put to bed she was still breathing, but had been unable to speak, and she had died shortly afterwards. On being questioned, McCriner stated that he was totally ignorant of how she had come by her injuries, saying he had been on good terms with his wife for a long time and that he had certainly *not* assaulted her with a poker some weeks ago.

The autopsy, however, described her numerous injuries in detail, and that she was also pregnant. The conclusion was that she could not have come by these injuries any other way than if they had been inflicted by another person. If she had fallen and injured herself, the type of injuries she had sustained were not consistent with such a fall.

What actually happened? There were many witnesses brought forward. John Addie was a farm servant who lived close to the Toll and he worked for John Johnston, tacksman of East Mains of Ballencrieff Farm. He had been at the steading of the farm about a quarter of a mile north of the Toll bar looking after the horses. On his way home, he had heard a man's voice on the road to Sunnyside and that voice was loud and rough and very angry. He was speaking to someone, but John did not know to whom. He had also heard a child crying off and on, but he could not say who the individuals were or what was actually happening.

Mrs Margaret (Peggy) Boyd was married to Robert Marshall, the miller at Sunnyside. She recalled how the McCriners and their visitors had first called on her at around six o'clock on the evening in question. She had gone to bed at around nine o'clock but had almost immediately been aroused by a knock at the door. Marion McCriner had shouted to be let in and she had her young daughter, who was crying bitterly, with her. Margaret didn't want to let them in, as she thought they had been at the Toll bar. Her husband agreed that they should be sent home as soon as possible. She was still wearing her nightdress when she opened the door, but Marion (who seemed only slightly the worse for drink) had pushed past her and sat on a chair. She had pleaded for Margaret not to let her husband in and to shut the door on him if he appeared. Margaret had refused, however, and when he had appeared he had proceeded to ask why Marion was sitting there. He had said that he would carry Isabella home, but when Margaret had gone to put the child on his back, the girl had started crying loudly. At Marion's request, Margaret had walked up the road a little with them – just to the gate - taking Marion's arm to steady her. Dundas did not appear to be angry, but he had told Margaret that she should return home, as it was a cold night. As the child would not go with him, Margaret had strapped her to Marion's back. Marion had wanted Margaret to come further, but Dundas had insisted that she go home. She had advised them to go away quietly and not to cause any disturbance and he had *assured* her that there would be none. Marion had explained that he was really quite good hearted and that she would *"face him up"* later. She was cheery when she said this. Margaret was afraid that the child would be hurt if Marion fell, so she had listened for a while as she went down to her own house, but hearing nothing untoward, she had returned home. She confirmed that she was aware that the couple had quarrelled many times before this.

At around ten past one in the morning Margaret was rudely awakened by Dundas McCriner begging her to come and help him. He said that he had been struggling to get his wife home, and in doing so her clothes had become torn. What Margaret saw, however, was Marion lying nearly naked, freezing cold and close to death. She was injured all over her body and blood was pouring from her head. McCriner could not understand what had happened, apparently. Margaret had shouted to her son to come and help immediately and he had carried Marion home. Margaret had then lit a fire, put hot irons in the bed and tried to warm the very injured Marion. She had shouted to Janet Tripney, the neighbour, to help, but that lady was far too frightened to see Marion in such a state. Only James Marshall, Janet's lodger, would come and help her. Marion's mother had arrived from Bathgate at approximately three o'clock in the morning and washed Marion, who had by now passed away. On going down to her own house with Janet Tripney, she had found rags of Marion's clothes and blood in the water by the gate and on the gate itself.

David Marshall, Margaret's son, was a labourer. He remembered that night and how Mrs McCriner had come back to their house at around nine o'clock asking to be let in, with her child crying beside her. He remembered the woman telling his mother not to let Dundas in and that she seemed to have been drinking. He also thought that she looked quite frightened. When Dundas had arrived and tried to carry the child, the girl had screamed and cried and would not go to him. He remembered that at around ten past one in the morning he had been called by his mother to help carry Mrs McCriner home. He had been told to hurry and that the woman had nearly all her clothes torn off. He had carried her home, but she had been almost dead by that point. His clothes, when he got home, were covered with blood. Mr Robert Marshall remembered the night and what had happened. He remembered thinking that although McCriner had seemed civil, his wife had seemed *very* afraid of him.

John Marshall, who was a distiller at Glenmavis, Bathgate, had been examining the water hole at the farm road to Mounteerie at around ten o'clock that evening. He had heard a child screaming and the cries were coming from the direction of the gate. He had heard McCriner, whose voice was very familiar to him, as he had worked for him five years previously for about six months. It was a very distinctive voice, with a bit of a "*burr*" in it. He did not like the man and did not employ him again, despite being asked. He had heard the man and exactly what he was shouting, which was that he would murder someone. He had also heard him urging someone to come with him. The child would start crying, stop and then start again. McCriner was swearing.

Mary Anderson, wife of Thomas Wardrop the weaver, recalled how on the morning of the 20th, at between two and three o'clock, David Marshall had come running to her house telling her she must come to Mounteerie, as her daughter was very ill. She had gone there immediately and found Marion in a shocking state, bruised, covered in blood and dirt. Marion could hardly speak and Mary had asked Dundas McCriner what had happened. He had told her that he had asked his wife why she had got drunk and she had taken offence and gone outside, but he didn't know what had happened to her after that. Mrs Wardrop had sent for her daughter, Agnes, and she had taken the child away to the Wardrop's house in Bathgate. The poor child's pinafore had blood on it. Mrs Wardrop was aware that McCriner had treated her daughter very harshly when they lived in Bathgate. She also recalled the incident five or six weeks ago when she and her husband had visited the couple, along with McCriner's brother, George McCriner of Mid Calder. Her daughter had been struck by her husband with a poker.

Even the four year old Isabella had been questioned as to what had happened between her parents. She remembered the day her aunts and uncle and Rob Davidson had visited and then they had visited Peggy Boyd (Mrs Marshall). She remembered when they had gone back to Peggy's and Peggy had carried her because her "*mammy*" had fallen with her. In fact, there was a most detailed description of everything that the child had seen and heard in respect of what her father had done to her mother, which painted a very gruesome and pitiful tale. She understood that her father was very angry, but her mother was not. She remembered how she herself had cried bitterly witnessing the events which had occurred.

This was indeed a very shocking incident which had taken place on the outskirts of Bathgate.

What happened to Dundas McCriner? He was found guilty of culpable homicide at Edinburgh Court of Justiciary on 24 July 1844 and sentenced for a term of 21 years in terms of his own confession. He was transported to Van Diemen's Land, now known as Tasmania. He was fortunately never heard of again.

What happened to Isabella McCriner, who was left orphaned? She was living with her grandparents – the Wardrops – along with her aunt Agnes at Livery Street, Bathgate in 1851 and working as a cotton winder. She married David Todd, son of David Todd and Agnes Crawford, on 18 June 1858 at Bathgate and Robert Davidson was a witness at the marriage ceremony. Isabella and David had several children and the family subsequently moved to Kilsyth.

Julian Wardrop married her sweetheart, Robert Davidson, on 8 September 1844 at Bathgate. The couple were happily married for many years and had several children.

National Records of Scotland reference AD14/44/374; JC26/1844/441

JANET CALLENDER OR HASTIE

THEFT AT CARRIDEN AND LINLITHGOW JANUARY 1845

It was on Wednesday, 15 or Thursday, 16 January 1845 at the house at Bridgeness, Carriden, Linlithgowshire when Janet Callender or Hastie had apparently stolen a printed cotton gown belonging to Ann Young, wife of Thomas Stewart, coal grieve. Also, on various occasions during the months of January and February 1845 Janet was accused of stealing three pieces of striped cotton cloth, one half of a pair of blankets and a brass candlestick from the house of her father - Alexander Callender, calico printer.

When Janet Callender or Hastie appeared at Linlithgow Sheriff Court on 27 February 1845 she was described as being born at Linlithgow, aged thirty, with dark complexion, light brown hair, grey eyes and had a mark on her lip. She was dirty, intoxicated, with ragged clothes and her occupation was a knitter. She had a previous conviction for theft which was dealt with at the Circuit Court of Justiciary at Stirling on 12 September 1843.

On 8 March Janet Hastie admitted to David Lockie, one of Linlithgow's officers, that she had stolen and sold the various articles belonging to her father in Charles Mackay's shop.

Janet was married to Alexander Hastie, who used to work with Mr Black at Avon Printfield, but subsequently worked at Paisley. According to her statement, he had left her about six years previously, having enlisted as a soldier. She herself lived in Linlithgow with her father Alexander Callender. She said that some five or six weeks previously she had bought a dress from a woman on the Toll Bar on Borrowstouness Road for a shilling, at around five o'clock that evening, but she had sold it to a woman in Linlithgow named McGuigan for a half crown on the same day. She denied that she had been to Bridgeness to the east of Borrowstouness. She had been in several houses in Borrowstouness that day, but the only one she could remember was that of Bell Aitkens. She denied ever having stolen the dress from Bridgeness or anywhere else. She stated that she had recently been in Perth Penitentiary, having been tried and convicted of theft and sentenced to fifteen months. She said she had never been tried for any other theft.

Ann Young, wife of Thomas Stewart, coal grieve Bridgness, Carriden, stated that on Thursday 16 January she had noticed a dark printed cotton gown was missing from her house. It had been seen the previous day and she had subsequently been informed that a woman named Mullrane had been seen wearing it. She informed the police constable at Borrowstouness immediately. Apparently this gown was almost new and had been hanging on a tent bed in a room on the second flat of the house, which had an outside door. She believed the theft had taken place when she was downstairs in the kitchen, saying it would have been easy for a thief to have entered, due to the fact that the doors were on opposite sides of the building.

Janet Stewart or Meikle from Grangepans, Ann's daughter in law, confirmed this was her mother in law's dress and she had seen it in the house on Wednesday, 15 January. James Mullrane, labourer of Borrowstouness, confirmed he had bought that dress from Agnes McGuigan on 29 January, paying four shillings and sixpence for it and he had given it to his sister. Agnes McGuigan, broker of Linlithgow, confirmed that the prisoner had come into her shop one evening and sold her a dark printed dress for two shillings and sixpence. She could not recollect the exact day, however, and only wrote the transactions in a book when she thought the client would return for the item. She seemed to recall it would be about a fortnight after buying the dress from the prisoner that she sold it again. Isabella Aitken, publican and wife of John Graves, cooper at Borrowstouness, stated that she knew the prisoner who had come into her shop a number of weeks previously for a whisky.

As regards the other articles Callender had been accused of stealing, she said they belonged to her father. She had taken them at different times out of his house in January and February and pawned or sold them in Charles Mackay's shop. She got thrupence for the striped cotton. She gave the material to a girl in the shop who subsequently gave over the money. Mr Mackay was present, but had said nothing. She had taken the blanket later and was given one shilling and thrupence for it. Lastly, she had taken the candlestick and got sixpence for it. She did not remember on which days she took the articles to Mackay's shop.

Charles Mackay, a labourer and broker in Linlithgow, confirmed that he had seen Mrs Hastie in his shop several times four weeks ago offering articles for sale, but could not say whether he had purchased anything from her. He *did* remember purchasing a candlestick, but couldn't identify it again. He did not remember the blanket, but said that the shop's management was essentially left to his wife and he paid little attention to the comings and goings there. His wife, Helen Boyle, said that she had been unwell for a number of weeks in January and February, when she was confined to bed. In January her husband and a girl named Elizabeth Fairnie attended to the shop. Elizabeth had brought the striped cloth pieces, each about a yard and a half in length, to her room saying a Mrs Hastie wanted to sell them and Helen had approved the sale. She did not recollect the other items particularly, but when she consulted her broker's book, she confirmed that there was an entry for sixpence for the candlestick and one shilling and sixpence for the half blanket.

Elizabeth Fairnie, servant of Peter McNeil, labourer at 84 Canongate, Edinburgh, said (on 6 March) that she had been a servant to Charles Mackay, broker in Linlithgow for a time until about four weeks previously. When being asked to identify the prisoner, she immediately recognised her as the individual who had repeatedly come to Mackay's shop to sell articles. She remembered that she had come in at least three times to sell some blue and white striped cloth. She confirmed Mrs Mackay's version of events.

Mary Callender, wife of George Buchanan, shoemaker at Linlithgow, and sister of the accused, said that she had lived with her father, Alexander, prior to marrying a year ago. She stated that Janet Hastie had been addicted to drinking for some time and frequently sold her clothes to procure liquor. Mary had only visited her father occasionally since she married, but recognised the candlestick as being very similar to one he had had in the house, but she could not say on oath that it was the very one, as candlesticks all looked very similar. On being shown the striped cloth, she had seen this type of fabric in her father's house and it was to be made into shirts for her two brothers and for Mrs Hastie's two sons. She could definitely identify the cloth as being that which was in her father's house. She also identified the blanket as being her father's.

In a letter from the Crown Agent dated 13 March 1845 it was noted that the previous conviction was under the name of Janet Hastie, Bartholomew or Barclay, being her mother's name. The woman was said to be addicted to drinking for some time past and her mind had been in such a deranged state that she could not be examined. Her father had said he paid little attention to what was in the house.

What happened to the unfortunate Janet Callender or Hastie after the trial took place on Monday, 12 May 1845 at the High Court? She was fortunately dismissed, having been found not guilty.

National Records of Scotland reference AD14/45/332; JC26/1845/399

MARGARET MACKENZIE OR BURNS (ALIAS ELIZABETH TODD/TORBET/ROBB/FRASER AND MARY GORDON)

THEFT WITH PREVIOUS CONVICTION AT KIRKLISTON AND DECHMONT 29 AND 30 MAY 1848

It was Monday, 29 May 1848, and twenty five year old Margaret Mackenzie or Burns had left her lodgings at the Saltmarket, Glasgow where she and her husband, George Burns, shoemaker, were living with Daniel Farrel, who was a hatter to trade. George had been in the infirmary for several months, but as his health was improving, he was now in employment. In her statement of 30 May given at Linlithgow, Margaret said that she had been working for a Mr Arcot, stay manufacturer in Glasgow, and with this experience she had gone to seek work in Edinburgh. She had worked there for two days with a Mr Darling, stay maker at the New South Bridge, but she had been obliged to leave due to work being scarce. On 29 May she had therefore quit his employment and set off back home to Glasgow. According to her, she had stopped off at Broxburn en route and slept by the side of the road, where she had later been taken into custody. Apparently, she had tried to escape a rain shower and a man who was sitting there had asked her to sit by him. Both Margaret and this individual had a bundle with them and a constable had requested to see what these contained. A woman had accompanied the constable, saying nothing, but had apparently accused Margaret of stealing a waistcoat. This waistcoat was found lying in a hedge right behind Margaret, but she had denied ever seeing it or knowing of its whereabouts. Margaret denied ever using the name of Mary Ann Fraser.

When Margaret appeared at the Edinburgh High Court on 21 July 1848, she was convicted of stealing a pair of stockings from a hedge or fence near the garden next to the house occupied by James Baillie, farm servant, at Haugh, Kirkliston on 29 May. She was also convicted of stealing a cotton bed gown belonging to Janet Douglas, wife of Thomas Kerr, from a field beside a house at Dechmont roadside, as well as stealing a waistcoat belonging to James Russell, labourer, from a garden next to the house of Alexander Kerr, labourer, with whom Russell was lodging – both on 30 May.

Agnes Spalding, wife of James Baillie, who lived at Haugh, Kirkliston, confirmed that her husband was farm servant to James Hunter, the farmer at Haugh, and their house was situated on the south side of the Turnpike Road leading from Edinburgh to Glasgow by Broxburn. Haugh itself was a mile and a half east of Broxburn. At about noon on Monday, 29 June, Agnes had washed her husband's dark worsted stockings with a number of other articles, and draped them over a hedge in the front garden, which was near to the Turnpike road, to dry off. On going back out at about six o'clock to collect the clothes, however, she had noticed that the stockings had disappeared.

Janet Douglas, Thomas Kerr's wife, who lived at Dechmont roadside, stated that her house was about one hundred and fifty yards east of Alexander Kerr's house (her son). On Tuesday 30 May she had washed and hung out the clothes to bleach in a small green to the east of the house of William Wilson of Dechmont (presently occupied by John Meikle, carter – his tenant). She had brought the clothes back inside in the evening, but had not thought to confirm what was there. She had heard that afternoon, however, that something had been stolen from her son's garden. She had then suddenly remembered that the white cotton bed gown which she had hung out was not amongst the clothes she had retrieved. She was able to identify the missing garment when it was shown to her later.

Cottage - Dechmont Main Street

Margaret Russell, Alexander Kerr's wife, who also lived at Dechmont roadside, described that her house was situated on the north side of the Turnpike road from Edinburgh to Glasgow by Uphall. On 30 June she had washed her brother's waistcoat, with two of her children's petticoats, putting them all out to dry on a hedge beside the house. They had only been out for ten minutes when she noticed that the waistcoat had disappeared. She had afterwards seen Sergeant John Kerr on the road and informed him of the theft and he advised her that he had seen a woman coming out of her garden. On following her, both noticed that she had sat down next to a man and pushed something into a hedge behind her. The item in the hedge was found to be the stolen waistcoat. On returning to the garden, Kerr and Russell had discovered bare footprints leading to and from the spot where the washing had been hung out. The thief had said she was named Margaret McKenzie. The man had shoes on and had had no chance of taking anything from her prior to her being arrested.

John Kerr, sergeant of the Edinburgh and Bathgate Railway Police, who lived at Houston Mains, Uphall, recalled that on 30 June he was walking along the Turnpike road from Edinburgh to Glasgow by Broxburn and Uphall and on arriving at Alexander Kerr's house at Dechmont Roadside, Kerr's wife had informed him that a woollen waistcoat had gone missing from her garden. He had told her that he suspected a woman who was about one hundred and fifty yards away, as he had seen her coming out of Kerr's garden. They had followed her to ask what her bundle contained, but Kerr had seen her pushing something into the hedge – which was found to be the stolen waistcoat. The waistcoat was very wet and the woman feigned surprise when she saw it. Her bundle contained a napkin, a pair of shoes and a pair of stockings. The man seated beside her on the road had a bundle containing a dirty striped shirt and woollen muffler. Footprints of bare feet had later been found in Mrs Kerr's garden, but Mrs Kerr was wearing shoes at the time.

Helen Douglas, James Burgoyne's wife who lived at Broxburn, kept lodgings. She had identified the woman who called herself Margaret McKenzie, saying that on the night of 29 June she had arrived at her house with a man who she described as her husband, mentioning that they had come from Edinburgh that day. They had only stayed for a night, setting off between nine and ten next morning. After McKenzie's husband had gone to bed, his wife had opened a bundle, taking out a shift (underslip), but said that it was rather damp and that she would have to air it. Helen, taking hold of the article, had noticed it to be extremely wet and had been informed that the rain had soaked it. McKenzie had proceeded to dry it in front of the fire, and put it on when it was still damp.

Susannah Hall lived with her husband, James Allison, Keeper of the Linlithgow Prison. She had examined Margaret McKenzie at Linlithgow and found in her possession a white cotton shift, a white cotton bed gown, a pair of dark worsted stockings, two printed cotton aprons, a single white worsted sock and an imitation ermine wrap. McKenzie's shift was worn in the usual way, but the bed gown, which was quite wet, had been wrapped around her waist under a piece of blanket. The stockings and apron were contained in a small bundle, the worsted sock was pinned inside her gown and she wore the imitation fur across her bosom.

Margaret McKenzie had previous convictions in that on 11 July 1842 (using the name Elizabeth Todd or Torbet when she lived at Ponton Street, Edinburgh) she had stolen a light coloured silk and cotton shawl from Margaret McInally's broker's shop at West Port, Edinburgh (*for which she was imprisoned in Edinburgh for ten days*); on 28 December 1842 (using the name Elizabeth Fraser/Lamb when she lived at Toddrick's Wynd, High Street, Edinburgh) she had stolen a pair of blue checked blankets from Martha Hunter's lodging house (*for which she was imprisoned in*

Edinburgh for 40 days); on 28 November 1842 (Elizabeth Lamb/Morgan) she stole a half blanket, tartan frock and silk handkerchief from Jane Davies/Elder at Rose Street, Edinburgh; on 14 December 1842 (Elizabeth Lamb/Morgan) she stole a pair of blankets from Michael Goodwin at Hastie's Close, Cowgate; on 18 December 1842 (Elizabeth Lamb/Morgan) she stole a pair of blankets from Lawrence Burgoyne in Cowgate and on the same date a damask towel from Margaret McBride at Cowgate (*the last four crimes for which she was imprisoned for 30 days*); on 11 October 1845 (Elizabeth Robb/Fraser) she stole a muslin morning cap, three cambric handkerchiefs, two muslin shirts, two lace cuffs, a linen cuff, a cotton apron and cotton handkerchief (*for which she was imprisoned in Edinburgh for 6 calendar months*); and on 4 June 1846 (Elizabeth Robb/Fraser) she stole a tartan plaid (for which she was imprisoned for 15 calendar months). She was identified as being the same person who had committed each of these crimes by various criminal officers.

What happened to Margaret Burns (with her various aliases)? She was found guilty of the crime of theft aggravated by previous convictions and sentenced to transportation for 7 years.

National Records of Scotland reference AD14/48/326; JC26/1848/495

ELIZABETH FORRESTER OF BATHGATE

WILFUL FIRE RAISING AT GLASGOW 18 APRIL 1849

It was Wednesday, 18 April 1849. Bathgate born Elizabeth Forrester, who was the daughter of Richard Forrester, a plasterer, had gone to work as a kitchen maid for William Kidston junior, an iron master and ship owner, at 4 Jane Street, Glasgow, which is off Blythswood Square.

Elizabeth was 14 years old at the time this event took place. William Kidston, son of Archibald Glen Kidston and Catherine Warden, was married to Hamilton Wallace and they had three children, ie Isabella, Archibald and Katherine. They had lived at Jane Street for around four years and William worked for A G Kidston and Company, Merchants, Great Clyde Street, Glasgow.

The Kidston's home in Jane Street was situated on the first floor of a tenement, which contained three dwelling houses and the property belonged to Mr Peter Allan of Holland Place, Glasgow. Mr Brown and family lived on the ground floor, whilst Mrs McRuer lived above the Kidstons.

On the night in question Mr and Mrs Kidston had attended a soirée meeting at the Trades Hall (only about half a mile from their home in the Merchant City), which started at around seven o'clock, and they had given permission for the cook and housemaid to attend also. The children had been left in the care of the nurse, with Elizabeth Forrester as a nursery assistant, that evening. The event finished at approximately ten o'clock. When they had left their home, there was a fire which had been lit very low in the drawing room and Helen Wilson, the housemaid, had confirmed that she would ensure that it would still be lit when they arrived home.

They had walked home, going up St Vincent Street, and Mr Kidston had seen a West of England fire engine driving past extremely quickly and had learned from a policeman that there was a fire at the corner of **Blythswood Square!** He had run ahead and seen – to his utter horror - a glare of light in his drawing room window. The glare of the fire lit up the whole square. A large crowd had gathered, which terrified him even more, but he was able to get into the house. There were several men in the drawing room, which was full of smoke. He had shut all the doors and by this time, thankfully, the fire engine had arrived. All the other rooms in the house appeared to be in order, and within a short time the smoke had disappeared. The firemen had to chip away the wood round the window with hatchets, however, and the blinds and curtains still had sparks flying off them. He had to carry out the furniture into another apartment with some friends and the fire brigade had left after ensuring everything was in order again and the fire had been completely extinguished.

However, about half an hour later Mr McKirdy, Mrs McRuer's lodger, came downstairs to say that the fire had now broken out upstairs. There was crackling below the floorboards and the fire brigade had to be called out yet again. When he had come downstairs again, he had encountered Elizabeth Forrester standing in the lobby of the house. She seemed very composed and unafraid. Mr Kidston had given her a bit of a push and told her that as far as he was concerned she appeared to be the culprit. Whilst the fire was burning, Elizabeth Forrester had stood in a lobby of the house. She had made no effort in assisting with the furniture removal, nor had she made any attempt to get away. She was removed from the scene by Messrs Cameron and Mackay of the police, taken into a room and questioned. She had denied any involvement, and had tried to say that it was the child's nurse – Elizabeth Gillespie – who had been at fault, but was later taken to Anderston Police Office.

Elizabeth Gillespie stated that she and Forrester had never got on since she had come to the house, because Gillespie had reason to rebuke her and find fault with her at work. At the time of the fire Gillespie was in a room with the youngest child, who had been ill, and Forrester had come to tell her that Archie had wet the bed. Gillespie had sorted out the child's clothes and bedding, which was at around seven o'clock in the evening. She had heard Forrester in the nursery again and had been told Archie had wet the bed once more. The bedding and clothes were renewed again. Then Forrester had come back saying that Isabella had done the very same thing. Gillespie had gone into the baby room again, seen Forrester standing in the centre of a lobby, but she could not understand why. She had told her to put some coals on the fire as master and mistress would soon be home. Gillespie herself had carried some cinders from the kitchen into the drawing room fire in a large shovel. She had heard Forrester in the nursery *yet again*, saying Isabella had once again wet the bed. On asking Isabella why she had wet bed again, she had been told that Nurse Elizabeth had put water out of her mouth onto her. On asking why she had done that, Forrester had denied it. She had left in a rage because Gillespie believed Isabella. The children were not in the habit of wetting the bed, so the nurse had smelt the children's bed gowns and satisfied herself that it was pure water they had been wet with. She had then smelt burning, but thought it might have been caused by singeing with the iron, as Forrester had been told to catch up with this work, so had paid no attention to the smell. When the fire had begun to blaze, Elizabeth Forrester had run out screaming. The nurse had quickly taken the children to another house for safety. It appeared that there was ill feeling between the nurse and Forrester, and the young girl had decided to do something about this which would then put Gillespie out of favour with her employers.

Forrester later confessed to having set fire to the house by applying a lighted piece of paper or match to the cover of a couch or other furniture in the drawing room, causing part of the roof of that room to be destroyed, as well as the shutters of a window, the couch and chair, and curtains and blinds of the window and the carpet.

What happened to Elizabeth Forrester? At her trial at the High Court of Glasgow on 12 September 1849 she was found guilty of wilful fire-raising and was imprisoned for 13 months.

She had obviously been sent home to Bathgate afterwards, and she was living with her parents at Hopetoun Street in 1851. She married John Goodlet in Bathgate in 1853, had several children and moved back to Glasgow to live.

National Records of Scotland reference AD14/49/347; JC26/1849/329

JAMES WATSON, GEORGE SCOULAR (OR SCHOULER) AND JOHN McNIE

ASSAULT AND ROBBERY AT BOGHEAD FARM STEADING, BATHGATE 28 NOVEMBER 1849

It was Wednesday, 28 November 1849, and forty nine year old David Black, a mason who lived at Crossroads, Whitburn, had gone to Bathgate, as it was market day. He *did* take a dram in the town, but by his own estimation he was certainly not drunk. He had left Bathgate, setting off at approximately eight or nine in the evening, but about three quarters of a mile up the Bathgate to Whitburn Road, two hundred yards south of the Boghead farm steading occupied by William Steven, he had come across two young men. No words had passed, but suddenly one of the men had struck him hard on the breast with a stone in his hand, completely winding him in the process and leaving him quite powerless. Standing on Black's left side, one of the men had proceeded to tear open his waistcoat and rifle the pockets, stealing about seven shillings and sixpence in silver money and about fourpence in copper, as well as an oblong brass snuff box and double bladed pocket knife with a buckhorn handle. Not satisfied with this, his attackers had gone into Black's trouser pockets, where he kept his silver fob watch and a brass chain. However, having come to his senses a little by this time, Black had grabbed the man's hand, but as his attacker continued to pull the watch, Black had taken hold of his collar with his left hand to stop him. This had infuriated his assailant so much that he had grabbed Black's thumb in his mouth, biting it severely in two places!

The other villain was behind Black and he had kicked him on the back and punched him in the face, stunning him and making him lose his hold on his first attacker. The two of them had escaped in the direction of Bathgate. This scuffle had lasted roughly five or ten minutes, so it seemed to Black, and due to the fact that he could hardly breathe, he could not call out for assistance. Black had also been holding a walking stick, but this was lost in the affray. It had been a clear moonlit night, so he was able to describe his attackers as being about twenty to twenty four years old, with both being approximately five feet seven and eight inches tall. They were both tradesmen of clean appearance, dressed in darkish shooting coats and cloth caps, but he had not heard them speak. He could easily identify his watch, which was a double cased silver watch made by Manton London - No. 5414 - as it had a crack on the dial plate. There was also a thrupenny silver piece and brass watch key with a steel pipe attached. Black subsequently identified James Watson as being his main attacker and robber and George Scoular as being the individual who had kicked him in the back.

John Rankine was a groom who worked at Hopetoun Street, Bathgate. He knew David Black and stated that at around half past eight on the evening of 28 November Black had come into the stable at the Bathgate Hotel and they had taken a dram there together. Black – who had his vest buttoned up - had certainly taken more than one drink by that time, but was perfectly competent. He had taken his watch out to verify the time and had given some of his snuff to Rankine. When Black had left the hotel, Rankine had walked with him along Hopetoun Street and Engine Street and they had parted near the Free Church. Black was going towards the Whitburn Road and they had certainly not witnessed any fighting in the streets along their way.

James Douglas, a mason who lived at Whitburn, had been in Bathgate on the evening in question. Having left there at around eight or nine o'clock, he had been walking home and about fifty yards south of Boghead farm steading he had heard a shout. When he was about two hundred yards to the south of the steading, a man had come walking towards him with a bleeding nose and a torn vest and he had recognised him as David Black. Black had then told him how he had been attacked and robbed.

Alexander Morrison Black, who lived with his mother, Jane Morrison or Black, a widow and hotel keeper in Bathgate, said he knew Watson, but Scoular only by sight. He had not seen either of them earlier that evening, however, but had gone to Watson's house with John Stewart, a millwright, about midnight when he was somewhat intoxicated. Scoular had been there with Watson and they were dressed in dark moleskin clothes and drinking whisky. Jane Fleming had also been present and, early in the morning, Alexander McDonald had arrived. Alexander Black stated that he had seen no watch and had heard no conversation regarding what had taken place earlier in the evening.

John Stewart, millwright, son of John Stewart weaver, who lived at South Bridge Street, Bathgate, confirmed that he knew the three accused – Watson, Scoular and McNie. He said that Watson had come into his father's house on the evening of the Bathgate fair, at about half past seven, and drunk a dram, remaining there for about an hour. John had not seen either Scoular or McNie then, but when he had gone to Watson's house in an intoxicated state at around two in the morning, Watson, Scoular, McNie and Jane Fleming had been present, as well as Alexander McDonald.

William Stewart, weaver, son of William Stewart, publican in Main Street, Bathgate, confirmed that he knew the three accused. He said that he had been in company with Scoular and McNie at Bowie's public house on the evening in question, but they had left the pub at approximately eight o'clock. He had gone to Watson's house early next morning, having met Watson and Alexander Black in the street. Scoular, McNie and John Stewart were already in Watson's house, and Alexander McDonald had arrived later. Scoular was wearing Watson's coat, but there was no blood on anyone. Due to being intoxicated, William had fallen asleep, and after the three accused had been apprehended, Jane Fleming had lent him a knife and snuff box, which had subsequently been handed over to Sergeant Kerr.

Jane Fleming, weaver, confirmed that she had been married previously, but had not seen her husband for three years and did not know his whereabouts. She had been living with Watson for about six months, but had known him for six months before that. She said that on the evening of 28 November Scoular and McNie had come looking for Watson after dark. They had waited for about an hour for him, but had given Fleming sixpence to buy a half mutchkin of whisky. When Watson *did* arrive, he was given the last glass. Scoular had put on Watson's coat and they had set off for Bowie's public house. Fleming had gone to visit a neighbour and Watson had come back around midnight to get the key to their house. When Fleming had returned home, Watson, Scoular (still wearing the coat) and McNie had been sitting talking and Scoular had taken a half crown from his pocket and sent for two bottles of whisky. Early in the morning Jane had gone to the well, McNie accompanying her, and Alexander McDonald had come back to the house with them. William Stewart, John Stewart and Alexander Black – all the worse for drink – had also arrived. She denied ever seeing any watch, hearing anything of what had happened earlier in the evening, or seeing any blood on anybody's clothes. She had heard of nobody named Wicket. She had borne a child on the Friday following the fair day and there had been no food in the house. Mary Arnot, daughter of Robert Arnot, weaver, of Gideon Street, Bathgate said that she had gone to Watson's house on the Friday after the Bathgate fair at approximately seven o'clock in the evening to see Jane Fleming, who was expecting a child. She confirmed that after about half an hour Watson, who had been drinking, had arrived and given her half a crown to get some meat, as there had been none in the house, and whisky.

Alexander McDonald was a labourer who lived with Agnes Anthony or McDonald, widow, in Bathgate. He said that he had been at the cattle market on the day of the Bathgate fair when he had seen Watson and McNie there together in the morning, as well as a man nicknamed "*Wicket*" – whose real name was John Wright. Wicket was a carter whose origins were unknown, but who had worked on the Bathgate railway the previous winter. McDonald had chatted to Wicket, with McNie at his side. At around noon he had once again seen Wicket in Bathgate town, in the company of David Dobbie, a carter from Bathgate. Later on in the evening, McDonald had been in Bowie's public house with Scoular, McNie, David and William Stewart and William Newlands. Scoular, McNie and the Stewarts had left at around eight o'clock.

McDonald had met Scoular on the street in Bathgate a week after the fair on the Sunday and as they were very close friends, Scoular had proceeded to tell him that after he had left Bowie's with Watson and McNie, they had gone up the Whitburn road to Boghead and witnessed Wicket fighting with an Irishman. After this scuffle, Wicket had walked on a bit further, where he had come across a man who was decidedly intoxicated. Seeing an opportunity, Wicket had knocked him to the ground and his friends had helped him to rifle the pockets of this individual. A watch and money had been stolen, but the watch had been sold to two boys from Edinburgh for twelve shillings and the money equally divided amongst Watson, McNie and Scoular. Scoular told McDonald that he had been wearing Watson's jacket at the time of the robbery.

Richard Forrester junior, a slater and weaver who lived with Catherine Martin or Rankine, a widow, at North Street, Bathgate, was acquainted with the three prisoners. He recalled that on the Thursday following the fair day he had gone into the shop where McNie worked and McNie had taken a brass snuff box and double bladed knife from his pocket saying "*Look at that!*" He had proceeded to explain how he, Watson, Scoular and a carter had stolen them, together with a watch and some money, from a man near Boghead steading. McNie had later attempted to sell the watch to a tailor named Izatt, but as *he* could not afford it, he had later sold it to another lad for ten shillings. McNie had explained that he and the others had *purposely* gone out on the Whitburn road with a view to robbing someone. He also said that they had attacked a carter at Engine Street with the same purpose in mind, but that man had escaped unscathed.

Young Jane McNie, who was the sister of James McNie, said that her brother had left the house on the afternoon of the Bathgate fair and had not returned until the Thursday morning, the worse for drink. On the following Tuesday he had given her a brass snuff box to keep for him and, on seeing her mother with a doubled bladed knife, Jane had bought this from McNie for sixpence. On the day that McNie was apprehended, William Stewart had asked to borrow the knife and she had given it to him. She had also given him the snuff box later on in the day. Next morning, Sergeant Kerr had come asking for these articles, but she had to tell him that Stewart had them and they went to his house to fetch them. Her brother had never informed her of the origin of the articles.

Alexander Izatt, the tailor who lived in Bathgate, knew the three prisoners. He had seen them on the afternoon of Thursday, 29 November, when they had tried to sell him a watch for ten shillings. They did not show him the watch, however, and he only possessed seven shillings, so had declined their offer. Watson had mentioned in conversation that they could always break up the watch and sell it for old silver, which had immediately made Izatt suspicious.

Seventeen year old David Scott was the son of David Scott, a dealer in the Old Tron, Edinburgh, with whom he lived at Aird's Close in the Grassmarket. He stated that he drove about the country on a horse and cart with his brother, Joseph, selling fruit and purchasing old iron and the like. They frequently visited Bathgate for this purpose and had been there on the day of the fair - 28 November. They had returned to Edinburgh next day, but had returned to Bathgate on the Friday with another load of fruit. That evening he had seen the three prisoners and Watson, to whom he had previously spoken on a few occasions, had asked him if he wanted to go to Mr Wallace's public house for a drink. They had all gone to a private room there, including young Joseph, and drunk whisky and Watson had proceeded to try to sell him a watch (without chain) for fifteen shillings. Scott had asked several times if it was actually Watson's own watch and he had been assured that this was the case. Watson had said that he would not have been selling his watch if it was not for the fact that his wife had recently borne a child and they had no money to buy necessities for it. Watson was so persuasive about the necessity of getting the money that Scott had agreed to lend him twelve shillings against the watch. When the money was given over, however, he had witnessed that it was split between the three individuals. Scott confirmed that he never actually bought the watch, but merely lent money on it. He had given it to his father as part of the money he should have given him for goods he had sold and when his father asked him where he had got the watch, Scott answered that he had purchased it from a man in Bathgate.

Thirteen year old Joseph Scott concurred generally with this account, saying that his brother had proposed to take the watch for twelve shillings, with Watson re-purchasing it later, with an extra couple of shillings to be thrown in. Watson had confirmed that the watch was his own, but had split the proceeds with his two friends. On 11 December Joseph's father had gone to Bathgate and asked Joseph to point out the man from whom David had bought the watch. He had then given the relevant information to the police, because it appeared that a man named Lawrence Spence had been arrested in Edinburgh for that very crime.

David Scott, the father of James and Joseph, stated that his sons had gone to Bathgate to sell fruit on the Friday and not returned to Edinburgh until the Tuesday. When his son, David, had handed over the money he had collected, he had also handed over a watch purchased from a man named Watson for twelve shillings, because his wife had had a child and they sorely needed the money. Mr Scott had kept the watch until 10 December, when he had bought a chain for it and sent his friend, Lawrence Spence, to pawn it at the South Bridge, so that he could buy some iron. After he had been waiting outside the pawn shop for Spence for about ten minutes, however, he had seen him being escorted outside by a policeman. Suspecting that the watch had been stolen, therefore, Scott had gone home immediately, fetched his son and set off for Bathgate. He had informed the policeman in Bathgate, telling him that his friend had been arrested for stealing the watch, but that his sons had bought it earlier from a man in Bathgate.

Lawrence Spence, a dealer in old iron who lived at Grange Court, Causewayside Edinburgh, said that he had not been to Bathgate for well nigh thirteen years. He confirmed that he had been given the watch by David Scott on 10 December. Scott and he were in the old iron trading business and they were to go to Mr Spence, coachbuilder at the Mound, Edinburgh, to buy some iron that day, but had been short of the necessary money to do so. Scott had devised a plan to pawn his watch to raise the shortfall and it was agreed that Spence would go to Thomson's Pawn Office on the Bridge to pawn it. However, in so doing, a constable had taken him into custody. Spence had been with Scott in Leith on the day his sons had come home with the watch, which young David had described as being purchased in Bathgate for twelve shillings.

John Donaldson Thomson junior was a clerk in his father's pawn broker's shop at South Bridge Street, Edinburgh and he stated that at about ten in the morning of Monday, 10 December, he had received information from the police that a watch "*No. 5414 Manton London*" had been stolen and it had been requested that if any person called offering it in pledge, he was to be detained. At approximately half past one that very afternoon, a man had called in requesting an advance of one pound for a watch and, on examining it, Thomson had discovered it to be the very article. He had asked the man how long it had been in his possession and had been advised eight days and that it had previously belonged to a man named Scott who lived at the Grassmarket. As this man seemed determined to get out of the shop and go down for his friend, young Thomson had got between him and the door and had been able to detain him. He had run immediately to the police office, but on going down the stair a strong, powerful, country looking man had been loitering there. John Amos was the constable who had returned with him and he concurred with Thomson's statement. Amos confirmed that Scott had been known to him for a number of years, but that he had never heard anything against him. As for Spence, Amos said that he had also been known to him for a number of years and that, although he bore a somewhat indifferent character, he had never been convicted.

What of the criminals themselves? John McNie was an eighteen year old weaver, son of James McNie, slater, and he lived at North Bridge Street, Bathgate. He was six feet four inches tall, with dark brown hair, brown eyes, round face, fresh complexion, stout build, and had a scar on the palm of his right hand. According to his statement of 11 December 1849, on the evening in question he had been in Bowie's public house with Scoular, Alexander McDonald, William Stewart and Robert Brodie. They had gone to James Watson's house at approximately eight o'clock and when they had left half an hour later they had met an individual named Wicket on the street. Walking along Whitburn Road near Boghead farm steading, Watson, Scoular and he had gone ahead. On hearing a cry from behind, however, they had found Wicket lying on top of a man on the road, rifling his pockets. McNie had joined in the robbery and found five pence, a double bladed knife and a box, which were subsequently given to his sister for safe keeping. They had all returned to Bathgate through the fields and Wicket had sold a watch he had stolen to McNie for five shillings. The watch was then sold on the following Friday to a lad named Scott from Edinburgh for twelve shillings and the proceeds divided amongst Watson, Scoular and himself.

In his following statement made on 22 December, however, McNie admitted that they had met Wicket opposite George Wallace's pub in Bathgate and had discussed going out on the Whitburn Road "*to see what they could get*". He said that Wicket had met up with Black about two hundred yards past Boghead farm, spoke to him and then jumped on him. Although they had planned to rob someone, the robbery itself had not been planned in detail, but they had all assisted in it. Apparently, the man named Wicket had left them opposite Bowie's pub in Bathgate on their return.

James Watson, a mason who lived at High Street, Bathgate was six feet tall, with light hair, grey eyes, round face, fair complexion, middling stout build, and had a scar on his right cheek. When he made his statement on 11 December 1849, he admitted that he knew David Black of Crossroads, Whitburn, but had not seen him on Bathgate market day of 28 November. At approximately eight o'clock that evening Watson had gone out with George Smith, who was working on the Bathgate railway, to Bryson's pub where they had drunk a toddy. Prior to that, however, Watson had gone out at about five o'clock and taken a drink with George Smith, a weaver, and his sons, John and James, and John Pender, farmer at Middlerigg, at John Stewart's house. He had become a bit tipsy at Bryson's pub, met up with Scoular and McNie in the street and had eventually gone home. They had met a man selling a watch and apparently it had been bought between Scoular and McNie, given to Watson to keep and then sold three days later to someone named David Scott, a fruit dealer from Edinburgh, for a profit of seven shillings. The transaction had taken place in George Wallace's pub. He confirmed that he was not married, but had lived with Jean Fleming for six or seven months and she had borne a child the previous week. He also said that he remembered a man called Wicket trying to sell a watch on the morning of 28 November. He denied robbing David Black and said that any blood on his jacket had been from separating Alexander Black and John Stewart who were fighting on the day after the market day.

In his subsequent statement of 14 December his story altered quite significantly. He stated that he had met Scoular and McNie coming out of Bowie's. They had gone down the street, walked along Jarvie Street once or twice, then along Engine Street, when they had come upon a man named Wicket. (He did not know Wicket, but had heard someone saying his name.) He described the incident at Boghead and how Wicket had struck Black. Watson admitted that he had put a plaid over Black's face to prevent him crying out, but he had stolen nothing. McNie had apparently stolen money and a snuff box and knife. All three – Wicket, McNie and Scoular had been rifling the man's pockets. When they had returned to Bathgate, Wicket had shown them the watch he had stolen. McNie and Scoular gave Wicket some money for the watch as his share of the robbery and that was the last they had seen of him. Watson, McNie and Scoular had gone to Watson's house and drunk two bottles of whisky which were paid for by Scoular, who had apparently worked hard for that money. The watch had been given to Watson, but McNie had kept the chain. The watch had subsequently been sold to Scott at Wallace's public house. Scott had asked no questions as to how the watch had come into Watson's possession.

When nineteen year old George Scoular, weaver, who lived with his father, James, in Bathgate made his first statement on 11 December, he said that on the evening in question he had gone to Bowie's at around seven o'clock with David Stewart, William Newlands and John McNie and they had stayed there for about an hour before they left to walk the streets. After meeting Watson and another man named Wicket, they had all gone down the Whitburn Road, where at some point near Boghead Wicket had started a scuffle with a man who was walking there. He had then walked along further and set upon a second man, pushing him to the ground. This individual had cried out, "*Mercy on me!*" as Wicket wrestled with him and stole his watch. Although Watson and McNie were standing close to Wicket, they had apparently taken no part in events and they had all eventually gone back to Bathgate through the fields. McNie had given Wicket five shillings for the watch and that money had been divided between the three prisoners. The watch had then been sold to a lad named Scott from Edinburgh for twelve shillings.

In his second statement of 22 December, however, Scoular related that he and McNie had been the only ones who had left Bowie's, after which they had fallen in with Watson on the High Street and having meandered the streets for half an hour, had met up with Wicket in Bridge Street. Wicket had knocked a man down beside the Free Church, because "*he had been tormenting him all night and he deserved what he got*". Scoular said that they had only gone down the Whitburn Road to get away from Wicket. He also said that he had been pretty drunk and had worn Watson's coat that evening. He had not known what Wicket was about to do and Scoular had taken no part in the attack. McNie had later told him that he had got a knife and five pence from the victim. When they had returned to Bathgate, Wicket had offered to sell the watch to the others, as he was impoverished at the time. Scoular had given him four pence and a half penny, McNie a shilling and Watson nothing, although he kept the watch. Wicket had disappeared thereafter and the three others had gone back to Watson's house.

What happened to the prisoners? All three were tried at the High Court in Edinburgh on 25 February 1850, found guilty and sentenced to transportation for ten years. They sailed on 30 December 1853 on the ship Sea Park bound for Western Australia.

Note: George Scoular had appeared at Linlithgow Sheriff Court on 22 July 1847 when he was described as being of clean appearance, sober and wearing good clothes. He had a dark complexion, with brown hair and grey eyes. His crime was theft of a white hen for which he was imprisoned for one week.

The Linlithgow Prison records indicate that James Watson and John McNie had never been in jail before. The three appeared before the Sheriff Substitute on 11 December 1849. On the same day, Lawrence Spence from Edinburgh – 5 feet 6 inches tall and a broker- was imprisoned for reset of stolen goods, but was liberated before trial by the Procurator Fiscal. His friend, David Scott, was treated likewise.

National Records of Scotland reference AD14/50/480; JC26/1850/590 JC26/1850/590/HH21/18/1

MICHAEL FANNON – ALIAS WILLIAM THOMSON

THEFT AT DRUMSHORELAND STORE, UPHALL 15 JANUARY 1850

It was very early on the morning of Tuesday, 15 January 1850 – and there was snow lying on the ground - when the Drumshoreland Store near Uphall was broken into. The store, owned by John Bruce who was living at Dirleton, East Lothian, was managed by John Ramsay. It sold all manner of goods, from clothes and shoes to food and utensils, and was always securely locked each evening. It had formerly been a stable and above it was a loft where various goods were stored, but the only way to gain entrance to it was by a ladder which was kept in an adjoining house owned by James Jamieson. The loft door was also locked and the door outside the store was locked by iron bars – on the outside. The windows were secured by iron stanchions.

On Monday, 14 January – *Old Handsel Monday* – the shop was closed. John Ramsay had secured the doors to the shop and loft on the Saturday evening previous, at approximately seven thirty, but had also gone round to check on the store at around four o'clock on the Monday afternoon. All was well and Adam Douglas, a timekeeper on the Clifton Section of the Edinburgh and Bathgate Railway, who lodged with George Douglas at Broxburn, had been present on both of these occasions when the premises were secured. On the Tuesday morning at around five thirty, however, William Jamieson had run along to Ramsay's house to say that the shop had been broken into. Apparently at three or four o'clock in the morning noises and voices had been heard in the store, which was in the same tenement as Jamieson's father's house, but these could not be identified. William had heard men going in and out, but was too afraid to venture out of his room. When he did eventually pluck up the courage to do so, he was trapped inside, as the men had tied his door from the outside! He had to shout to some passersby to free him when all had gone quiet, whereupon the break-in had been discovered.

Ramsay had identified what was missing from the loft and had gone immediately to Sergeant Kerr's house at Houston Mains to report the incident. He and Kerr, constable on the Edinburgh and Bathgate Railway, had come back to investigate and it had been obvious that there were marks of forced entry on the outside doors and the loft door had been broken open. The missing items consisted of two velvet coats, four shirts, two pairs of stockings, three pairs of drawers, two pairs of braces, eight vests, a blue cloth cap, two slopes, three pairs of socks, pair of shoes, 6lbs of tea, 48 lbs of bacon, 12 lbs butter, 12 lbs sugar, 2lbs candles, 2 lbs tobacco, 6 loaves, one shilling in copper money, sack or bag and two handkerchiefs.

John Baird was a farm servant working for Joseph Alexander, a farmer at Broxburn. On Tuesday morning at around six o'clock he was going with Thomas Readdy to the farm steading, which was around three hundred yards from the store. He had seen two men and two women coming from the stackyard, walking very briskly in the direction of the houses which were about sixty yards from the store, occupied by

Barclay or Bartholomew Kilboa, James Ivers and Timothy Lavan- three Irish families who were known to take in numerous lodgers. The four looked highly suspicious. With the snow being thick on the ground, their footprints could be traced right back to the stackyard. Some loose straw was lying on the west corner and Baird and Readdy had found a linen slope filled with several articles underneath the straw. They had also found other bundles containing various objects matching the description of those stolen from the store and Ramsay and the policeman had come along and taken these. Unfortunately, neither Baird nor Readdy could identify the men, but could only state that one wore a hat and the other a bonnet. Although the houses of Bilboa and the others had been searched, nothing had been found there.

Thomas McQuillen, a constable in the Edinburgh Police Establishment, lived at 22 High Riggs, Edinburgh. At the trial at Edinburgh High Court on 11 March 1850 he stated that he had gone to the police office on Thursday, 17 January, when it had been reported that a person had been trying to pawn a coat at the South Loan office at 39 South Bridge, Edinburgh. He and his colleague, John Amos, had proceeded there immediately and seen William Slack standing outside the door. Michael Fannon was standing inside the office, at the counter, with the coat and was subsequently questioned as to its origins. Fannon insisted that it had been in his possession for three months, having purchased it in Newcastle, but both he and Slack were taken into custody and charged with theft, which they had vehemently denied.

John Muir, police constable, 4 St Leonard's Lane, Edinburgh, concurred in that on 17 January Fannon and Slack had been brought to the police station in the custody of Amos and McQuillen. Fannon had been wearing an apparently new striped shirt, a pair of new worsted stockings and pair of white worsted braces without buckles, which matched the description of some of the stolen articles from Drumshoreland Store. When the two labourers were charged with theft, however, Fannon denied ever having been in Linlithgowshire, having only arrived from Newcastle a fortnight previously, and Slack said that he had only arrived in Edinburgh the previous night from Broxburn. The pair explained that they had only met each other accidentally that day. Although Fannon said he had never known Slack before, Slack said he had met Fannon when working at Broxburn at the last harvest.

After he was taken into custody, twenty three year old Michael Fannon, who was born at Roscommon, and had been lodging with Bartholomew Kilboa at Broxburn, made two statements - on 18 January and 1 February. He stated firstly that he was a labourer on the Bathgate railway at Broxburn. He admitted that he had broken into the Drumshoreland Store on the night of Monday, 14 January, by forcing open the door, and that he had stolen a black velvet coat, a blue striped cotton shirt, a pair of worsted stockings and a pair of braces, but he had no accomplice.

In his second statement Fannon described William Slack as being the son of Bartholomew Kilboa's wife by a former husband. He also described Kilboa's house as consisting of only one apartment, where all of his fourteen or fifteen lodgers (including two women) and his wife lived! According to him, Fannon used the alias of William Thomson at work and in Broxburn, because it was more easily pronounced and understood than that of the Irish '*Michael Fannon*'. He admitted that he had gone from Kilboa's to the store at approximately nine o'clock on the Monday evening with the intention of breaking in. He had entered by a ladder to the loft, after forcing open the door, and had then gone through a trap door to the apartment below. He denied, however, that he had gone into the stackyard and concealed any stolen articles there, or that he had been in the company of another man and two women. He said that the only other things taken from the store were two loaves of bread and the stolen articles had been hidden in the planting on the moor beyond Broxburn, near the railway station, where they had lain until the Wednesday night. He said that he had been in Kilboa's house all Tuesday and Wednesday until six o'clock in the evening. William Slack had gone to Edinburgh on the Wednesday and the two had met on the street accidentally on the Thursday morning at about nine o'clock. He had asked Slack where he could find a pawn broker and had been directed to the shop, where he had afterwards been arrested.

Statements given by Agnes Cunningham, Bartholomew Kilboa, Patrick Kilboa, Francis Lacey, Patrick Kildare, Bridget Early or Kilboa, wife of Bartholomew, William Lacey, Betsy Lacey and Roger Tansey were not used, as they were found to be unreliable. (The Kilboas were known to the police. For example, twenty one year old Thomas Kilboa, a "*navvy*" born in County Leitrim, had been convicted of theft of a quantity of coats on 29 December 1849 and sentenced to 60 days in Linlithgow Prison.)

At the trial, John Ramsay was able to identify Fannon as a man who worked on the railway at Broxburn, who went under the name of William Thomson, and was frequently in the store. What was the outcome of this case when it was heard at the High Court in Edinburgh on 11 March 1850? Michael Fannon, alias William Thomson, was found guilty in terms of his own confession and sentenced to transportation to Van Diemen's Land for 7 years.

National Records of Scotland reference AD14/50/467; JC26/1850/598 JC26/1850/598

ALEXANDER GRAHAM

ASSAULT AT CAIRNIEHEAD, WHITBURN 28/29 SEPTEMBER 1850

It was either on the evening of Saturday, 28 or the early morning of Sunday, 29 September 1850 when Alexander Graham, a pitsheadman, had severely assaulted John Corkle, a miner, at his house at Cairniehead, Whitburn. Corkle had been wounded and bruised "to the effusion of blood and danger to his life".

John Corkle was a thirty five year old miner who lived at Cairniehead with his wife and family. He worked at the same location as Graham, which was Number Six Crofthead Pit. Graham lodged with Barney or Bernard Lafferty at Blackfaulds, Whitburn. According to Corkle, after finishing work at the pit on the Saturday in question, he had come home with his pay and then stopped in at John Reid's Public House near Fauldhouse, along with a man named Spiers and Robert Mansefield. Prior to leaving, Alexander Graham and Thomas Wilson, two other miners at the pit, had come to the same pub and taken a drink by themselves. Spiers, Mansefield and Corkle had left at approximately eleven thirty that evening and Graham had followed them, saying he would contribute a sixpence to buy something in a bottle. They had all counted their money, returned to Reid's and two bottles of whisky had been purchased for three shillings. Mansefield and Corkle had paid a shilling each, and Graham and Spiers sixpence. They had gone to Widow Bell's house (who lived in the street between Reid's house and Corkle's house at Cairniehead) where they had drunk one of the bottles, along with a number of other men who were there.

At about one o'clock on the Sunday morning, after the first bottle had been drunk, Graham had come to Corkle's house - about half a mile away - with the other bottle. Graham had informed Corkle that he'd had no supper, so Corkle had invited him home, saying that his wife would give him a cup of tea. When Mrs Corkle had been brewing the tea, the men had drunk three glasses of whisky. Graham had then enquired of Corkle, *"Are you not going to get your wife to get the beefsteaks ready?"* and Corkle had retorted that she was making them as quickly as she could. All of a sudden, Graham had jumped up and grabbed Corkle by the hair. A stone breaker's hammer had been lying at the fire side, which was for breaking up coals, and this weighed about a pound and a half and had a handle about a foot long. All Corkle could remember was his wife screaming, *"You are not to strike him with the hammer!"* and then Graham had done that very thing! Corkle had become unconscious and could remember nothing more until he awoke in bed, when Dr Grosset had been attending to him. As well as the hammer blow to his forehead, Corkle had a cut behind the ear, another on the crown of his head and severe pain in his right leg. By 7 November he had quite recovered, however, and had been working for three weeks, although he had been off work for ten days, and for a fortnight after the incident he was only able to work half days.

Jean Corkle, John's wife, stated that her husband had returned from work on Sunday, 29 September, at approximately one o'clock in the morning, together with a man who introduced himself as Alexander Graham. Although her husband had seemed quite drunk, Graham had seemed sober enough. Whilst the tea was being made, she had prepared three glasses of whiskey toddy for them. She had a mutton chop in the house, but Graham had mentioned that her husband had promised him beefsteaks. She had been reluctant to cook at this late hour, but as her husband had asked her kindly, she had proceeded to heat the chops. An argument had developed between the two men, however, regarding a shilling which had apparently been paid by Graham for whisky. Suddenly, Graham had exploded in anger and Corkle had been grabbed by the hair, flung down beside the fire hearth-stone and hit on the forehead with the hammer which was lying there. She had begged Graham not to hit her husband, but he had carried on with the assault. When she had tried to run for help, he had pushed her to the floor and had continued to kick Mr Corkle, who was already unconscious, trampling his stomach with his feet. A furious Graham had shouted, "*By Jeese, I'll take you both out before I go!*" He had still been grasping the hammer when he went outside, but had returned almost immediately and looked at her husband's head wounds. Williamson, who lived "*but and ben with them*" (next door) had then ran to the house and Graham had immediately fled the scene of the attack. Mrs Corkle described how Graham had kicked her husband all over his body and that she had actually been holding her two month old child when he had thrown her down on the floor. Her husband had been insensible for several hours, but Mrs Corkle was unsure if the whisky had contributed to this state of affairs.

John Williamson, miner, confirmed that he lived right next door to the Corkles. On the Sunday morning in question he had heard shouting and swearing, coming from his neighbour's house, followed by Mrs Corkle shouting, "*Don't hit my husband with the hammer!*" A blow had been heard, however, and Mrs Corkle had shouted out, "*Murder!*" followed by, "*You surely will not kill me and the infant!*" Although undressed, Williamson had dashed next door and witnessed John Corkle lying on the floor, blood flowing from a wound on his head, with Alexander Graham standing beside him holding a hammer in his hand. After hurriedly putting on his trousers in his own house, Williamson had gone back to the Corkles' house, but Graham had disappeared. Williamson had pulled up Mr Corkle – who appeared at that time to be quite dead - from the fireside. On returning next door to fetch his shoes, Williamson had seen Graham standing by the door breaking a whisky bottle, and then going back into the Corkles' house, whereupon he had shouted, "*By Jeese I'll take them both out*". He had then heard Graham saying that he had done nothing, but that Corkle had merely fallen by accident and struck his head. Williamson had gone to fetch some neighbours and Corkle's brother and when they arrived, Corkle had thankfully regained consciousness. On further examination, Williamson had stated that it was the noise of men talking which he had first heard next door – sometimes high and sometimes low. He had not paid much attention to it, however, as apparently this often happened on pay nights! There had been no noise of actual fighting.

Margaret Findlay, Williamson's wife, concurred with her husband's statement in that Mrs Corkle had shouted out for someone not to strike her husband with a hammer and then there had been sounds of a scuffle, followed by, *"You have done for him now!"* She had rushed next door and seen the apparently dead Mr Corkle and then a man, with a bottle in his hand, had been seen in the passage coming from the house. She had heard Graham saying he would *"take them both out"*. Corkle had seemed the worse for drink, but Graham had no such appearance.

Robert Mansefield, who lodged with John Corkle, recalled the evening of the assault and how he had been in Mrs Bell's house with Corkle, Graham and some others. Although Graham had taken a dram, he had *"known what he was about"*, although Corkle had been quite drunk. Mansefield had gone home about an hour afterwards and found Graham sitting with Corkle by the fireside, chatting away amicably. About the time when Mrs Corkle had starting preparing the tea, however, Mansefield had fallen fast asleep. When he had awoken to the noise of shouting and screaming, all he could see was John Corkle bleeding profusely, saying that Graham had attacked him with a hammer.

James Bell, a miner, who lived with Widow Bell at Crofthead, recalled that Corkle, Graham and some others had been in his mother's house on the evening in question. One bottle of whisky had been drunk there and Corkle and Graham had taken away another. Corkle had been rather the worse for the drink, but Graham had appeared sober enough, and both had been on good terms. Widow Bell concurred with this statement.

James Watson's note of 29 October 1850 stated that Alexander Graham had absconded, and although every effort had been made, he had not been apprehended. He had left the scene of the crime before it had been reported to the police and had never been seen again since. William Grossart's Medical Report dated 10 December 1850 stated that John Corkle's life had been in danger from the probability of inflammation of the membranes of the brain following fracture of the skull.

What was the outcome of the trial which took place at the High Court in Edinburgh on 27 January 1851? Alexander Graham, fugitive, was outlawed and put to the horn.

Note: John Corkle, a pauper formerly a miner, widower of Jane Hutchison died 9 March 1887 at 19 Clyde Street, West Calder when he was aged 75 years of natural causes *(National Records of Scotland death reference 701-30)*

National Records of Scotland reference AD14/51/557; JC26/1851/502

MARY HUNTER AND JEAN ANDERSON
THEFT AT COCHRANE STREET, BATHGATE 9-10 JULY 1851

The trial of Mary Hunter and Jean Anderson took place at the High Court, Edinburgh on 10 November 1851. Whilst they were awaiting trial, however, they were incarcerated in the prison of Linlithgow.

Witnesses included Adam Colquhoun, superintendent of police of Linlithgowshire, Christian Wardrobe, merchant, Christian Russell or Taylor, a widow Bathgate, Jean Stewart or Easton, wife of John Easton, weaver Bathgate, Thomas Anderson junior, a weaver in Bathgate, Peter Tennant, a flesher in Bathgate, William Stevenson, overseer at Balbardie Estate who lived at the gatehouse there, David Alexander Sheriff Officer of Bathgate and Mary Cameron or Alexander, wife of David Alexander.

The prisoners were advised, *"Theft especially when committed by means of housebreaking and by a person who is habit and repute a thief and has previously been convicted of theft is a crime of an heinous nature. In so far as 9 or 10 day of July 1851 or June preceding or August following you both did break into and enter the shop in or near Bathgate occupied by Christian Wardrobe, merchant there, by opening a window of the kitchen communicating with the shop, and having obtained entrance, you did steal:*

16 shillings and 8d sterling in silver money, 10 ½ copper money, 3 purses, 3 small merino shawls, 3 silk handkerchiefs, 5 cotton handkerchiefs, 3 pairs worsted stockings, pair of cotton stockings, 2 paper boxes, hair pins, pins in papers, 4 pieces sewed muslin, 17 yards printed cloth, 2 pieces of cotton cloth each a yard in length, 7 pieces of cotton cloth, a night gown, 4 yards pink cotton cloth, 2 pairs small worsted stockings, 2 pairs gloves, 4 pieces of tape, 11 pieces of braid, 10 finger rings, a stay lace, 3 yards tape, 3 yards braid, a needle case, 2 pieces of cotton or cloth for petticoats, a yard linen, 2 pairs stays, pair of scissors, 2 pounds of tea, 5 pounds sugar and 20 yards cotton shirting – all the property of Christian Wardrobe."

Christian Wardrobe, daughter of Alexander Wardrobe, a cooper, and Margaret Wardrobe, had a general store in Bathgate. She was living at Kamehead, Bathgate in 1851 when she was aged seventy seven.

Who was Mary (Robina) Hunter? She was the illegitimate daughter of Mary Anderson (who later married William Anthony, coal banksman, and had three children with him by 1841). William Anthony was Mary Hunter's step father and by the time the 1851 census was taken the Anthony family was living at Cochrane Street – the same street where Christian Wardrobe had her shop. Mary Hunter sometimes lived with her grandmother, Marion Anderson, an embroiderer, at Cochrane Street.

Young Mary Hunter had previous convictions of 14 April 1848 and 13 November 1848. She had been sentenced at the Sheriff Court Linlithgow on 14 April 1848 to one month's imprisonment for the theft of a frying pan whilst she was living with William Anthony, a weaver in Bathgate. She was subsequently imprisoned in the Prison of Linlithgow.

She had also been sentenced on 13 November 1848 for the theft of sixteen shillings and sixpence in silver money, which was aggravated by the crime being committed by means of opening a lockfast place and by a person previously convicted of theft. For this she was sentenced to be incarcerated in the Prison of Linlithgow for four calendar months. Her description stated that she was five feet tall with a mole on her left arm.

Mary's declaration of 10 July 1851 included the fact that she could not write, that she was an eighteen year old weaver and lived with William Anthony, a weaver in Bathgate (her step father). She stated that she had gone to Christian Wardrobe's shop in Bathgate either late on the night of 9 July or early morning of 10 July with Jean Anderson - daughter of Alexander Anderson, a slater. They had gained entry by lifting the sash of a window in a back kitchen, taking a number of articles from the shelves there. Money had been stolen from a purse on a shelf, but she didn't know the actual amount. She had taken lots of items from the shop and brought them along to Jean's mother's house. They had subsequently taken three bundles of items to Balbardie Plantation in the neighbourhood of Bathgate and hid them there. Seeing an opportunity, they had quickly made up some petticoats and aprons with the cloth and trimmings, but had been taken into custody sometime in the morning – before they had the chance to sell the items.

Her declaration of 21 July 1851 stated that she had been taken into custody and searched by Mary Cameron, wife of David Alexander, Sheriff of Bathgate. Mrs Alexander had taken away a yard of linen, a pair of scissors, a checked cotton petticoat, a striped gingham apron and a pair of stays from the thief, who admitted that they were part of the articles taken from Christian Wardrobe's shop and that the petticoat and apron were merely made out of the cloth that had been taken from those premises. Also, John Kerr, police constable, had taken two dress rings off her fingers, which were also taken from the same premises. Mary and Jean had put the purse with the money in it under a bed in Jean Anderson's mother's house and hidden the rest of the articles among some nettles, covering them with tree roots at Balbardie.

Who was Jean Anderson? According to the 1851 census she was aged seventeen, a pirn driver, daughter of Alexander Anderson, slater. She lived with Jean Stewart or Easton, wife of John Easton, weaver in Bathgate.

The declaration of Jean Anderson taken on 1 July 1851 mentioned the fact that she could not write. She had also been searched by Mrs Alexander, who had taken a pair of grey worsted stockings, a pair of jane stays, a gingham apron and a striped cotton petticoat from her. She denied that she had put a purse under a bed in her mother's house and she said that she did not see anyone searching there after she was apprehended. She confirmed that a brass ring had been taken off her finger, although she could not remember who had taken it off. She also confirmed that tuppence half penny had been taken from her, but that this money had been given to her by her Mistress the night before. Some bundles had been made up of the things taken from the shop, she said, but they had been made up by Mary Hunter, with no involvement by herself. She stated that she didn't know who carried the bundles away or to where they were carried. She did not know what the bundles consisted of exactly, but confirmed that there were several pairs of cotton worsted and cotton stockings and silk and cotton handkerchiefs. She could not have identified any of the articles, however, as they had all been taken in the dark. She confirmed that there were other articles taken from Miss Wardrobe's shop such as babies' caps, gloves, and a piece of pink cotton cloth, as well as a large piece of blue printed cotton. She also confirmed that she and Hunter had agreed to hide the articles somewhere after they had taken them.

The statement of 10 July 1851 confirmed that she was aged sixteen, a pirn driver, daughter of Alexander Anderson, a slater in Bathgate. She admitted to being in Christian Wardrobe's shop in Bathgate on the night in question with Mary Hunter, who had persuaded her to go there. Mary Hunter had gone in first by a back window, which was found to be open, and Jean had followed. She did not recall the window being opened forcibly. She admitted that they had both taken goods from the shelves out of the shop, but she had not seen any money or any purse being taken. She could not recall all of the things that were taken, but that bundles had been made up at the back of her mother's house. Some of the articles had been made into petticoats and aprons by both of them.

What happened to Mary Hunter and Jean Anderson? Mary Hunter was convicted at the Edinburgh Court of Justiciary for a term of 7 years on 10 November 1851. She was one of 220 convicts transported to Van Diemen's Land (Tasmania) on the Sir Robert Sippings or Seppings on 17 March 1852. Mary Robina Hunter married William Kilby on 3 September 1863 at Launceston and died in 1920. Jean Anderson was convicted on the same date for the same term and was transported on the same ship.

Christian Wardrobe died of old age on 12 February 1856.

National Records of Scotland reference AD14/51/456; JC26/1851/605

Information on transportation courtesy of The Female Convicts Research Centre

MARY PATERSON

CHILD MURDER OR CONCEALEMENT OF PREGNANCY AT HOUSTOUN HOUSE 29 OR 30 MAY 1852

It was during the evening of Saturday, 29 or the early morning of Sunday, 30 of May 1852 at Houstoun House, Uphall - the residence of Norman Shairp Esquire - when Mary Paterson had borne a female child, which she had subsequently killed and hidden. Twenty two year old Mary was a children's maid in the service of Lieutenant Charles Taylor Leckie of the Royal Navy, who was abroad. Mrs Elizabeth Binning Leckie was the daughter of Norman Shairp Esquire and she lived with him there in her husband's absence, together with her children.

Mary Paterson had entered service there on 22 January that year. Norman Shairp, when questioned, stated that some months ago Mary had come to be a child's maid to Mrs Leckie and *"she was a remarkably kind, affectionate and attentive person with the children."* As far as he was concerned, there was nobody who could have been more kind or careful than she had been and he had not been in the least suspicious that she had been pregnant – nor had any other members of the family. On the Saturday evening in question, he had been advised by another servant that it was suspected that Mary had borne a child and Mr Shairp had immediately sent for Dr Dick, who had arrived after midnight. After examining Mary Paterson, the doctor had come to Mr Shairp's bedroom and confirmed the situation and the location of the corpse, whereupon notice had been sent to the Procurator Fiscal. The key to the chest where the child had been found had been handed to Doctors Dick and Baird on the Sunday morning.

Dr John Dick stated that he had arrived at approximately one or two o'clock on the Sunday morning and had seen Mary Paterson in bed and another servant had been present during the whole time he had been there. Mary had at first only said that she had felt unwell and had gone to bed, but after examination by the doctor, it had been obvious that she had recently given birth. Dr Dick had asked her where the sheet of her bed was and she had refused to tell him, but had eventually got up, showing him that it was in a trunk in the room. She had quickly closed the lid, but the doctor had gone there afterwards and found not only the sheet, but the body of a female child which was hidden underneath it. The sleeve of a nightshirt had been wound round its neck. He had then told Mary Paterson, *"You can see what you have brought yourself into by your folly"*, but she had said nothing in response.

The infant's body had been placed in the bathroom, the key of that room had been given to Major Shairp and the doctor had told him that the authorities should be informed immediately. The doctor's report dated 31 May 1832 said that on the Sunday 30 May Dr Dick had been called by the Procurator Fiscal of Linlithgowshire to visit a woman at Houston House, said to have given birth to a child under suspicious circumstances. After having made the necessary investigation, Dr Dick had been satisfied that delivery had recently taken place and he had been shown an infant child said to be hers. It was a new born female, full time and plump, with a mark round the neck. His opinion was that the child had been born alive, but had died soon afterwards, as a result of strangulation. The report was signed by John Dick MD and George Dallas Baird, surgeon.

Elizabeth Black was the cook at Houstoun House and she stated that Mary, who had her own bedroom, had been children's maid to Mrs Leckie for the last few months and had come from Edinburgh. The cook had only been with the family for two weeks, but had suspected Mary was with child, although she had said nothing to her about it. Mary had complained to the cook of pain in the stomach on Saturday 29 May and she had gone to a bed in another room upstairs (where the other servant girls slept) to take a nap. However, on going to that bed later, Black had found that she had left that room and gone back to her own room. The cook had seen marks of blood on the bed tick and had suspected something was amiss. She had been in the room with Dr Dick when Mary had said she had been unwell and suffering from stomach pains. When he had said that it was suspected she had suffered a miscarriage, Mary had at first denied it. He had asked where the sheet was and told her that he would not leave on any account until he had seen it. She had then risen from the bed, taken out the blood-marked sheet from the chest, and tried to hide something else which was there.

The doctor had subsequently reopened the chest and found, to his utter dismay, the dead infant. Elizabeth Black had carried the child to the bathroom and laid it down there. Mary had told her that she was so very sorry she had not told anyone about the pregnancy or the birth, but Black had retorted that it was a pity she had not spared its poor life. Mary had explained that she had not known rightly what she was doing at the time and that the child's father was a shepherd in Peebles and he had not acknowledged her letters. Black had sat with Mary all night and the girl had seemed very remorseful. She had told nobody in the house of her pregnancy.

The only other servant who had seen Mary in bed was Jean Pane, who had gone to the room to dress on the Saturday evening. She had asked Mary Paterson if she was feeling better and had been told that she was. It had been a quarter to seven in the evening and Mary had not seemed to be in any pain at this time.

Houstoun House, Uphall

Mary Paterson stated that she had been delivered of a full term child on the Saturday afternoon between five and six o'clock. Prior to her service at Houstoun House, she had been in the service of Mr Henderson, Coates Crescent, Edinburgh. During the summer, Mr Henderson's family had been at a place called Elibank, near Walkerburn in Peeblesshire, and Mary had met a lad named Thomas Dalgleish, who she confirmed to be the father of her child. She said that she had told him of the pregnancy before she left the area and before she came to Houstoun House she had written him several letters. In one of the letters from Edinburgh she had definitely told him that she was with his child, but she had received no response from him. She explained that the reason she had not mentioned her situation in more than one letter was because she had been afraid that the letters might be intercepted. She had told nobody else of her situation and when she had gone into labour she had not told any of her fellow servants, or asked for their assistance. She had often intended to tell Mrs Leckie that she was with child, but had felt ashamed and terrified of the consequences. The housemaid had actually been dressing herself in the room when the child was delivered, but Mary had been in bed and had said nothing about it. She had only told the servants during that day that she felt unwell and when Jean Pane had asked how she was feeling she had replied, "*A good deal better*". The child had not cried and as Mary had been ill, she could not say whether it had moved or not. She admitted that she had put the sleeve of her nightgown around its neck, but she had been in such a state that she had not known what she was doing. In the course of the evening, when it was getting dark, she had carried the child from that room to the room where the doctor had examined her and had put the body into a chest, with a sheet on top. In the early morning, Doctor Dick of Mid Calder had visited her, as he had been sent for, but she could not even remember what he had said or what she had replied.

During the course of the investigation, nineteen year old Thomas Dalgleish of Thornlee, Innerleithen, had been located. He had stated that he was a shepherd working for Mr James Roxburgh, farmer at Thornlee, and had been in his service for two years. He had become acquainted with Mary Paterson during the course of the previous summer, when she was servant to Mr Henderson and living at Elibank. She had left there about three weeks before last Martinmas term 1851. He denied, however, that she had neither informed him that she was pregnant before leaving, nor had she ever hinted at such a thing. He only confirmed that he had never seen her since then and had received no correspondence from her. He did admit, however, that he had had sexual relations with her when she lived at Elibank.

Mary Paterson was incarcerated in Linlithgow Prison on 5 June. She was described as being born in Edinburgh, having lived there for most of her life. She was a member of the Free Church of Scotland and was unwell when she was admitted to prison. What happened to Mary Paterson at her trial at the High Court of Edinburgh on 21 July 1852? She was found guilty in terms of her own confession and was sentenced to one year's imprisonment at Linlithgow Jail. She served a total of 411 days in prison.

National Records of Scotland reference AD 14/52/311; JC26/1852/436

ALEXANDER ALEXANDER AND HIS DAUGHTER, MARY ALEXANDER PASSING COUNTERFEIT MONEY AT BROXBURN 22 NOVEMBER 1852

It was Wednesday, 22 November 1852 at Broxburn when a mould for making counterfeit money was found in the house of Alexander Alexander, although his daughter had also been accused of passing over the counterfeit coins to purchase goods prior to this. Alexander Alexander, a fifty year old labourer who was living at Broxburn, was accused of having made seven shilling coins, using a crude plaster cast. He had a previous criminal past, and this time he was arrested for passing a counterfeit shilling to Mary White, daughter of William White, a carter in Broxburn to pay for some tobacco. He had also passed a coin to Agnes Gilmore, the wife of William White, to pay for some bread, tea and sugar. Alexander was accused of having made the coins resembling a shilling piece of the Queen's current silver coin.

Alexander was a widower, who occasionally took in lodgers. His daughter Mary lived with him and he had only been released from prison a month before. He was not a particularly upright citizen and one of his previous arrests had been on 23 March 1845 when he was described as being a labourer with a sallow complexion, light blue eyes, and a dirty, ragged appearance – but sober. On this occasion he was arrested for breach of the peace and assault.

His version of the events which had taken place was that on the Monday previous to the date the crime had been committed, he had taken in two lodgers by the names of James and John – their surnames having been forgotten by him. The lodgers stayed for several days and by the Saturday only John had come back to his house. Although Alexander had not actually seen these men passing money to his daughter, he had seen Mary coming back to the house on the Monday evening and giving two bottles of whisky to the man named John. On that evening another local, Stephen McKay, a labourer, had come to the house and the four men had sat drinking. Mary had been sent out for further supplies of the drink, but had returned saying that Agnes Lowrie, Mrs Fraser's daughter, had refused to sell her any more whisky, as her shilling was a fake one. Agnes had also warned Mary that the police would be sent for. Apparently this had resulted in James leaving immediately and John leaving the following afternoon at around three o'clock. Neither lodger had informed Alexander where they were going and neither paid for their lodgings, meat or drink.

Alexander also stated that he had sold a shirt to John for a shilling and, using that very coin, he had gone to William White's shop to buy a loaf, sugar and a quarter ounce of tea. He was given change by Mrs White, who served him, as well as some money owed to him. After Alexander had sat down to chat to Mr White, Mrs White had come into the room to say she had examined the coin carefully and found it to be "*bad*". After the police had come to Alexander's house and found various items including a mould, he said he had never seen this before, never seen the lodgers making anything, had never taken any *"bad"* shilling to a shop for a mutchkin of whisky or given one to his daughter.

Mary Alexander was accused of having tendered a counterfeit shilling to Thomas Kerr on 18 November 1852, knowing it to be false, followed by a similar crime on 20 November, when she tried to pass a coin to Esther Sanderson Cooper, wife of Thomas Barclay, blacksmith, and daughter of Helen Cooper who had a grocer shop in Broxburn. The money was for payment of sweet oil and tobacco. She had then passed another shilling at Andrew Hunter's draper and grocer shop at Broxburn for butter and dye on 22 November and one at William Fraser's public house for some whisky and one to Agnes Lowrie Cunningham for the same drink.

Because of the seriousness of this crime, many witnesses were asked to give statements. Thomas Kerr, grocer, confirmed that he knew the prisoner and his daughter well. Mary had often come there to purchase groceries. The shop at Broxburn actually belonged to his brother, Daniel Kerr, who was now a farmer in Canada and had been for several years. On the evening of Thursday, 18 November, he recalled that Mary had come in to purchase bread, tea and sugar and passed over a shilling in payment. He did remember that the coin looked odd but had said nothing, giving her change in coppers. Having shown this to his wife later and tried it in his mouth, he realised that it was counterfeit and went to Alexander's house where he confronted Mary and a man seated by the fire. This short Irishman, wearing moleskin clothes, had taken the *"bad"* coin and given Kerr a legal shilling. Kerr's wife, Helen Bryce, recalled the incident but she was *"ben the hoose"* (next door) when the coin was passed over. She recalled that two counterfeit coins were found in the till after Mary had come into the shop on another two occasions.

Esther Barclay (daughter of Helen Martin, widow and grocer in Broxburn and wife of Thomas Barclay, blacksmith) said she was well acquainted with the prisoners. She remembered that Mary Alexander had come for a half gill of sweet oil on 20 November 1852 at around four o'clock in the afternoon and paid with a shilling, with change given. Mary had forgotten to get some tobacco and paid for this with the change. On the morning of Wednesday 24th, Officer Anderson had come into the shop asking if she had got a counterfeit shilling and he had located one in her till. On the previous Monday morning a short Irishman wearing a blue jacket and dirty moleskin trousers had come into the shop enquiring if there was any stucco for sale for a sore foot. She had none, but the stranger had seen some whitening in a barrel and had remarked that this was exactly what he wanted, but she had replied that it was not appropriate. About a quarter of an hour later, Mary Alexander had come in asking for the same stucco and was given the same response. She had not returned.

Mary White, daughter of William White, carter and grocer Broxburn, described her father's shop and house as being a single apartment. On the evening of Monday, 22 November 1852 – when it was dark outside - Alexander Alexander had come into the shop and bought half an ounce of tobacco, paying for it with a shilling, with change given. He had sat by the fire and smoked for a while, left, returning later when her parents were there. He had bought a loaf, paying for it with a shilling, following which he had bought tea and sugar with the change he had been given. Mary's mother had examined these coins and informed him that they were fake, whereupon Alexander had told her he knew the person who had given them to him to pay for a shirt, but was unaware that they were counterfeit. Agnes White, William's wife, concurred with this, saying she had examined the coins by candlelight. He had assured her that he would return with genuine coins – but he had not done so. William White, on returning from work at approximately six o'clock in the evening, had seen the dirty coins, brassy in the centre and obviously counterfeit.

Andrew Hunter, grocer and draper in Broxburn, knew the Alexanders. On Monday morning, 22 November, Mary had come into to the shop asking for a penny worth of butter dye, which she paid for with an obviously fake shilling. Mary had informed him that it had been given to her by a Mrs Linn, who was known to him, so he had told Mary to take the item to her and he would get the money another time. Mary had taken the shilling, saying she would return, but had run in the opposite direction of Mrs Lin's house. Hunter had heard about counterfeit money being passed in town the next day and Officer Anderson had come along and shown him the fake 1816 coins, which Hunter recognised as being the same as that which Mary Alexander had tried to pass to him.

William Hunter, a Broxburn baker, had described that his shop adjoined that of his brother, Andrew. He knew the prisoners well. Shortly after Alexander had been liberated from prison, he had come into his shop asking for some cement. On being asked the purpose, Alexander had replied that he had fallen over the basket of a man selling statues, knocking off some of the heads, so needed cement to mend them – a likely story! On Saturday the 20th, Mr Hunter noticed he had base coins in his till and on showing them to his brother was told he had also been passed one. The coins were passed to Officer Anderson. Two other individuals remembered Alexander had been looking to buy stucco and cement – Jessie Gorman, niece of Jane Neil or Mather, innkeeper, and Margaret Black, wife of James Wallace, a carpenter.

Agnes Lowrie Cunningham, who lived with her step father, William Fraser, cement maker and publican at Broxburn, confirmed that she was often left in charge of William's small public house. She knew the prisoners well. On Saturday, 20 November, Mary Alexander had called in for a pennyworth of cement for her father, but could not be sold such a small quantity. On the previous day an Irishman had requested some stucco for heartburn. On the Monday evening 22 November at around ten o'clock Mary had arrived at the public house with two bottles in her hand, requesting a gill and a half of whisky in each. She had stood outside until the bottles were filled, paying with a shilling. Agnes had been suspicious and on examining the coin, it was found to be slippery and of bluish appearance. She had wrapped it in paper, putting it in her pocket. Mary had returned at around eleven o'clock for the two bottles to be filled again, but Agnes had insisted that she come in this time. She had examined the obviously fake second shilling, which apparently had been given to Mary by a man named Pat. The coins were not properly moulded and she took them to Officer Anderson.

William Fraser's wife, Margaret Gowans, recalled that on Monday 22 November Agnes had given her a shilling, which Margaret had subsequently used to send out for some articles, but which coin had subsequently been returned as being fake. That same night her daughter had informed her about Mary Alexander and the incidents of the whisky and base coins. Apparently Margaret had even joked with Mary saying, *"Is this a new trade you've begun to?"* referring to the counterfeit money. The coins were very badly finished off round the edges and discoloured.

Matthew Gemmell was gamekeeper to the earl of Buchan and lodged at Clapperhouse Hall in Uphall with Thomas Thomson, farmer. He recalled that he had been in the company of John Thomson and Matthew McMillan on Monday evening, 22 November, in the Fraser public house. At approximately eleven o'clock Mary Alexander, who was well known to him, had come to the door requesting some whisky from Agnes Cunningham. The whisky had been given and the door barred shut. She had returned twenty minutes later for more whisky, but had been informed by Agnes that the coin she had passed previously was fake, as was this one. Gemmell could hear the conversation very distinctly and he had been shown the very badly made coins afterwards. This story was confirmed by John Morrison, a gamekeeper, who lived at Broxburn Railway Station.

Margaret Mitchell or Linn, a widow in Broxburn, stated that she knew the Alexanders, who lived nearby, very well. She recalled that Mary Alexander had called at her door one evening asking for a shilling for two sixpences that she had, which was for a lodger. Being suspicious, she had shown the sixpences to a neighbour to ensure they were legitimate and then she had given the girl a shilling.

Mary Ann Gordon or Berry, lodging house keeper – next door neighbour to the Alexanders for eleven years - stated that her husband had left her about ten months before and was believed to be in England. On the day before Alexander was released from prison (25 October), John - a short Irishman in a blue slope - had lodged with her for two nights. The next night, Alexander had come to her house and slept with the Irishman, but she had not heard their conversations. Mary Alexander had come the next night asking for a bed, saying she would pay for it. Mary Ann had heard the men talking in the back room the next morning. She had heard Mary Alexander mention fake money, but had not associated this with counterfeiting and she had not witnessed anything suspicious taking place. Alexander had asked his daughter to buy some provisions with a shilling and, after breakfast, the three had gone into Alexander's house. On Friday, 19 November, a stout Irishman, wearing a blue flannel shirt and white moleskin trousers, had come looking for lodgings, but no name had been given. Her room - costing three shillings - was too expensive for him and he had gone to Alexander's house. The two Irishmen were gone by Tuesday 23 November. On that same morning, at around eleven o'clock, Alexander had come to her house, sat down and produced a piece of an old yellow handkerchief containing a large stucco mould in two halves, which he had said was for making money. Inside was a shilling and he had tried to get her to buy provisions with it, but she had had grave suspicions, particularly when he had proceeded to take out a knife and trim the edges! She had hurried him and his mould away. Apparently Alexander had never worked since leaving prison and was receiving thrupence a day from the parish.

Robert Alexander, assistant game keeper and assistant constable in Broxburn, confirmed Alexander Alexander to be his uncle and that he was a criminal who had frequently been in custody for theft. He had even heard him boasting some years ago that he could counterfeit coins or *"make money"*, as he termed it, although he had not embellished on the procedure. His uncle had been apprehended about seven months before, and Robert had assisted Constable Anderson in taking him to Linlithgow. Once again, the subject of counterfeiting using a stucco mould was mentioned. Robert confirmed that he had been in Alexander's house after he was freed and had seen Mary, his cousin, with an orange half handkerchief round her shoulders. He explained that the house in which Alexander lived had once belonged to an aunt of his and that Alexander did not pay rent for it.

John Anderson, District Constable of police for Broxburn, recalled that Agnes Cunningham had come to him on Tuesday morning, 23 November, with three fake shillings. That evening he had gone with Mr Colquhoun, Superintendent of police, and James Allan to Alexander's house at approximately eleven o'clock, when the door was forced open. Alexander and his daughter were asleep in the small apartment and John had taken hold of Alexander by the wrist until a light was struck. A thorough search had been conducted and, after Allan had gone up into the loft above the bed, an orange coloured napkin containing a stucco mould in two halves, with the figure of a shilling, was discovered. Alexander had protested his innocence and although enquires had been made about the two Irishmen, they had never been located, although a man answering the description of one was seen at Queensferry and, once again, some counterfeit shillings had been left behind.

According to records for the Linlithgow Prison, Alexander appeared at the Linlithgow Sheriff Court on 8 July 1849, having already been in the prison three times. On this occasion he was sentenced to 6 weeks in prison for theft. He was in Linlithgow Prison again, having come before the Sheriff on 16 March 1852 – for theft with previous conviction – and was sentenced to 6 months imprisonment. The trial took place at the High Court Edinburgh on 14 February 1853. His daughter, Mary, appeared before the Magistrates on 21 September 1852 for assault, for which she was imprisoned for 14 days.

Alexander Alexander was found guilty of the crimes against him and sentenced to transportation for 7 years. The case against his daughter, Mary, was dismissed on the recommendation of the Advocate Depute.

National Records of Scotland reference AD14/53/436; JC26/1853/480 JC26/1853/480

THOMAS SCOTT

THEFT FROM A ROYAL MAIL BAG BETWEEN TORPHICHEN AND LINLITHGOW 11 JUNE 1853

It was on the morning of Saturday, 11 June 1853 when Thomas Scott had found a mail bag on the road between Torphichen post office and Linlithgow and subsequently stolen a pound note from a letter. He was charged with the crime of contravention of 1 Vict., c. 36, ss. 27 & 28 (Post Office Act) and for this crime he could have been transported beyond the seas for life. The mail bag had contained approximately fourteen letters and, although not all of the addressees were known, one envelope had certainly been addressed to *"Mrs Magdalen Reddoch at Mr John Kane's, 21 Court, Chisenhale Street, near the Clarence Dock, Liverpool"* and this was the one which contained the bank note.

Daniel Friel stated that he had been working for James Bowie, a tavern keeper at Bathgate, since the previous Martinmas. Mr Bowie had the contract for taking the mail bags from Bathgate to Linlithgow and bringing them back again to the post office at Bathgate and Friel was employed to do this. He generally left Bathgate with the two mail bags early every morning on horseback, going by Torphichen Road, stopping off at Torphichen post office to collect their bag and subsequently delivering all three bags to the Linlithgow post office. He would put the three bags – all sealed - in his saddle bag for security.

Torphichen Post Office today

On the morning in question, he had left Bathgate, as usual, at approximately five or six o'clock. It was a wet day and John Roberts, the postmaster at Torphichen, had come out with the mail bag in his hand and, to avoid Friel having to dismount, Roberts had put it into the saddle bag. It was a leather mail bag, with a brass plate on it engraved "*Torphichen and Linlithgow*". Whilst Roberts had been doing this, the horse had shied slightly, and Friel had not actually seen the bag being put in, as his saddle bag was behind him. He had merely stood up in the stirrups without turning round. He had gone on his way, passing Wallhouse Lodge, and when he was about a mile away from Linlithgow, he had come off the horse for a couple of minutes, but the bridle reins had never been out of his hands. Having remounted – without checking the bags in any way – he had continued on his journey to Linlithgow post office. When he had opened the saddle bag there, however, he had been astounded to find that the Torphichen/Linlithgow bag was missing. He had immediately advised the postmistress, got back on his horse and returned to Torphichen, where enquiries had been made, to no avail.

He had returned to Linlithgow, then Bathgate, which was at around nine o'clock. He was mortified to have to report this loss to his master, Mr Bowie – cap in hand. Friel stated that the road coming from Wallhouse North Lodge was exceedingly steep for a few hundred yards and when he was riding down there, his legs could not clasp the saddle very tightly, which may have resulted in the mail bag falling off. As far as he was concerned, this could be the only explanation for its loss.

John Roberts senior was a blacksmith and post office keeper at Torphichen and had kept the post office for around eight years. His house *was* the post office and he made up the mail bags every evening at approximately ten o'clock, and these were then conveyed by Daniel Friel to Linlithgow. Roberts recalled making up the bag as usual on the Friday evening of 10 June and it had contained fifteen letters. William Bruce had come in to the post office with a letter, and Mrs Roberts had handled the transaction. The only addresses he could remember were those of Magdalen Reddoch at Liverpool, Mr Dickson at Edinburgh, Mr Learmonth at Linlithgow and Mr Dymock at Linlithgow. The letters, having been prepaid with postage stamps and imprinted "*Torphichen 10 June 1853*", were enclosed, as always, in a way bill which he made up and wrapped with a piece of string.

The following morning, Friel had come to collect the bag, asking if Roberts would place it into the saddle bag, as it was wet and miserable outside. It was the first time he had ever asked him to do so, but Roberts distinctly recalled having put the mail bag safely beside the others in the saddle bag. Shortly afterwards, however, a worried Friel had returned with the news of the lost bag. On the following Monday, Mr Colquhoun, superintendent of police, had shown Roberts a portion of the mail bag and the relevant way bill, which the postmaster had recognised as being his. On being further questioned, Roberts had then recalled that one of the letters had been addressed to "*Miss Wilson, Edinburgh*", as it had come up on the Friday from

Linlithgow and she had left Woodcockdale by then, so he had written *"try Bathgate"* on it.

Margaret Fleming, wife of John Roberts, stated that she was generally in the house at Torphichen. She had taken some letters on the evening of Friday, 10 June, one of which had been brought in by Mrs Purves, addressed to her son, David, and John Lindsay's niece had also brought one. She had put stamps on both and William Bruce had arrived later with another letter for Liverpool, asking her to put a stamp on it. All had been placed in the letter box that evening, after which her husband had made up the bag and sealed it. Marion Speeden, postmistress Linlithgow, confirmed that letters posted at Torphichen were sent to Linlithgow in a mail bag, which was subsequently opened by her. They were subsequently sent to their proper destinations. Daniel Friel had brought the mail bags on the Saturday in question, telling her that the Torphichen bag was missing.

John Alexander senior, who lived at Broompark, Torphichen, had sent for William Bruce, overseer at Broompark Brick and Tile Works, to come and write a letter for him to his daughter in Liverpool. He was replying to her request for money, as she was due to leave for America, so he had given Bruce twenty shillings in silver, to have it changed for a pound note to be enclosed with the letter. After having it read to him, Mr Alexander had signed the letter and the envelope had been addressed to *"Mrs Magdalen Reddoch at Mr John Kane's, 21 Court, Chisenhale Street, near the Clarence Dock, Liverpool"*.

William Bruce confirmed this and that he had gone to David Morrison in Torphichen, where he had been given the pound note, which he had then put inside the letter. His wife had been there when he did this and sealed it afterwards. He recalled it being an oldish note and that he had taken the letter to Mrs Roberts at Torphichen post office, where he had bought the stamp at approximately nine o'clock. David Morrison, the grocer and publican at Torphichen, was able to confirm the transaction which had taken place and described that the old and oily pound note had been either of the Union Bank or the British Linen Company and he had been passed it the same day by a collier.

Agnes Bruce Alexander stated that her husband, John, had come in on the Friday night in question at around nine o'clock, saying that he was going to post a letter for his father, Mr Alexander senior. The letter containing the pound had been put into an envelope and sealed with wax. Mary Ann Masterman, gatekeeper at Wallhouse North Gate Lodge, stated that the gate was about quarter of a mile north from Torphichen and she had written a letter that Friday afternoon to her cousin, Miss Smith, addressing it *"opposite the Horse and Farrier, St Nicholas Street, Butcher Gate, Carlisle"*. Having put a stamp on it, she had then sent her six year old daughter to post it. Grace Masterton, who said, *"I cannot read writing yet"*, confirmed that her mother had sent her to the Torphichen post office and she had given the letter to Mr Roberts.

Alexander Kirkpatrick junior, who was an assistant teacher living with his father, a gardener, at Broompark, Torphichen, confirmed that he had written a letter to *"Messrs Dickson & Company, Nursery Seedsman, 1 Waterloo Place, Edinburgh"*. He had then posted it at Torphichen at approximately seven o'clock that evening, having given Mr Roberts a penny for postage. Rachel Purves, a widow, had asked James Martin to write a letter for her that Friday to David Purves, her son, who was a joiner at Duntocher near Glasgow. Martin had read it over, the gist of which was to request David and his wife to visit her on the Torphichen Fair Day of 24 June. The letter had been addressed and sealed with wax and she had taken it personally to Mrs Roberts at the post office at around eight o'clock that Friday evening. Mrs Purves explained that she was going to live with her son - George Purves, another joiner working with Messrs Lyon and Lawson, at 730 Gallowgate, Glasgow - the next month and that his house adjoined a new church, and had a public house beneath it! James Martin, a labourer in Torphichen, confirmed that he had written the letter.

Agnes Pringle of Carribber, Linlithgow had written a letter addressed to *"Mrs White, Mackenzies Lodgings, 111 George Street, Edinburgh"* that Friday and it been given to her brother, David Pringle Esq. of Carribber, to be posted. William Arthur, labourer at Torphichen, and employee of Major Pringle, had posted it at Torphichen that evening and had remembered the address, as he had posted another for it previously.

Helen Eliza Cowe Scott or Gillon, widow of William Doune Gillon Esq, who was living at Cathlaw House at the time, stated that she frequently wrote letters and sent them to Torphichen post office. On the evening of Friday, 10 June, she had written to Mr Dymock and Mr Learmonth – both at Linlithgow - enclosing both in one envelope and addressing it to Mr Dymock, a grocer. She had written another to Andrew Gillon, her son, addressing it, *"the New Club, Edinburgh"*. She had prepared the envelopes with stamps and sent them to Torphichen post office *"by some person"* but she could not remember his name. Andrew Summers, the butler at Wallhouse, Estate, *was* that person and he confirmed that Mrs Gillon, the mother of the proprietor of Wallhouse, sometimes lived at Cathlaw. When he had been there that Friday evening, she had given him two letters to be posted and he had put them in the letter box at Torphichen at about ten o'clock.

Helen Gillon or Wardrop, wife of William Macfarlane Wardrop Esq of Bridghouse, had written a letter that Friday to Mr Robert Learmonth, butcher at Linlithgow, and had sent a servant boy, John Martin, to post it. She had heard the following Sunday that the mail bag had been lost, and when Mr Learmonth had been at Bridgehouse on the Monday, he had informed her that he had never received the letter. Likewise, Walter Gillon, a labourer, had written a letter to his sister in Edinburgh, addressing the envelope to *"Miss Jessie Gillon, 112 Lauriston Place"* and sent it with Jane Calder to the post office, giving her a penny for postage. The letter had never been received, however.

What of the prisoner – Scott? Thomas Scott, five feet eleven inches tall, a thirty year old labourer living at Hillhouses, Muiravonside with his mother, Elizabeth Marshall, had been cautioned and interrogated on 13 June at Linlithgow. He stated that he had been going to work early on Saturday morning 12 June and was on the road leading from Linlithgow to Torphichen and Bathgate, when had spotted a bag lying on the road about a hundred and fifty yards south of the lodge leading to the house of Mr Gillon of Wallhouse. He had lifted the sealed bag, which had a brass plate marked "*Linlithgow and Torphichen*", and had carried it along the road. He explained his actions by saying he had been the worse for drink and had not known what he was doing. However, he had torn up the bag up after seeing that there were a good many letters in it. There had been something like an old note in one and he had taken it and put it in his pocket, whilst throwing away all of the letters. He had then torn up the bag about a couple of miles from where he had come across it and gone on his way to work on the road leading from Bathgate to Edinburgh, where he was breaking up stones.

It was around noon when he had seen Mr Young, the farmer at Caputhall, on the road with another person called Anderson or Aitken. Scott had been looking at what he had found when they had approached him. He had asked Young to identify the paper and it had been recognised as a pound note. Young had said he would give him five shillings for it and "*take his chance*" with it (if it was counterfeit), saying he might not pass it successfully by itself, but he might if it was in a bunch with some others. Young's companion had lent him two half crowns, which had been given to Scott, and Scott had then given the pound note to Young. About two hours later, Young had passed by again, telling Scott that he had received full value for the note, having changed it at Deans or Uphall. Scott had admitted that he had thrown away part of the bag and the brass plate and the remaining part of the bag had been put in his pocket and taken home. He had hidden it afterwards in a dyke, but could find it again, if requested to do so.

On being questioned again, Scott stated that he had later shown the superintendent of police, in company of George Watt, sheriff officer of Linlithgow, and another person calling himself the Inspector of the Post Office, where he had found the bag and where he had opened it. The location was a planting in Torphichen. He had taken all the letters out of the bag, put them in his pocket there, opening them as he walked along the road, but had subsequently thrown them away. He had opened the one letter containing the pound at a place called Bellmount or Bailie Mount, where Mrs Russell lived. Some pieces of the letters had been discarded there, with others being strewn along the road. He had then called in on Mrs Donaldson, who lived at Drumcross, a mile south of Bellmount, and "*taken a smoke*" there He had shown her the note, having dried it at the fire, telling her that he had found it. He had asked her if it was a pound, but she had given no satisfactory answer. He had later shown the superintendent the place where the remainder of the bag was concealed and it had been extracted from the dyke. The pieces of letters had also been retrieved.

Elizabeth Marshall, who lived at the cothouse on the Hill Farm, Muiravonside, was aged 55. She stated that Thomas Scott was her illegitimate son and he lived with her. Prior to his apprehension, he had worked on the Edinburgh, Bathgate and Glasgow Turnpike Road – several miles away - and he went to work every morning early, returning in the evening. She had been in bed on Saturday, 11 June, when he had left for work at six o'clock that morning. He had returned at approximately ten o'clock in the evening, producing a portion of a leather bag, saying he had found it on the road. She had washed it and hung it up to dry. The next day the officers had come to her house and she had given it to them. (There was a note written on the bottom of the page of this statement which said, *"Scott is a bad character and has been several times in custody for various offences."*)

William Russell, who was ten years old and son of Thomas Russell, dyke builder at Bellmount, or Bailie Mount, Bathgate - two miles south east from Torphichen - described that there was a farm road which passed the house, but the road had no name other than *"the Rigghead Road"*. This road only led to Drumcross and to the Edinburgh and Bathgate Turnpike Road. He had become acquainted with Thomas Scott several days before the Saturday morning in question, as he had frequently passed the house going to his work in the morning and returning in the evenings. Young William had seen him on the road that morning, a little east of the house, tearing up some letters and trampling them beneath his feet.

It was a wet morning and William had been putting the cows into a field at the time. Scott had gone eastwards to work at around seven o'clock and after he was out of sight, William had gone up to the place and found fragments of letters lying on the ground. Having picked up a portion of a letter and part of a way bill, he had shown these to his mother. His young brother had been with him, but he was far too young to be questioned. Two envelopes and the last letter had been burned, as it was thought that they were useless. On the Tuesday evening following, his mother had asked him to fetch the other fragments, which he did, and further east, near Rigghead Planting, he had found an envelope and five small pieces of letters, which had been retrieved. The next day, the officers had arrived and taken everything away.

William's mother, Margaret Russell, stated that she knew Scott by sight but she had not seen him that Saturday morning. Her son had come to the house with some letters that he had found near the house, some of which were burnt, but on the Tuesday evening following, she had gone out with her son and husband, Thomas, to see if there were any others lying around. They had afterwards located the fragments and pieces of envelope, which were then given to the officers. Her husband concurred with this, adding that he had heard about the lost mail bag on the Tuesday, which had led them to search further. His son, William, had gone on to Rigghead Plantation, where the envelope addressed to Magdalen Reddoch had been found, along with some additional fragments, which had been trampled into the soil.

Mr Russell said that his house was situated two miles south east of Torphichen, with Caputhall being two miles further south. The three parishes of Linlithgow, Torphichen and Bathgate were near to Silvermine, which was in the vicinity of his house, and an individual leaving Torphichen going to Caputhall would need to go through these three parishes. He was familiar with the Rigghead plantation, near to Torphichen, the south portion of which formed part of Wallhouse estate.

James Young, farmer at Caputhall, stated that at approximately eleven o'clock on the morning in question, he had been walking with Mr Fraser, innkeeper at Broxburn, along the part of the Edinburgh to Bathgate Turnpike Road which passed through his farm. He had met Scott, with whom he was acquainted, and the lad had been looking at a piece of paper which had *"blown onto his feet"*. Scott had wondered if it actually might be an old pound note and had offered to exchange it. Young had suggested a crown, saying he would *"take his chance of it"*, as it might have been a forgery. Fraser had loaned Young the money, which was given over for the pound note and this had been changed in less than half an hour at the house of Mrs Kerr, a publican at Dechmont. William Fraser, cement manufacturer at Broxburn, concurred with this, saying that he had come to see Mr Young by the morning train. He had warned him that the note might be a fake, but Young had been persuaded that it was genuine and it had been changed by Mrs Kerr, who had now moved to Edinburgh.

Jane Marshall, a widow who lived at Drumcross, stated that her house was a mile south of Bellmount. Scott had been in the habit of passing her house when going to his work and she recalled that he had done so on the morning of Saturday, 11 June, at around seven o'clock. He had been sober and had asked for a light for his pipe, which he had then smoked while asking her to identify something. He had produced a pound note, pretending that he was unsure what it was. It was a damp note of the British Linen Company Bank and Scott had told her that he had been given it the previous night by a man *"a good way from here"*. He had dried it at the fire, put it in his tobacco box and said that he would change it at Dechmont. When she had asked him if he had actually *found* it, he had vehemently denied this.

David McNair, a slater and builder at Dechmont, who lived at Torphichen, stated that he knew Scott, as he had formerly worked for him. He had encountered him on 11 June and had asked him if he had seen the missing mail bag. Scott, however, had said that if he had, he would have given it to Mr Bowie for a reward.

Adam Colquhoun, superintendent of county police, stated that on the Saturday evening, 11 June, he had been informed of the loss of the mail bag by John Alexander, one of Mr Bowie's men. He had offered a reward, intimating that anybody who kept it would be prosecuted. Colquhoun had made enquiries and received information about a possible suspect who had been asking about the reward. He had then met George Watt, sheriff officer in Linlithgow, and Sergeant Kerr on the road between Torphichen and Wallhouse, having ascertained that Thomas Scott was the suspected party. They had all then walked to The Hill at

Muiravonside, where Scott lived with his mother. Only Scott's mother was at home, but on searching the premises, the officers had located the lower half of a mail bag, which they had taken away. They had then located Scott – who had denied everything - and charged him. Even when he had been shown the portion of the bag, he had denied having ever seen it. On being taken to Bathgate, however, he had then admitted voluntarily that he *had* found the bag, saying that he could show them the location. He also admitted that he had known it was a post bag, as he had seen the brass plates. The following Wednesday, Scott had directed them to the place, which was along the road to Bellmount, and various fragments of the letters had been found. Afterwards, they had gone to the dyke near the adjoining farm of Drumcross, where the prisoner had produced the upper portion of mail bag, which was wet and damp from exposure. They had searched for the string in vain, but other pieces of letters had been located on the road heading east from Bellmount. Sergeant John Kerr and George Watt concurred with this statement.

What was the outcome? Thomas Scott was tried at the High Court on 11 November 1853. He was found guilty and sentenced to 4 years penal servitude.

National Archives of Scotland reference AD14/53/423; JC26/1853/548

DAVID DRYSDALE

THEFT OF A HORSE FROM EASTER INCH, BATHGATE, AND A DOG AND ROPES FROM BATHGATE 14/15 OCTOBER 1854

It was during the night of Saturday, 14, or the morning of Sunday, 15 October 1854 when a horse had been stolen from Plain Park or Lawn Park, Easter Inch, Bathgate. This property belonged to James Fleming Esquire of Craigs, who lived at Woodhead Bathgate, but the field was occupied by John Pollock junior, grazier and farmer, who lived at Easter Inch.

John Pollock stated on 25 October that he was the occupier of the large field on the farm lands of Easter Inch called the Plain or Lawn Park, which adjoined the farm house and steading immediately on the east, measuring 52 Scotch acres. The steading was about a mile and a half to the south east of Bathgate, away from the public road. Pollock owned the twelve year old dark brown mare (valued at about £20) and its foal, which was born at the end of the summer past and was not yet weaned. Both had been in the field on the Saturday evening, as he had been responsible for putting them there and shutting the gates properly. At approximately eight o'clock next morning he had been advised that the mare was missing and he had hurried to the field with his men, finding the foal standing by a gate which was shut. The gate at the west side was standing open, but it was assumed that this had been done deliberately to mislead, as the foal would have gone to that gate had the mother been taken out by it. He had gone to Bathgate and informed Sergeant Kerr of the theft. On returning, his men had discovered the direction towards which the mare had been taken, which was across another two fields to the Livingston road. Mr Pollock had ridden off to find the mare with some of his men in a gig, tracking her steps away to the east. Several people had informed him that they had seen her and on arriving at around nine in the morning at Howden foot toll, west of Mid Calder, the mare had been found in the keeping of the toll people, tethered up in a park. The mare was rolling around badly and it was evident that she had been overridden, was heated and quite bare. Having left her in the care of Gideon Paris, the toll man, Pollock had gone east with Sergeant Kerr in search of the man described as having been seen at Burnwynd, as well as other places. He could not be found, however, so the mare had been brought back to Easter Inch and had not been well since.

John Pollock senior, a grazier or quarryman at Easter Inch, stated that he owned a house there, whilst his son "*had the grass*" of Plain Park. He often helped his son and had assisted in carting the potatoes on the Saturday in question, when the mare had been used. He corroborated his son's statement, and also stated that after the gates had been shut, he had seen a man heading east with a dog. On the Sunday morning he had challenged his son's employees as to what had happened with another mare in the stable, whose blinders had been taken off, but was now wearing them again. There were also three belly band ropes lying there which had not been seen before. Apparently a man had come into the stable during the night and it could only be assumed that he had brought these with him. A small black dog had come to the door scraping for food when the stranger had been in the stable and the beast was easily identifiable by the white markings round its neck and on the tip of its tail. The ropes had later been claimed by Henry Fairley.

Henry McKnight, who had been a labourer with John Pollock junior, but was now at Caputhall, Bathgate in the employment of James Young, stated that he used to sleep in the stable at Easter Inch steading. He had seen the mare and foal on the Saturday night at Plain Park and he had gone to bed as usual. During the night he had thought that someone had been meddling with his boots and then he had heard a dog scraping at door, wanting to be fed. His feet had come upon some ropes when he had gotten up and he had struck away the dog. When he had returned, someone had been lying in his bed and, on asking who he was, he had been told that he was a fellow on a tramp, who had been at the Falkirk Fair and had come to get a nap! The two had conversed for a while and the man had stayed for roughly an hour. He had mentioned that he had been *"in the fuddle"*(drunk) and tried to persuade McKnight to go for a whisky, saying he had two shillings in his pocket, but McKnight had refused the offer. He appeared to go by the stack yard - not towards Plain Park. McKnight could not identify him, as it was dark, but he had confirmed that the stranger was a big man with a slouching appearance. In the morning he had discovered that the mare was missing and he and Mr Pollock had found its tracks on the east side.

William Michael, another servant who had worked for John Pollock junior for two years, confirmed that the dark brown mare in question was called Bet and had been used along with another mare named Nancy in carting potatoes all day on the Saturday in question. He said that old man Pollock would put Bet in the Plain Park at night. Michael had slept in the stable that night, where Nancy was kept, and he had taken the blinders from her and hung them up. He hadn't seen anyone coming in, but had heard someone talking to Henry McKnight during the early morning. On questioning McKnight as to his identity, he had been informed he was *"a man on a tramp, who was wearied and cold"*. Bet had been missed on the Sunday morning and marks of her hooves, which had been recently shod, had been located at the east gate. The tracks went directly towards the right, to Mr Russell's field to the Livingston end and Michael had been there with Sergeant Kerr, Constable Robertson and George Watt on the 28th, but could not identify either Drysdale or his dog.

John Fairley, blacksmith at Livingston Village, had been up at around six o'clock in the morning of Sunday 15 October and had seen a man on horseback about forty yards east of his house, coming from the west. The dark brown horse – bare backed, with a colt halter - was walking, the man's back had been facing him and a small black dog with white markings was walking along with him. The man was a coarse, drover-like person, dressed in a square tailed coat and moleskin trousers. When

Sergeant Kerr and Mr Pollock had arrived at approximately ten o'clock, they had described the horse, man and dog, which appeared to be those which Fairley had seen. Fairley identified the prisoner on 28 October.

Gideon Paris was a labourer and the toll keeper at Howden Bridge, Mid Calder, but his wife generally attended to the toll, which was a mile from Mid Calder and six miles east from Bathgate. A surgeon had passed by his toll on the Sunday in question at around five o'clock in the morning and then Paris had heard horse's hooves at about a quarter to seven. A coarse looking man dressed in an old square tailed coat, moleskin trews and a cloth cap, had come from the west on a dark brown mare. On questioning him as to where he was going, the man had merely put his head down and given no answer. He had paid his one and halfpenny, asked for water, but had been told there was none, and had then asked for whisky, but had been refused, as there was none kept at the toll. The man had mentioned that he had been at the Falkirk tryst the previous day, had been *"on the batter"* (drunk) and was dry. He had subsequently taken a drink at a spout which was one hundred yards east and Paris could see that the mare *"had milk on her"*, so must have foaled recently. At approximately ten o'clock that morning, the same horse had come back alone and he had caught it, put it in his field and tied it to a tree. Sergeant Kerr had arrived shortly afterwards with Mr Pollock, who had claimed the mare as his own. Paris later identified the prisoner. His wife, Barbara Strachan, corroborated his statement and said that she had also seen the prisoner passing through the toll on the Friday afterwards – 20 October – with a small black dog and on the next morning with the same dog and a large dark greyhound. Although he had kept his head down and was whistling, she had recognised him from the Sunday.

Thomas Gibson was a miller who worked for Robert Smith, farmer and miller at Mid Calder West Mill, which was roughly four hundred yards north of the village. A large park called Markets Park stretched the whole length of the village behind it and he had seen a dark brown mare there at around nine o'clock on the Sunday morning, when he was going to the washerwoman's. On going to Bathgate and returning home at around two in the afternoon, he had seen the same beast tied at the back of Howden Toll.

Thomas Buchanan, innkeeper at Burnwynd, Kirknewton had seen the same man passing by east at around nine o'clock that Sunday morning, accompanied by a small black dog. He had returned fifteen minutes later, asking for a glass of spirits, saying that he had come from Falkirk. Buchanan could absolutely identify the man and his dog. Isabel Scott, the sixteen year old daughter of Alexander Scott, toll collector at Kiershill Toll, Currie, which is about two miles east of Burnwynd, said that the same man had come to her door just after nine o'clock on the Sunday morning. He had asked the time and had left with his little dog.

Thomas Clark, labourer at Cochrane Street, Bathgate, stated that Drysdale had lodged with him for a fortnight previous to the Saturday in question and he had come from the Edinburgh area with his small black dog named Bess. Drysdale had been working on a railway bridge near Bathgate, where Clark worked. Having only received five shillings for his pay that Saturday, which was to tide him over until the Monday, Drysdale had not been pleased. He had not returned to Clark's after he was paid and the next time Clark had seen him was on Monday, 23 October, at the railway station, when he was accompanied by his own dog and John McDonald's dog. All that Drysdale had said was that he had been in Edinburgh.

Thomas Gowans, the farmer at Adambrae Mill, Mid Calder, had been in Bathgate on business on Saturday, 14 October, and had taken some toddy at the Commercial Hotel, following which he had gone to Mr Johnston, publican, to meet some people there. Drysdale had come in and during their conversation had told Mr Gowans that he was a ploughman from Glasgow and was looking for work. He had named several people he had worked for and wondered if Mr Gowans would employ him. They had made a "*sort of arrangement*" and Mr Gowans had given him a shilling, but afterwards Drysdale had given such incredible stories about himself that Gowans had become suspicious about his character and he had taken back the coin.

As far as the ropes were concerned, Henry Fairley junior, who lived with his father, Henry, at South Bridge Street, Bathgate, stated that he was a carter and the carts usually stood in the street opposite their stable near the house during the night. He had left them, as usual, on the Saturday evening in question and there had been two belly band ropes tied to the carts, but these had disappeared by the next day. He had been at Easter Inch on 17 October and when he had been speaking to Mr Pollock, he had been advised that the ropes had been left there by a man. James Fairley – Henry's brother – added that he had been in Johnston's public house on Friday, 20 October and had seen Drysdale with two dogs tied together, one of which he recognised as John McDonald's. Drysdale had left the pub in rather a cantankerous mood!

As far as the theft of the dog – Springer - was concerned, John McDonald, miner, Robertson's Square or Baillie's Close, off Main Street, Bathgate, stated that he had a large black dog which was a cross between a pointer and greyhound and it had been in his possession for three months. He had left it at the mouth of the close on the Friday evening, 20 October and when he had gone out and whistled for Springer, the dog had disappeared. He had advised Sergeant Kerr of the theft next morning, but the dog had appeared at his mother's house on the Monday following. The beast appeared to be jaded, hungry and exhausted. Apparently, a boy had told him that Drysdale had been seen with it, but Drysdale had explained that it had followed his own dog, which was in heat.

James Walker was a coal drawer lodging with James Brown, but who had previously lodged with John McDonald. He said that Drysdale used to call in at McDonald's house, wanting Springer back, as the dog had formerly belonged to him. However, McDonald would not return it until Drysdale paid what had been spent on its keep.

McDonald had been offered a shilling, but had refused it. Walker had seen Drysdale with McDonald's dog on the Monday, 23 October, and had tried to entice it. Eventually Drysdale had let Springer go, saying it had followed his own dog.

Drysdale had been seen by Robert Orr, the toll collector at Livingston Toll Bar, four miles east of Bathgate, on Friday, 20 October, when he had been accompanied by his small black dog. He had then been passing through the toll the day after with two dogs – one being the greyhound cross. Orr had also seen him on the following Monday with the same two dogs. His description of Drysdale was that he was a peculiar looking person with some disability in one of his arms.

Sergeant John Kerr described the sequence of events concerning the missing mare, culminating in its being found at Mr Paris' toll, where it had been neighing piteously. The marks of the mare's hooves had been irregular, going from one side of the road to the other, as if the rider had not proper control of it. He and Mr Pollock had visited all of the tolls Drysdale had passed through and had eventually gone to Edinburgh to find him, but had been unsuccessful. When he had seen Mr Pollock on Wednesday 18th, Kerr told him that he suspected a man named Robert Meikle as being the culprit, as he was a criminal from Edinburgh, and reputed to be a horse thief. As Kerr had become ill that evening, Adam Colquhoun had obtained a warrant against Meikle. He knew the Meikle family – criminal characters all – and had gone to Edinburgh to find Robert Meikle, but he had not been of the opinion that any of that family had fitted the description of the thief in question.

Constable William Robertson, railway policeman, on hearing the description of the thief, had said that he recognised him as being David Drysdale. He had known him for ten years, and that he had lived at Carrington, Edinburgh during that time. Drysdale, who had a bent arm, was known to be a poacher, but had been working at Bathgate since the early summer and was known to have poached with John McDonald. As Sergeant Kerr's health had improved by Monday, 23 October, he had gone into Bathgate and seen Drysdale speaking to someone in the street. He was instantly recognisable, with his small black dog with the white markings. Kerr had pretended to question Drysdale about the missing dog and had taken him to his house, but had needed another officer to assist, as he was still feeling very weak. Drysdale was charged with the three thefts, which he had denied. He did admit that he had gone east by the road past Livingston, through Burnwynd, to see friends on the Sunday in question. Sergeant Kerr had noticed brown horse hair on Drysdale's coat, but Drysdale could say nothing about it.

David Drysdale's father, when questioned, had said that his son, David, had visited him on Monday, 16 October, and left on the Wednesday. Nothing had been said about a horse, however.

What had David Drysdale, the 21 year old mason, to say about the matter? He stated that he had lodged with Thomas Clark and had worked in Bathgate for three months.

He admitted that he had left Bathgate on Saturday, 14 October at approximately eleven o'clock in the evening – when the pubs shut – and had gone to a toll to the east of Bathgate, where he had promptly fallen asleep at the back of a dyke. He had a dog with him and had been somewhat the worse for drink, with a bottle of whisky in his pocket. He had apparently wandered around in the dark, eventually finding himself at Burnwynd at around seven o'clock next morning. He had no knowledge of a place called Easter Inch, had not gone to a farmhouse, had not taken any horse or been riding. He had visited his father at Temple, Midlothian on the Monday and had told his employer's son, Murdoch McLean, that he was going there. As to the dog, he knew McDonald's dog, but he had not had it with him. It had merely followed him into the street after he had been at Johnston's pub.

David Drysdale had been committed to Linlithgow Prison on 23 October 1854. What happened to him when he was tried at the High Court in Edinburgh on 18 December that year? The jury found it established that he had taken away the mare, but not with a theftuous purpose. David Drysdale was therefore freed.

National Records of Scotland reference AD14/54/404; JC26/1854/443

Note: In a History of Easter Inch in the Courier of 8 September 1877 it was stated that these lands had been purchased several years ago by John Waddell Esq, contractor, formerly the Provost of Bathgate, who now lived at Edinburgh. The previous proprietor had been the late Mr Fleming of Craigs, who had succeeded his uncle, Mr Robert Douglas of Blackburn House. Mr Waddell had improved the lands greatly and erected new fences throughout, as well as building a steading *"rivalling any in the kingdom in point of situation and commodiousness"*. This consisted of a front of two storeys, and two wings of considerable height, with the front elevation containing an archway in the centre and surmounted by a fine turret. The old steadings on the hill to the east, and at the Dubs on the west, had been completely removed. Mr Waddell had at one time contemplated building a fitting mansion on the east side, which could be approached from the turnpike at Kirkton. He had even had a few of the stones taken away from the old demolished College of Glasgow and brought to Easter Inch in preparation for this, due to his love of antiquity. The writer of the article stated, *"I am satisfied whenever he feels leisure he will carry this enterprise into effect, as he is a gentleman not easily baulked in his purpose."* The mansion, however, was never erected.

MATTHEW BOYD

ASSAULT AND ROBBERY AT THE MEADOWHEAD TAVERN, BATHGATE 17 NOVEMBER 1854

It was Friday, 17 November 1854. Laurence (Larry) Hart was a licensed hawker of soft goods who lived at 315 Coull's Close, Edinburgh, which was his own house. He sold his goods around a 12 mile radius of Edinburgh, visiting Bathgate and the surrounding area once a month. Having left Edinburgh with his packs on Tuesday, 14 November, he lodged with a Mrs Learmonth in Bathgate. He had a large amount of goods wrapped in a larger pack which consisted of an old shawl with an oilcloth cover on the outside, bound with a leather strap. This larger pack was carried on his back, but he also carried a small pack by hand and this held smaller items such as scarves, mufflers, spun silk handkerchiefs and the like.

He recalled that he had met Matthew Boyd and they had gone into a tavern at Meadowhead, Bathgate, kept by Robert Whitehead on the afternoon in question at approximately four o'clock – when it was not yet dark. Hart had tried to bargain with the owner and was eventually paid six shillings for ten yards of wincy. However, the hawker had become somewhat befuddled due to the amount of alcohol he had been drinking with Boyd (which Hart had mostly paid for). Hart recalled that Boyd had asked to look at a chocolate-coloured handkerchief in the bundle and asked what the price might be, but eventually Hart had felt that it was time to leave and Boyd had offered to carry his pack on the road, to which Hart had replied, *"Friend, if you wish me well, let me go. I can find the road myself."* However, about one hundred yards along the road, Boyd had tried to grab the pack by pushing Hart and making him fall onto the muddy road. Boyd had come down on him, seizing him by the throat, trying to strangle him. Hart had implored Boyd to take his hands off him and spare his life, telling him to take everything. His violent attacker had struck him on the jaw with a clenched fist and Hart had cried out, *"You've killed Larry Hart!"* He had then sunk into insensibility.

The road had been wet and muddy and, on regaining consciousness, Hart had found several people gathered round him with a light. He had informed them that he had been attacked and robbed – well nigh murdered. He had asked them to look for his bundles, but nothing had been found. His hat was missing. He had then proceeded to Bathgate for Sergeant Kerr of the police and had subsequently been taken to a lodging house, where he had seen Boyd sitting with the bundles. He had taken Kerr, the policeman, to the location of the assault – about one hundred and forty yards from the tavern, away from the houses - and the marks where he had fallen could be seen clearly. The value of the goods stolen was approximately sixteen pounds. Hart had been examined by the doctor and said that he had a sore mark on his leg where Boyd had kicked him, as well as marks on his face. On the Saturday, Hart described that he had fallen several times *"as if the breath would leave me"* and had pain on drawing breath. He had been sore and pained for days.

The medical report dated 23 November 1854 signed by J Balfour Kirk MD was used as evidence against Boyd. Hart had been examined on the evening of the attack, when his external appearance indicated that a severe struggle had taken place. His face and clothes were covered with mud, and blood from the right cheek was oozing through the mud at a great many places. A great number of abrasions of the cheek and nose were present and Hart had complained of tenderness of the throat.

Robert Whitehead, the tavern keeper, described that his premises were a few minutes' walk going west from Bathgate. On being questioned, he said that he knew Larry Hart, who had come into the tavern at around three or four o'clock in the afternoon on the day in question, carrying a large bundle. Hart had taken a drink and bargained about a muffler, but a price could not be agreed upon. He had drunk several half gills of whisky, but was not drunk when he left. Around fifteen minutes later, he had returned with Boyd and each had paid thrupence for a gill. He had overheard Boyd saying that he would like to travel with Hart, and he had lots of money of his own. Boyd had even mentioned going into business with Hart and the pair had continued to drink. The *"packsman"* was by this time beginning to get rather the worse for drink. Whitehead had witnessed Boyd taking out a note from his pocket, giving it over to Hart, and a bullet had fallen out with the paper. Boyd had mentioned that he had a small pistol at home. Hart had tried to conduct some business again with Whitehead and opened his pack, whereupon the cloth had been purchased for Whitehead's wife. He recalled Boyd asking about the chocolate coloured handkerchief and that by this time Hart was *"pretty stupid"*(drunk). An individual named Turnbull had come in to the premises, requesting Boyd to come away, but he had refused. Apparently Boyd lodged with Sandy Rintoul in Bathgate. Hart always gave the name John when speaking to Boyd and used an Irish surname for him – not Boyd. Whitehead mentioned that Boyd had said that he was born outside Belfast, but he certainly had a North Country accent now. It had been a dark and dirty night and although Hart had tried to leave, Boyd had persuaded him to come back and drink some more. On leaving, Hart had given him his small bundle to carry, but the two had sat down again. Boyd had gone out for a minute and Hart had whispered to Whitehead that he would just like to slip away. When Boyd had returned, Whitehead said that *he* had tried to distract him by asking him to take a smoke with him, but this suspicious looking individual had shook his hand on leaving the premises, saying, "Good night. I'll do that bugger before he goes many yards!" Whitehead had shut the door as Mrs Johnston came in.

About ten minutes later John Johnston had come to the door asking for a lantern, as he had heard cries of *"murder!"* outside. On opening the door, Whitehead had heard the screams of a man being throttled coming from the easterly direction. The poor man was crying out pitifully, saying that he had been robbed. Whitehead, along with his brother-in-law, had come across poor Hart, who was crawling along the road, bedraggled and covered in mud. No packs had been found – only a muffler. They had gone for Sergeant Kerr and found Boyd sitting very comfortably at Rintoul's, whereupon he had said pleasantly to his landlady, "*Didn't I tell you that a man would call in for his bundles?*" On being questioned for a second time, Robert Whitehead recalled that Boyd had said that he lived with a widow and they were on friendly terms and he had even asked Whitehead to call on them some time. He remembered that Boyd had plied Hart – who seemed like an honest enough man - with drink and that he had tried to cheat him over the purchase of a handkerchief. Whitehead stated that due to the darkness of the night, he did not think that Boyd would have realised that houses were nearby. Although Hart was drunk when he left the tavern, Boyd had not taken very much alcohol, but had taken enough to loosen his tongue, making him reckless about what he said. Whitehead had also noticed a slight disagreement about who was to pay for the alcohol and that Boyd had become a bit piqued about this.

Helen Cant was Robert Whitehead's wife and she confirmed most of what had been said. She had seen no bullets, but had witnessed Boyd plying Hart with alcohol. She had not in the least liked the look of Boyd, who appeared highly suspicious - and she could see that eventually Hart had been trying to get away from him. Boyd had mentioned buying trousers from Hart's pack, but had been told that was not the type of garment he sold. She could see that Boyd was "*meditating some kind of mischief.*" The morning after the assault had taken place, Hart had been brought out to Meadowhead and his face was scratched and bruised all over. She said that when he had left the tavern the night before, he was perfectly clean and now his clothes were soiled and covered in mud.

May McLean was the wife of James McLean, mason, who was at Inverary searching for work. She had been lodging with John Johnston until her husband returned, but gave the address of her uncle, Charles Jackson, boot and shoemaker, at 49 Cambridge Street, Cowcaddens, Glasgow, as a contact. She recalled that the packsman had come into Meadowhead tavern with his packs at around four o'clock in the afternoon. She said that he had chatted and said that he took spirits to drink rather than anything else, because he was afraid of catching cholera. He tried to sell her some cloth, but she was not interested. He told her about a frightening dream he had experienced the night before and had gone to purchase more alcohol, whereupon she had advised him to go back to his lodgings. He had not left, but had fallen in with the prisoner, Boyd. She had subsequently heard the cries of "*murder*" outside at around seven o'clock and sounds of a man being choked. The cries had become louder and eventually when she had gone outside she had seen the packsman coming from the east, saying that he had been robbed. His packs were nowhere to be seen.

John Johnston, a hammerman at Heather Cottage, Meadowhead, described that he had come home from work at around six o'clock on the evening in question and, as he was eating his supper, his wife had gone to Whitehead's for some spirits. He had heard a man outside asking another to come for a drink, followed a while later by sounds of a scuffle, and a man shouting out, "*Are you going to murder me?*"

Johnston had then gone outside, but prior to that, his wife had let Mrs McLean out, as she had been sitting *"ben the hoose"* (through in another room). He had seen Whitehead coming out of the tavern and the pair of them had gone eastwards, where they had found the packsman bare-headed, robbed and injured. Margaret Johnston was the wife of John Johnston and she described the location of her house, which was situated a few yards east of the tavern. She had witnessed Larry Hart coming out with packs at approximately six or seven o'clock on the evening in question, the worse for drink. She had seen another man coming behind him, speaking in a threatening way, and had later heard sounds of quarrelling near to her house. There was then some swearing, with sounds of a struggle, and she could hear someone being knocked against the hedge. She then heard, *"Dinnae murder me!"* and pitiful cries of choking. As the sounds had become louder and more distressing, her husband, John, had searched for a lantern, but she had become rather impatient with him and had run towards the tavern, subsequently finding the packsman who had been robbed. The next morning, Sergeant Kerr had come along with Hart, who looked dreadful.

William Cant, who lived with his father, Thomas, a carpenter at Meadowhead, was described in the court records as being aged 13 – *"a smart and intelligent boy"*! He described that his house was next door to the tavern and he had been out working all day on the Friday in question. At approximately seven o'clock that evening, however, he had heard the cries of *"murder"* and had gone out to find Hart, covered in mud and injured, and had been informed that he had been robbed. The poor man wore no hat and seemed very confused. Cant had run east to see if he could see the thief, but was unsuccessful. He had only found two mufflers near the footpath, and a blue silk handkerchief – both of which were soiled – and which were later handed over to Sergeant Kerr. Francis McIntosh, a miner at Hopetoun Lane, described that Hopetoun Street was located in the line of the road coming from Armadale. On the Saturday morning after the attack, he had been out for a message with his child and had seen a woollen muffler lying in the street. This had subsequently been given over to the sergeant.

Mary McGregor Rintoul, wife of Alexander Rintoul, weaver in Mid Street, related that Boyd had asked if she could take him and his brother, John, as lodgers, they having left another house which they did not like. They had apparently been working on the railway near Aberdeen. Both spoke with a North Country accent, but when asked if they originated from the Highlands, they had replied in the negative. Although they worked some days on the railway, they sought other employment and on Thursday, 16th, Matthew Boyd had told her that he had saved ten pounds, but only had six pounds left. His brother had left her premises that morning. On the Friday, he had gone looking for work at the pit and she confirmed that he had behaved quite well during the time he lodged with her. She had seen no pistol, however. At around six or seven o'clock, Alexander Turnbull had called, mentioning that Boyd was drinking with the packman at the Meadowhead Tavern and a short while later Boyd had made his appearance, carrying a large pack and a smaller bundle. When Boyd had arrived, he had been a bit tipsy and she had informed him that he was to bring nobody back to her house. He had flung down the bundles, saying that a man would come for them, and had gone to wash before having supper. There seemed nothing suspicious about his behaviour. He wanted steaks for his tea and she informed him that she would not go out for them, as the house was quite remote and not near any shops. He was quite jovial when he threw down lots of silver on the table, saying he would buy steaks for them all, but telling her to keep his money for him. However, Sergeant Kerr had come along at this point, taking the bundles and some silk handkerchiefs from Boyd's pockets. Boyd had been taken to the "*lock up*" and Kerr had taken the silver away, but she had given the notes to Turnbull. She informed Kerr of this later. Alexander Rintoul concurred with his wife's statement and added that he had said to Boyd (who was drunk and covered with mud), "*You are so dirty as having been down the pit!*"

Alexander Turnbull, a labourer who lived at South Bridge Street, stated that the Rintouls were relations of his and he sometimes lodged with them. He knew Matthew (and John) Boyd and Matthew had always called himself by that name. Boyd had told them that he had worked on the Aberdeen railway and at Ayrshire and had saved up several pounds. Turnbull recalled seeing Boyd at the Meadowhead Tavern on the evening in question and he was asked if he wanted a dram. There had been a hawker sitting by the fire with his pack and bundle and he appeared drunk. Turnbull had tried to entice Boyd to come home, but had been told that he would be there in about half an hour and he had asked Turnbull to inform the landlady. On going to Rintoul's, Turnbull had changed his clothes, telling her about Boyd. He had gone into a nearby shoemaker's shop and heard a crowd of people walking along and then going into Rintoul's. He had witnessed the packman covered in mud, Sergeant Kerr taking Boyd away and Mrs Rintoul appearing very worried about some money Boyd had passed to her (five North of Scotland Bank pound notes rolled in a bunch). After passing these notes to Turnbull, they had subsequently been given over to Kerr.

John Kerr, Sergeant of Police in Bathgate, had seen Hart on several occasions. He had particularly remembered when Hart had come to him at around eight o'clock on the Friday in question, bare headed, stupid with drink and crying that he had been robbed. Mr Whitehead had also come to confirm what had happened. Kerr had gone to Rintoul's, found Boyd and charged him with assault and robbery, although this had been denied by the prisoner. As well as the packs, two handkerchiefs, a scarf and a bullet mould had been found on Boyd, as well as thirteen actual bullets. Boyd had apparently talked and laughed a great deal and had been "*bold and impudent*", whilst denying any knowledge of what had transpired. Some of Hart's pockets had been torn, as though someone had rifled them, and Kerr had seen marks of a struggle at the scene of the crime. Kerr had returned to Bathgate and put Hart to bed and had been told about Boyd trying to strangle him. He had asked Turnbull for the notes, but had first been told that he had none, but had then been given them. Hart had also showed Kerr his injured and discoloured leg. The only thing which had gone in Boyd's favour was that he had taken the bundles to his landlady's house, saying that they were to be given to the owner, but he had not informed her who the owner was or how the packs came to be covered in mud. It was quite obvious that Boyd had been planning to rob Hart, whilst looking at his bundles and plying him with drink. Several people in the tavern had witnessed them together and that a slight disagreement had come to pass during the evening. Kerr stated that the Rintouls had given false statements about what had happened and they could well have given false statements about what Boyd had actually said when he arrived with the bundles. They should have informed the police about the incident immediately, but had not done so.

What had Matthew Boyd to say about the attack and robbery? He was a 26 year old labourer and had come to Bathgate looking for work around 9 November from Ayrshire, where he had been working at the ironstone pits near Old Cumnock. He was originally from Aberdeen and was five feet nine inches tall. According to him, he had been to several pits around Bathgate looking for work on 17 November, one of which was called Whiteside. He said that he had gone into a public house on the road from Bathgate to Glasgow, by Armadale - just to the west of Bathgate – at about three o'clock in the afternoon. He had met a soft goods hawker at the door of the pub and they had gone in together. They had taken some drinks and the landlord and a man coming home from work had joined them, following which Boyd and Hart had left in rather an intoxicated state. He said he did not bargain for anything with this man. Hart and Boyd had shared the costs of the drink, according to Boyd, as he had been well paid by James Campbell, contractor on the Great North of Scotland Railway. Boyd recalled that both he and Hart were very drunk and that is how they both came to be covered in mud, having fallen down several times. There was no attack. Although he could not remember how he had come by the packs, he had taken them back to Rintouls for safekeeping. Sergeant Kerr had come along later and taken him away to the lock up. He confirmed that he had a pistol and bullets at his lodgings, saying that a chap at Stonehaven had made him a present of them, and that he had given over his paper notes into Mrs Rintoul's care.

What happened to Matthew Boyd following the trial at the High Court of Edinburgh on Monday 29 January 1855 when he was accused of assault to the effusion of blood and injury of the person, as also of robbery? He was found guilty and sentenced to 4 years penal servitude.

What happened to Lawrence Hart? Lawrence Hart, an unmarried hawker aged 56, died on 7 August 1867 at the Royal Edinburgh Asylum, Edinburgh. The cause of death was *exhaustion from mania* which he had suffered for 3 months.

National Records of Scotland reference AD14 55/295; JC26/1855/300

Death of Lawrence Hart: National Records of Scotland reference 685-01 798

PETER MCLEAN, WILLIAM MANSFIELD, CHRISTINA PETERS OR MCLEAN

MURDER AND ASSAULT AT BATHGATE 15 NOVEMBER 1856

It was late in the evening of Saturday, 15, or the early morning of Sunday, 16 November 1856 when the assault of brothers, John and Thomas Maxwell, occurred at Bathgate. Peter McLean, Christina Peters or McLean and William Mansfield were charged with the assault, which took place near the public road leading from Bathgate to East Whitburn, near the Boghead Bridge. They were accused of attacking Thomas Maxwell, a miner who lodged with Alexander Crey, a miner, at Durhamtown, knocking him down to the ground, kicking him and striking him with a stone near his chest, which resulted in him being mortally injured and murdered. Also, they were accused of attacking his brother, John, who lodged with Thomas Comisky, a miner, at Durhamtown, knocking him down, striking him on his head or face and stabbing him with a knife on the leg.

John Maxwell, in his statement, said that he and his brother had been in several public houses in Bathgate on the Saturday night, the last one being Thomas Chalmer's. By this time, John had become very drunk, but he recalled that Neil McMullen had been there at the time. He had no recollection of being in the Railway Tavern (Taylor's) or Rosina Devellin's house. Because of the condition he was in, he could not remember seeing his brother on the road, but had no doubt that they were together. On his way home, between the Railway Bridge and Boghead Bridge, he had quickly come to his senses, however, when Peter McLean had accosted him and threatened him, whilst trying to strike him. At this time, John recalled seeing Mansfield, with his wife and daughter nearby. William Mansfield had then joined in the affray by hitting John on the back of his head with a stone, felling him to the ground, whereupon he had become unconscious. When he was still feeling drowsy, but just regaining consciousness, he had heard Mansfield tell Peter McLean to come away, but the latter had replied, "*Not until I kill him!*" When questioned, he confirmed that he had not actually seen his brother attacked. John had managed to get home, but on reaching the house, his right leg was found to have been severely cut and there was a huge quantity of blood in his boot. He could only think that he had been stabbed when he was lying unconscious, but he had no earthly idea why he had been attacked.

There were many witnesses to the events which had led up to the attack. Edward McGlachan, who lodged with James Gray in the last house in Bathgate on the Whitburn Road, said that at around eleven thirty on the Saturday night he had gone out of the house and seen a man, woman and girl (who was holding a bundle) standing on the road nearby. Another man had come along saying, "*We shall do the buggers in tonight!*", whilst the woman had replied, "*You must do it, sure and quietly.*" It was a moonlit night, but because McGlachan had been hidden by the retaining wall of the house, they had not seen him when he went back into his house. He had then seen two men coming out of Devellin's house, which was in the same tenement, and they had proceeded south. McGlachan had peeped through a chink in the window, observing the four original people moving off in the same direction, but had gone back to bed.

Daniel Fern stated that he had been out in Bathgate on the night in question and when he had come to the railway viaduct around a hundred yards north of Boghead Bridge – which was at around eleven o'clock – he had seen James Pollan and passed a few words with him. However, between the two bridges, he had heard some people running after him. Mansfield was one, and McLean, who had seized him, had seemed infuriated, saying, "*You're not the man I want*!" On McLean quickly turning around, Fern had distinctly seen a weapon in his hand and observed a woman standing near the viaduct. The two incensed men had set off for Bathgate. Fern confirmed that later on he had seen the body of Thomas Maxwell in his lodgings.

Rosy Devellin said that between ten and eleven o'clock that evening Neil McMullen had come to the house, where Thomas and John Maxwell were drunk and talking of leaving. James Pollan had appeared and Rosy had gone to the door and seen a woman and girl on the road opposite the house, the latter with a bundle. The Maxwells had departed a few minutes later and then James Mullen had come along, saying that there had been cries of, "*murder*!" on the Durhamtown Road. They had all hurried to the door and on hearing the cries for themselves, McMullen and Pollan had gone to see what had happened. The Maxwells were, at that time, in perfect health. This statement was corroborated by James Mullen, who also stated that he had actually gone to the door with the Maxwells, seeing them off down the road to Durhamtown. He had heard a noise of quarrelling shortly afterwards, mentioning this to the others.

Patrick Cairney, John Sinclair junior and John Armstrong had left Durhamtown for Bathgate at approximately half past eleven on the night in question and met the Maxwells, who were setting off home, about a hundred yards north of Boghead Bridge. Although John Maxwell had seemed extremely drunk, Thomas appeared sober. Then further along the road, north of the viaduct, McLean and Mansfield had been seen walking very fast towards Durhamtown. McLean had been heard to say, "*They are on afore us*". After John Armstrong had left the others, he had met Thomas Comisky and Alexander Crey on the road and they had asked if he had seen Thomas Maxwell. It was only after proceeding a little further that Armstrong had seen Thomas Maxwell lying on the roadside and later witnessed his dead body being taken to Alexander Crey's house.

Neil McMullen described that he had been with John and Thomas Maxwell at Chalmer's pub at around ten o'clock that evening, but did not think they had been particularly drunk at the time. They had all gone to the Railway Tavern with James

Pollan and, whilst there, Mansfield and McLean, along with Jane McLean, had left and McMullen had gone on to Rosy Devellin's house, where once again he had met up with the Maxwells. He recalled the Maxwells leaving a minute or two after he arrived, although James Pollan had stayed. Hearing a noise from the road outside, McMullen and Pollan had run away in the direction of cries of *"murder"*. On arriving between the viaduct and Boghead Bridge, they had seen some people standing around, and recognised Mansfield and McLean (with his wife). They had seen these two men lying on top of two others, who they later learned were the Maxwells. McMullen and Pollan had chased Mansfield and McLean, but on being threatened, they had run back to the two men, who had been lying prostrate on the ground. John Maxwell had by this time disappeared, but his brother, Thomas, was lying there covered in blood, with a chest wound. The body had been taken to Alexander Crey's house on a cart and the police, who had been alerted, had apprehended Mansfield and the two McLeans. When McMullen had helped the police to take the prisoners to Bathgate, he had witnessed a clasp knife covered with moist blood being found in the female's possession and heard her saying it was her husband's. James Pollan corroborated this statement.

Thomas Comisky confirmed that John Maxwell had lodged with him for a considerable time and on the evening in question he had come to his house drunk and injured, with his trousers cut below his knee and a severe cut on his right leg. Maxwell had explained that Peter McLean and William Mansfield were guilty of the attack and Comisky had immediately hastened to fetch a doctor with Alexander Crey. On doing so, they had met a boy who had informed them that a man was lying on the side of the road. They had subsequently found the dead body of Thomas Maxwell. Alexander Crey confirmed that Thomas Maxwell lodged with him. Having heard on the night in question that John Maxwell had returned from Bathgate without his brother, Crey had gone to James Comisky's house, where he had seen John wounded and had heard that McLean and Mansfield were the perpetrators of the crime. He confirmed that the body had been located and brought to his house until James Balfour Kirk and another medical person had been able to inspect it. He also said that on the 16th John Murray had found a stone (on which there was blood and hair) which was later delivered to John Kerr.

Daniel Mooney had been standing with some other men a little to the north of Durhamtown, between eleven o'clock and midnight that night, when he had heard cries of *"murder!"* He had hurried along the Bathgate Road with the others to see what had happened, met Peter McLean, with his wife and daughter, and asked who had been shouting. They said the cries were theirs and that McMillan and Maxwell had been abusing McLean and Mansfield. When Mooney and his friends had followed them home, they had seen Peter McLean's hands covered in blood and had been told that McMillan's knife had caused this. MacLean had gone to wash his hands and after Mooney had left, he had seen the body of Thomas Maxwell being brought to Durhamtown.

But what of the prisoners? William Mansfield stated on 16 November that he was a twenty seven year old miner who lodged with James Hamilton, miner, at Durhamtown. He had met up with Peter McLean the night before and they had been drinking in Bathgate at Bryson's pub with Richard and John Pake, who worked with him, and McLean's wife and daughter. Then they had taken another drink at Richard Pake's house. Not content with this, he and the McLeans had drunk at Taylor's pub, and they had left at closing time, when Mansfield had spoken briefly to William Low. Mansfield's version of events was that he had come upon some people at the Railway Bridge near Durhamtown and these people had been quarrelling and hitting Peter McLean. Daniel Harn was with Mansfield and they had tried to stop the fight, whereupon they had been struck themselves. Mansfield said that John Maxwell had been fighting with McLean and Neil Mullen was there with another six or seven men, but, being afraid, Mansfield had run away. McLean had apparently been using "*rash*" words, saying he had something on him which he would use if they would not leave him alone. Mansefield said that he had gone straight home, but was soon taken into custody.

Peter McLean was a twenty nine year old miner who lived in Durhamtown. He was five feet seven inches tall, born Antrim. He confirmed that he had been in Bathgate with his wife and daughter on the night in question, having been paid by George Snadden, contractor, his employer. His wife had bought some provisions at Ferguson's grocer shop whilst he had waited for her at Bryson's pub, opposite the hotel, at the corner of Jarvey Street. He had taken two half mutchkins of whisky and a quart of ale. Richard and John Pake and William Mansfield – all miners – had drunk with him there and his wife had joined them, taking a drop, as had his young daughter. They had left (without the Pakes) for Durhamtown at approximately eleven o'clock, but nobody was the worse for drink. On the road, they partook yet again at Taylor's pub. By the time they had reached the Railway Bridge there were around six or seven men, all very drunk. Neil Mullen and one of the Maxwells were there and one of them had shouted out, "*To hell with your yellow soul*", whilst striking McLean and getting on top of him. His wife had helped him to get free and he had run away. He had apparently been followed by the men, but he did not recall what had happened next. He denied having any weapon with him or threatening anyone with a knife.

When questioned as to how he had come by a cut on his right hand, McLean was unable to answer, other than to say that this must have occurred when the men were on top of him. He said that he had been obliged to kick and struggle to get free from his attackers. Shortly after he had arrived home, he had heard some people trying to get into his house, so he had locked the door, as he had apparently already been attacked two or three times since coming to the area. He had identified the boots, trousers and shirt shown to him as those he had been wearing and which Sergeant Kerr had taken from him. He further explained that he was an Irishman and a

Protestant and Mullen and the Maxwells were Irish Catholics, intimating that this had been a fight of a sectarian nature.

Christina Peters, the twenty nine year old wife of Peter McLean, was born at Stirling and had lived most of her life there. She confirmed that she had been in Bathgate on the night in question with her husband and daughter, Jane. After buying some provisions, she had joined him at Rankine's public house, where he was sitting with Mansfield and the Pakes, following which they had gone to Richard Pake's house, then Taylor's public house and had drunk some more at both places. She had headed for home with her daughter, and both were carrying bundles. They had seen the people quarrelling at the Railway Bridge, where they had waited for Mansfield and her husband. She said that she had seen two men running after them, however, and Mansfield had shouted that they were going to be beaten, so had run away. Neil Mullen and another individual had apparently set upon Peter McLean, who had been pushed down and kicked several times, according to her, and she had roared out, "*murder!*", as had her daughter. She had seen no knife in her husband's hand. Her husband had been lying on the road for fifteen minutes before he was able to get home. She confirmed that a crowd had come to their door, which was locked.

Sergeant Kerr had taken her into custody just as she was cutting a piece of beef for supper, so she said that she had thrown the meat on the bed, putting the knife in her pocket. That knife belonged to John McLean, her brother in law, but she did not have it with her on the night in question, when the attack took place. She further described that the piece of meat was actually a piece of cow's head which was being cut up, accounting for the blood on the knife and on *her*. She explained that the spots of blood on her cap and basket had come from her husband when he was bleeding and she was assisting him. She had not noticed that her husband's hand was cut, as he had gone to bed immediately on reaching home. She was unable to name the butcher shop where she had purchased the meat, but described its location as being near the railway station, the first butcher going into Bathgate from Durhamtown.

John Kerr, Police Sergeant, confirmed that he had been called out on the morning of the 16th in connection with the assault and murder and that Doctor Kirk had been sent for. He had seen the dead body of Thomas Maxwell with the wound on his chest and his clothes soaked with blood. He stated that the prisoners had seemed very anxious and there was a good deal of blood on Peter McLean's hands and his clothes, as well as a cut on his hand. A basket had been found in the house, the handle being covered in moist blood, as were a pair of boots, and the basin was full of bloody water. A half cow's head was found - just as it had left the butcher shop. Kerr described the locations where the assault had taken place and the body had been found, together with the state of the ground. The prisoners had been taken to Linlithgow prison that morning. Mrs Kerr, Sergeant Kerr's wife, had been present when the women were searched and she said that Mrs McLean seemed very nervous indeed when the knife was found in her possession, explaining its presence by saying that she had been cutting up a cow's head with it when arrested. The cow's head had been shown to Peter Russell, the butcher, who lived with James Russell, farmer at Dykehead, Bathgate, and he confirmed that Mrs McLean had purchased this from him and it was in the same condition as when it had left the shop.

What happened to the prisoners at their trial which took place at Edinburgh High Court on 12 January 1857? William Mansfield was found guilty of assault and sentenced to 2 years imprisonment at Perth, the case against Christina McLean was not proven and she was dismissed, although she had spent 53 days in Linlithgow Jail. Peter McLean was found guilty of murder and although there had been a recommendation for mercy, he was sentenced to death by hanging by the public executioner.

The council of the Royal Burgh of Linlithgow held a meeting on 15 January 1857 and had been aware that there was every possibility that a huge number of colliers, miners and other workmen *"of that class"* would amass for the execution at Linlithgow. There were, after all, mineral works at Bo'ness, Bathgate, Armadale, Whitburn, Fauldhouse, Crofthead and other places in the county as well as Airdrie, Gartsherrie and Dundrydon in Lanarkshire and Redding, Slammanan, Polmont and other places in Stirling. Meaningful of the character of these people and that there was no police force which could deal with them should they become riotous, it was decided that application should be made to the proper quarters for the presence of a military force. Robert Glen, Town Clerk, noted this in the Minutes.

Peter McLean was executed at Linlithgow on Monday, 2 February 1857. Prior to his execution he urged those present to **avoid alcohol and bad company and to uphold the Sabbath**.

Note: Peter McLean's was the last public execution in Linlithgow. The Linlithgow Treasurer's account for 3 February 1857 lists:

Cash paid for executing Peter McLean £75 1 shilling 11d.

Note: Death certificate for Peter McLean states that he was married, a coal miner aged 30 but his parents were not known to the informant. He died at the Cross, Linlithgow – hanged and buried at the precincts of Linlithgow Prison by David Lockie sexton. *[National Records of Scotland reference 668-01 16]*

National Records of Scotland reference AD14/57/254; JC26/1857/339 JC26/1857/339

Linlithgow Treasurer's Accounts for this period held at West Lothian Council Local Archives, Linlithgow

WILLIAM MANSFIELD

ASSAULT NEAR RUSSELL'S ROW, ARMADALE 7 AUGUST 1859

It was in the early morning of Sunday, 7 August 1859, at around six o'clock, near the turnpike road between Blackridge and Bathgate, opposite Russell's Row, when an attack of a sectarian nature took place. This row of cottages had been built by Messrs Russell and Son for their mine workers. A party of young men – around fifteen or sixteen of them – were walking from Airdrie to Berwickshire to assist with the harvest shearing and they were passing through the village of Armadale en route. They had started their journey on the Saturday evening, but as the weather was pleasant, they had decided to keep walking during the night. Several were carrying "*walking*" sticks. On reaching Russell's Row, they had noticed several miners standing in front of their houses there, but the Airdrie lads had carried on walking.

According to those who were assaulted later, however, it appeared that one of the miners had shouted out an insulting, "*To hell with the Pope!*" Most of these lads from Airdrie were of the Catholic religion, and it became obvious that the miners were **looking for trouble**.

Luke Haughey was one of those who had been severely assaulted. He was a miner who lodged with Patrick McMullen, a shoemaker, at Rawyards near Airdrie. According to him, he had left Airdrie on the Saturday night with his friends, the McAlinden brothers, ie Lawrence, Patrick and Michael, together with Patrick McLauchlin. Haughey had heard the miners shouting these sectarian insults and then one of them had made his position very clear when he shouted, "*We are Orangemen*", whilst running towards them and grabbing their sticks. One of the miners had proceeded to strike him repeatedly over the head with a stick or a poker, felling him to the ground and, whilst lying there, others had kicked him for nearly five minutes, so it seemed to him. Stupefied, he had eventually risen to his feet and staggered to a nearby field, where he was able to rest, albeit the blood was running profusely down his face and he felt faint with the loss of it. Haughey had then walked to Bathgate with his companions, who had joined him on the road. He could not go on to the harvesting, however, and was obliged to return to Rawyards on 13 August. He had only been able to work for a few days afterwards, due to the injuries he had sustained. As to identifying any of the accused at the trial, he was unable to do so with any accuracy, since his arms had been firmly held over his eyes and face to ward off the attack.

The medical report dated 9 August signed by James Longmuir, surgeon, confirmed that although Haughey had complained of general soreness, his wounds had been mainly confined to his head. There was one wound so deep that a part of the bone was exposed. There were two cuts on the back of his head and one over his left eyebrow. These injuries were obviously of a very serious nature and appeared to have been inflicted by a dangerous weapon.

Lawrence McAlinden, a drawer from Airdrie, concurred with Haughey's statement *"down to the letter"*. Dressed in a blue shirt, black cloth vest, cap and corduroy trousers, he had also been grabbed by two of the miners, who had told him that they were Orangemen, whilst wrenching his walking stick from him. The miners seemed to think that one of the Airdrie party had shouted out, *"To hell with you!"* after the insult regarding the Pope had been made, but McAlinden had vehemently denied this. They had retorted, *"You bugger, you ARE the man who said it!"* This had resulted in a severe attack on McAlinden, when several of the miners had punched him on his face, neck and body, pushing him to the ground. He was extremely traumatised, but his brother, Patrick, had come to his rescue. After being lifted from the ground, Lawrence and his brother had gone into a field by the roadside and walked to Bathgate with the badly injured Luke Haughey, who was losing blood at an alarming rate. Fortunately, the McAlindens were able to proceed to Berwickshire that day. Dr Longmuir's examination of Lawrence McAlinden found that although he had a wound on his nose and upper lip, with the right nostril slit and his upper lip swollen, these injuries were not of a serious nature. As far as recognising any of those who had attacked him was concerned, only Mansfield could be named, although McAlinden could confirm that the first attacker had certainly had red hair and whiskers (Thomas Branagan).

Patrick McAlinden concurred with his brother's account, stating that he had also been struck repeatedly on the face and body. He was unable to identify Mansfield and seemed amazed that the miners had known of their religious persuasion. His twenty one year old brother, Michael, also concurred with the description of events made by his brothers, whilst twenty nine year old Patrick McLaughlin, a drawer, confirmed that one of the attackers was the ferocious Branagan, of the red hair and whiskers, who had brandished a poker whilst shouting, *"Where are you going to the harvest, you Papish buggers?"*, whilst saying he would knock out their brains!!

And what of the miners? What had they to say about the events which had taken place that morning? Henry Robb from Armadale had been awoken at approximately six o'clock by the noise outside. Standing at his window, he had witnessed some miners at Russell's Row repeatedly striking two men on the ground with sticks and he was able to identify William Mansfield as one of the assailants and Patrick McAlinden as the person who had assisted one of the victims. James Cunningham said that he had seen Mansfield running back and forwards between the two men on the ground, but had not actually seen him striking anyone. Cunningham had seen Thomas Branagan and Samuel Burnet in the group of miners, but had only actually seen Branagan hitting anyone. He had seen Lawrence McAlinden, one of the shearers, bleeding profusely, but although Mansfield was there at the time,

Cunningham had not seen him strike anyone, although he certainly had not stopped those who did.

James Naysmith stated that his house was situated three hundred yards east of Russell's Row and he had heard a fracas coming from the road to the west. He had seen the party of shearers, roughly fifteen in number, going eastwards opposite his door. They were running and five or six miners, one of whom was Mansfield, were in hot pursuit. He had heard Mansfield, who was brandishing a stick, saying that they had better turn round, as *"they"* were too strong for them and shortly afterwards a young man with blood on his face had come running past. This man was identified as Luke Haughey. Thirty year old Henry Burnet confirmed that Mansfield lodged at his house, although he knew nothing at all about this incident. He had heard a disturbance outside at approximately six o'clock that morning, and Mansfield had been outside, but he had come back inside the house shortly afterwards, going straight to bed and saying nothing. Naysmith was able to say, however, that Mansfield was *"a little affected with drink"*.

A labourer, Alexander Chisholm, who lodged with Thomas Martin, a plate layer in Blackridge, had been passing Russell's Row at around six o'clock when a party of shearers had been passing by. He had heard the insult regarding the Pope, but had also heard one of the shearers retorting, *"To hell with you"*, whilst running away. Whilst the miners had pursued them and wrenched away their sticks, they had subsequently attacked them. Chisholm had shouted for help and some of the miners' wives had come out and dragged their errant husbands away. There was one of these shearers who had been very badly injured and was bleeding heavily. William Mansfield was certainly one of the attackers and Chisholm was able to confirm that it was Mansfield who had taken the most active part in the assault. The miners had cursed and swore, making a terrible din, and, according to Chisholm, the shearers had been in no way to blame for what followed. On being questioned further, he admitted that some of the miners had grabbed him by the throat and told him that if he did not shout out the insult regarding the Pope, they would knock out his brains. It was only when he said that he would comply with this request, being terrified of what they might do to him, that they had let him go. He had then seen Mansfield striking a man with a blue coat, who was later identified as Lawrence McAlinden.

William Robertson was the district constable in Armadale and he had heard a disturbance at Russell's Row at approximately six o'clock that morning. The miners had quickly dispersed when he had gone outside and he had been informed that a fight had taken place there. He had seen both Mansfield and Branagan, the former standing in a field opposite with a stick in his hand, the latter standing outside a house. Witnesses had given statements to him on Monday, 8 August, but Mansfield, Branagan and Burnet were not to be found.

When William Mansfield, a miner of no fixed abode, gave his statement on 13 August at Bonnyton, near Linlithgow he stated that he had lived at Armadale for several months prior to the incident, and latterly he had lodged with Henry Burnet at Russell's Row. According to his version of events, he had been awoken at around six o'clock that morning by a number of men arguing and fighting outside, some of whom were Thomas Branagan, John McCallum, William Michael and James Houston. He had seen some strangers passing by on their way to the harvest, but had not seen anybody near them and he had certainly not attacked any of them. He had left Armadale on the Monday night, along with some others, heading for the east country, and on reaching Edinburgh he had enlisted with the 26th Regiment. He had subsequently been apprehended. To confirm this statement, W McLemerty of the Adjutant General's Office in Edinburgh had written to J Watson, Procurator Fiscal in Linlithgow, on 21 November. He had the honour to enclose a Protecting Certificate for *"recruit William Mansfield of the 26th Foot"* and he had written that he would be obliged for this to be given to the keeper of the prison for Mansfield on his release from confinement.

William Mansfield was no stranger to fighting. He had a previous conviction of 12 January 1857, when he was living at Durhamtown, for the assault of John Maxwell by means of stones or other instruments at Boghead Bridge, public road from Bathgate to East Whitburn, for which he had been imprisoned for two years with hard labour. (*His accomplice, Peter McLean, was hanged at Linlithgow 2 February 1857.*) Thomas Branagan, born County Tyrone, had been incarcerated in Linlithgow Jail on 20 May 1854 for fourteen days, for assault and malicious mischief, along with other Irishmen – William Haggerty, Robert Miller and John Baxter. He was incarcerated again at the same jail for six days on 4 April 1855 for assault, along with John and Henry Burnet, William Bell, John Russell, Robert Gilbert, Samuel Burnet and James Bell.)

William Mansfield's trial for this particular assault took place at the High Court in Edinburgh on 10 November 1859. What was the outcome? The first charge of attacking and assaulting Luke Haughey with fists and stick or poker, striking several blows to his head, face other parts, throwing him down and repeatedly kicking him to the effusion of his blood and serious injury to his person was found not proven. He was, however, found guilty of assaulting Lawrence and Patrick McAlinden and due to his previous conviction he was sentenced to four years imprisonment.

National Records of Scotland reference AD14/59/360; JC26/1859/379

THOMAS CRAWFORD OF LIMEFIELD BATHGATE

LITIGATION – 4 JUNE 1863

Thomas Crawford was born at Bathgate in 1825 to Abraham Crawford, a lime merchant, and his wife Agnes Carlaw and was living at Petershill Limeworks - situated north of Glenbare Quarry - Bathgate in 1841. Thomas married Ann Lochead on 28 July 1857 at Tradeston, Glasgow, but prior to this he was living at Limefield Farm, Bathgate, (*tip of the Puir Wife's Brae*) where he farmed 113 acres and by 1863 was father to four children – Abraham, Thomas, Agnes Carlaw and Catherine McEwen Crawford.

An action was taken at the instance of Thomas Crawford, farmer at Limefield, "*to whose great hurt and prejudice was made*" and this was heard on 4 June 1863. The action was against Jane Kerr or Neilson, wife of David Neilson, miner, formerly of Blackbraes, Muiravonside - now at Grangemouth (with whom Jane had married on 17 October 1856 at Bothkennar) – and she was charged with David Neilson and Alexander Kerr, miner, living at Skinflats near Grangemouth, her father.

It had previously been established that Thomas Crawford was the father of an illegitimate child (Alexander) who had been born to Jane on 15 April 1853 and costs had been agreed as to the inlying charges and maintenance payable until the child was nine years old, together with legal expenses. However, the findings had been obtained by "*false, feigned and fabricated, simulated and devised statements and depositions made up collusively and emitted by the defender, the said Jane Kerr or Neilson, and others illegally conspiring with her in rearing up fictitious and unfounded claims against the pursuer*". In other words, they had committed perjury in this action of paternity and aliment. It was stated that the pursuer was not the father of her child and he should be discharged of all claims, demands and allegations and £500 in compensation and damages should be paid to him, together with £100 expenses. Crawford wanted all the defenders arrested and their movable goods seized.

Thomas Crawford had apparently had the misfortune to become acquainted at Shotts Market with William Donaldson, who was tenant of the small farm of Kendieshill, Muiravonside a good many years before. (Kendieshill was situated at Muiredge, Muiravonside, which was about four miles from Linlithgow and Falkirk. As well as arable land, the lands of Kendieshill contained coal and ironstone and, according to the Caledonian Mercury of Saturday 2 and 9 January 1813, there was a "*commodious dwelling house upon the premises*".) This had led to a relationship developing between the parties, with Thomas Crawford occasionally supplying Donaldson with considerable quantities of oats as a change of seed and getting in exchange payments in cash or delivery of stock, produce or farm implements. Donaldson always seemed to be in poor circumstances and was ultimately ruined by litigation with the landlords - the Carron Company - who refused to re-let him his farm. His crop, stock and effects were ultimately sold off to pay for the arrears of rent, damages and expenses.

On Martinmas 1851, Jane Kerr had been engaged as a servant by Donaldson at his farm, which was near to her father's house at Blackbraes. Donaldson was said to be a bachelor and *"so great an admirer of the fair sex as to render women of character averse to associate with him,"* whilst there was a danger that young girls would become in danger of unprotected communication with him, however innocent. In other words, they would be seduced! It was stated that if Jane had been properly cared for at home, she would never have been allowed to enter the service of Donaldson – who was obviously a philanderer of the highest degree. The result was as expected - she became pregnant and was delivered of a son on 15 April 1853, with the child being procreated around July/August 1852. As far as the claim being made against Crawford was concerned, however, and the dates given, there would have been 280 days between conception and birth of this child!

Crawford stated that had such claims been founded in truth they would have been immediately enforced and not allowed to lie dormant from the birth **15 April 1853 to 9 February 1860,** when the first summons had been served on him. He had been astounded by the allegation. He had apparently had no previous acquaintance with her and between the middle of April and the end of October 1852 he had been seized with rheumatic fever due to drinking cold water, when he was overheated in sowing one of his fields at House Park. He had then been confined to bed for several months when he had been attended to by Dr Dickson, surgeon at Bathgate, who had ordered him to be swathed in flannel, rubbed with turpentine and his head bathed with vinegar to reduce the fever. As a consequence, he had been unable to go out again until the beginning of November. Even after that, he could not have gone any greater distance than the town of Bathgate – which was one mile away - even by the spring of 1853. Alexander Stewart, his farm grieve, and William Roberts, ploughman, had confirmed this and that he was never away from his farm during that time. They had seen him morning and evening each day confined to the house. When his sister, Jane Crawford or Millar, and his mother had visited him at home, he had been consistently in bed from June to August 1852, which completely destroyed Jane's credibility.

After being questioned on 9 April 1860, Jane had said that Thomas Crawford was often at Kendieshill during the time she had been a servant, but she had given two conflicting stories about how the alleged incident involving him had happened. Crawford had obviously been confined to his own bed at Limefield eight miles away, which was backed up by his family and servants. On being cross-examined, Mary Marshall, another servant of Donaldson's, had stated that her master had defrauded her of a large sum of money which she had set apart for support in her old age. She now had no hope of ever recovering it!

This was indeed a sorry tale and several cases of litigation were brought about by Thomas Crawford after this one. The next year he disputed the amount owed by him for iron railings provided by the foundry of the late James Hosie of Falkirk. He sued James Christine Hart of Kirkton and Drumcrosshall for damages, claiming that he was entitled to abatement of rent, reparation for the injury done to his crops by the defender's game, and damages. These actions appear to have ruined him, as he was subsequently sequestrated in 1864 under the 1856 Bankruptcy (Scotland) Act.

Thomas lived at Marjoribanks Street, Bathgate in 1881 with his wife and two daughters, when he was described as being a retired farmer. He died at Glasgow at the age of 83.

National Records of Scotland reference CS228/C/30/31; CS284/10; CS228/C/31/9); SC66/7/1859/21

DONALD MCLEOD ALIAS JAMES STEWART/JOHN STEWART/JAMES CAMPBELL/ALEXANDER CAMPBELL/JOHN MACLACHLAN OF NO FIXED ABODE

A VAGRANT COMES TO TOWN – FRAUD AND WILFUL IMPOSITION

LINLITHGOW 16 NOVEMBER 1869 AND BATHGATE 18 AND 19 NOVEMBER 1869

It was Tuesday, 16 November 1869, when Donald McLeod, a labourer, arrived at Linlithgow on the train from Edinburgh. Unbeknown to the locals, Donald (who used various aliases) was a vagrant of no fixed abode, who spent his time travelling the country, eating and drinking at various inns and lodging houses, purporting to be able to afford it. In truth, he had not sufficient funds to pay.

On the day in question he had arrived at the Star and Garter Hotel in Linlithgow, representing himself as a railway contractor. The proprietor of the hotel at that time was Mary Rintoul or Maddox, a widow. McLeod was shown into No. 7 Room where he asked employee, Michael Kavanagh, to bring him something hot to eat. It was a cold day, after all. He wanted hot soup which was not available, so had then proceeded to order steak and potatoes and a cup of tea. Kavanagh had become suspicious (probably due to McLeod's appearance) and mentioned that such a steak would cost him one shilling and thrupence. However, the stranger was undaunted and said that he knew well enough the price of such an item in small towns and he could easily afford it. Thus reassured, Kavanagh had brought him the meal, as well as a cup of tea, two glasses of whisky and a pint of sweet ale. The total cost of this food and drink was two shillings and thrupence.

During the time he was eating and drinking, McLeod had started talking to Thomas Rintoul and others, who were in the same room. Kavanagh had overheard him telling them that he was a railway contractor, who sometimes dealt in ponies. Having finished the food, whisky and ale, McLeod had ordered another bottle of ale, but Kavanagh was by now becoming extremely worried, so had insisted that the money was paid over first. McLeod had merely retorted that Kavanagh would get the money when HE got his ale. After a heated discussion, McLeod had said that he wanted to see the landlady, as he actually had no money at all, whereupon Kavanagh had threatened to fetch the police. The fraudster had replied, "*I don't give a damn about the police*", so Kavanagh had gone to fetch a constable immediately. Apparently, during the time he had been away, McLeod had sold his bonnet to another man in the room for a shilling, immediately grabbing it back and placing it on his head. He had kept the money, however, defying any man present to try to retrieve the hat again! Constable John McLeod had arrived and taken him into custody. Unfortunately, the money for the food had to be taken out of Kavanagh's wages, so it was actually him who was defrauded.

When questioned at the trial, Thomas Rintoul, a huntsman living at Linlithgow, brother of Mrs Maddox, the proprietor, confirmed that he had seen McLeod, the prisoner, in No. 7 Room at the Star and Garter. He had seen him eating and drinking. The prisoner had struck up a conversation with him, telling him that he had a contract with Mr Waddell, between Monifieth and Forfar, but had lost approximately twelve pounds in this transaction. From his appearance, Mr Rintoul had taken him to be a drover, but McLeod had mentioned that he sometimes dealt in ponies. Rintoul had been treated to ale by him, but had left the hotel shortly afterwards, telling Kavanagh that he had grave suspicions about this stranger.

Another witness, Thomas Baird, head ostler of the hotel (*who fed, watered and stalled the customers' horses*), also confirmed that he had seen the prisoner in No. 7 Room. He had witnessed him selling the hat for a shilling and then McLeod had placed it on Baird's knee, snatched it back again, put it back on his head and kept the money. He confirmed that he had heard Kavanagh asking for payment and being refused.

John McLeod, police constable, now at Coatbridge, confirmed that he had been called out by Kavanagh and he had apprehended the prisoner, conveyed him to the police office and searched him. The prisoner had no money whatsoever on his person, but when he was about to be taken to the cell to be locked up, he had taken a shilling out of his mouth and passed it over. No convictions were known to exist for him at that time and after reporting the case to the Burgh Procurator, the latter declined to prosecute him and the prisoner was freed the next day.

Having been jailed for a day, he had then proceeded on his way to Bathgate on the Thursday. First, he went to the public house of William Wallace in Jarvey Street at around three or four o'clock in the afternoon, partaking of a glass of whisky. He had obviously been drinking prior to this, as he had become unruly, starting to sing, and was eventually thrown out. According to Margaret Newlands, who lived at her half brother, William Wallace's house there, the prisoner had then returned at around nine or ten o'clock that evening, in an even more inebriated condition. Wallace had ejected him, but had been threatened by the prisoner, who had shouted, "*I'll make sure you'll remember me the next time I return.*" He had been standing at the kitchen door on one occasion when McLeod had come to the house, and it was only on Sunday 21 November that a pair of elastic boots - the property of Margaret's brother - had been found to be missing. They had been sitting on either the kitchen dresser or in the cellar, which could be accessed from the lobby, with the door always being open. One of the boots had been mended above the instep and Margaret confirmed that those boots being shown to her at court were definitely those of her brother.

Samuel Newlands, who was twelve years old and who also lived with William Wallace, confirmed that the boots shown to him were his. He explained that he only wore these on a Sunday and, having worn them on 14 November last, he had not noticed that they were missing until the following Sunday.

Sarah McKechnie, wife of James Strathearn, pawn broker at Main Street, Bathgate, gave a statement to the effect that on the same Thursday at about three or four o'clock in the afternoon, the prisoner had come into the shop and offered the boots for sale, asking a price of five shillings. She had offered one shilling and nine pence and he had eventually accepted, giving his name and address as *"Donald McLeod, Robertson's Square, Bathgate"*. She had entered the transaction into the Broker's Book, and the boots were sold on to a William Ferguson for three shillings the following Saturday. William Ferguson, a bricklayer at Bathgate Muir, confirmed that he had purchased the boots for three shillings, but that Constable Sinclair had subsequently taken possession of them on Tuesday 23 November. The constable concurred with this.

Another theft was committed on Friday, 19 November. Twelve year old Alexander Dickson, who was the son of Peter Dickson, carter in the High Street of Bathgate, gave a statement at the trial. He confirmed that he worked as an apprentice to Donald Tulloch Sutherland, clothier and draper in Jarvey Street. Dickson had been in Mr Sutherland's shop at two o'clock that afternoon, when the prisoner had come in. Dickson had been concealed from view by some bales of cloth on the counter and McLeod had entered the shop, looked about and left again, looking furtively both ways along the street. He had put something under his coat, which Dickson had suspected was a pair of plaiding drawers –costing five shillings and sixpence - which had been hanging outside on an iron rod by the door. Calling for Robert Leith, the foreman tailor, Dickson had rushed out with him to the door where the prisoner was standing with his coat buttoned up. On seeing them both, McLeod had dropped the drawers from under his coat. After Leith had retrieved them, James Mackay had come forward, saying that he had seen McLeod stealing them – which was strenuously denied by the prisoner. The constable, Alexander Mackay, had been fetched and McLeod was subsequently taken into custody. Robert Leith of Marjoribanks Street confirmed what had happened.

James Rutherford Mackay, a draper who lodged with John Mackay, gave a statement to the effect that he had been in his father's shop, which was immediately opposite Mr Sutherland's shop, when he had observed the prisoner loitering there for ten minutes or so. He had witnessed the theft taking place and had run across the street to inform Dickson and Leith, but the prisoner had merely alleged that the theft had been committed by another man, who had run away and dropped the garment on the street.

As far as previous convictions were concerned, McLeod had a string of them over a number of years all over Scotland. Various well respected persons such as police constables, sheriff officers and prison governors, had come from their localities to testify that McLeod had committed similar crimes of fraud, mainly for being unable to pay for food and drink which he had consumed. He had received the following sentences:

At Campbeltown on 20 May 1853 under the name of John Stewart (four days hard labour) and on 20 October 1853 under the name of Alexander Fraser (thirty days hard labour). At the Royal Hotel Stirling on 5 July 1857 and at Inversnaid Inn, Buchanan, Stirling on 12 December 1857, for which he was sentenced to fifteen days imprisonment for the former and sixty days imprisonment with thirty days hard labour for the latter.

At Kilmarnock on 31 July 1857 and 11 September 1857 when sentenced to ten days and sixty days imprisonment respectively under the name of John Stewart and Alex Campbell alias John Stewart respectively.

At 6 Market Street, Greenock on 12 November 1857 under the name of Alexander Campbell for which he received twenty days imprisonment.

At Inverness on 14 June 1859 under the name of John Stewart (sixty days imprisonment) and 1 May 1863 under the name of James Stewart alias John McLachlan alias James Campbell (three years penal servitude).

At the Stag Hotel, School Wynd, Elgin on 3 April 1858 under the name of John Stewart for which he was imprisoned for five days.

At Elgin on 1 May 1858 under the name of John Stewart for which he was imprisoned for five days.

At the Inn at Minnlochy, Knockbain on 23 June 1858 under the name of Alexander MacDonald for which he was imprisoned for fourteen days.

At the Inn near Swiney, Latheron, Caithness on 31 July 1858 under the name of Alexander MacDonald for which he was imprisoned for thirty days.

At the Inn at Invergordon, Ross and Cromarty on 27 November 1858 under the name of John Stewart for which he was imprisoned for four months.

At Ross and Cromarty on 11 January 1859 under the name of John Stewart alias Alexander Macdonald alias Alexander Campbell for which he was imprisoned for four months.

At Ayr on 16 October 1860 under the name of James Stewart for which he was imprisoned for twelve months at Perth.

At the Old Kirn Inn in Dunoon on 19 October 1861 for which he was imprisoned for twelve months.

On 1 May 1863 using the name of James Stewart alias John MacLachlan alias James Campbell for which he was sentenced to three years penal servitude.

At the Grant Arms Hotel near Rothes, Elginshire on 11 July 1866 and at the Plough Inn at Rothes on 12 July 1866. After being apprehended for these crimes of fraud, he then aggravated the crime further by assaulting a warder and the governor of the Prison of Elgin on 18 July, when he struck them about the chest and throat and injured them. For these two crimes he was given a sentence of two years imprisonment.

At Fort William on 6 October 1869 under the name of James Stewart for which he was imprisoned for nineteen days.

Donald McLeod

It was obvious that this was a man who moved around the country habitually – a vagrant. A letter from the Procurator Fiscal's Office of Linlithgow dated 31 December 1869 noted that the convictions were so numerous and, having been obtained in the courts all over Scotland, the prisoner had not been specifically identified as to each particular conviction, but had been identified generally and there was no doubt that all the convictions applied to him.

As far as his own statements were concerned, the prisoner made two prior to the trial which took place at the High Court of Justiciary on Monday, 28 February 1870. In the first, given on 20 November 1869, he stated that his name was Donald McLeod and he was aged forty two, a labourer of no fixed abode. He said that he had arrived in Bathgate about two or three days previously and whilst standing outside a shop there, he had taken a pair of flannel drawers, which were hanging outside. He did not know what he was going to do with them, however, or what had induced him to take them. A man had then taken them from him, but McLeod did not run away from him.

In his second statement of 8 December 1869, he said he was aged forty. He remembered going into the Star and Garter Hotel at Linlithgow, but couldn't remember the date. He stated that he had only eaten a small piece of beef and some potatoes, maybe drunk some whisky, and given ale to some person, but had not paid for any of it. He had gotten a shilling from a drunken man, who had wanted him to leave his bonnet for him, but because he did not want to go out bareheaded, he had retrieved it from him. He denied telling the waiter he was a contractor, or eating steak, or that he was going to buy ponies. He said that he was drinking in Bathgate the following day and did not know what he was doing. He denied taking any boots from a house and said he had only sold his own boots.

What happened to Donald McLeod, alias James Stewart/John Stewart/James Campbell/Alexander Campbell/John Maclachlan following the trial at the High Court of Edinburgh on 28 February 1870? He was sentenced to 7 years penal servitude. There would be no more wandering the country for a long time!

National Records of Scotland reference AD14/70/291; JC26/1870/277

Acknowledgements for photographs used

Linlithgow Bridge – West Lothian Local History Library

South Bridge Street, Bathgate, Ballencrieff Toll – by kind permission of Dorothy Cook

Dechmont Cottage – by kind permission of West Lothian History and Amenity Society

Hartwood House – by kind permission of Acredale Camera Club

Photograph of Donald McLeod (Linlithgow Rogues Gallery) Courtesy of Edinburgh City Archives

Printed in Great Britain
by Amazon.co.uk, Ltd.,
Marston Gate.